HIGHER

GROUND

Higher Ground: How the Outdoor Recreation Industry Can Save the World is published under Erudition, a sectionalized division under Di Angelo Publications, Inc.

Erudition

Erudition is an imprint of Di Angelo Publications.
Copyright 2024.
All rights reserved.
Printed in the United States of America.

Library of Congress
Higher Ground: How the Outdoor Recreation Industry Can Save the World
ISBN: 978-1-955690-75-1
Hardback

Words: Luis Benitez, Frederick Reimers
Cover Design: Savina Mayeur
Interior Design: Kimberly James
Photographs: Didrik Johnck
Editors: Matt Samet, Willy Rowberry

Downloadable via dapbooks.shop and other e-book retailers.

For educational, business, and bulk orders, contact distribution@diangelopublications.com

1. Political Science --- Public Policy --- General
2. Sports & Recreation --- Extreme Sports
3. Business & Economics --- Conflict Resolution & Mediation

HIGHER

GROUND

HOW THE OUTDOOR RECREATION INDUSTRY CAN SAVE THE WORLD

LUIS BENITEZ
with FREDERICK REIMERS

CONTENTS

FOREWORD

SEN. JOHN HICKENLOOPER

Luis Benitez is that rare athlete who has made their sport part of their mission in life.

Luis is half Missourian and half Ecuadorian, which meant spending many summers of his youth visiting his father's family on their farm in Ecuador, surrounded by some of the highest volcanoes in the world. While he mastered the traditional values of hunting and fishing with his mother's family in Missouri, it was in the high Andes he experienced the awe and exhilaration that comes when facing dangerous routes at high altitudes.

Calling on his early passion for the glory of the outdoors, Luis spent a decade managing the legendary leadership organization Outward Bound, where he developed both the moral training and fundamentals of successful teamwork necessary to summit the world's highest peaks. While still a young man, he accomplished feats many adventurers could only dream of: climbing the highest peak on every continent, and summiting Mt. Everest not once, not twice, but six times.

This journey is described in gripping detail in this book you are about to read (or listen to). But what really sets this work apart from other accounts of mountain conquest is the passion that came to Luis from various combinations of circumstance and achievement.

Luis came to see how the lives that people live when engaged in outdoor adventure, or more broadly, in Outdoor Recreation, creates a complex but unique value chain. Whether it's simply hiking in a local park or one of our majestic National Parks, or skinning straight up a mountain before skiing back down, humans are doing much more than just exercising their bodies – the health benefits, both physical but also mental, are prodigious. Numerous studies over the years demonstrate that consistent exercise is without a doubt the most cost-effective pathway toward dramatically reducing our nation's soaring health care expenditures.

People climb mountains and navigate wild rivers not just for the health benefits or the thrill, but to see nature in its purest state. Many of the greatest religious leaders in history at one time retreated into the wilderness to "hear God" and later brought back the wisdom to their people. For many indigenous groups around the world, tribal lands remain sacred and the very source of religious belief.

For millions of Americans, too, public lands of all sorts are sacred. From Niagara Falls to the Grand Canyon to the Rocky Mountains, from wilderness to urban green space to grand bodies of water, their most intimate and most precious experiences are tied to public lands. This connection cannot be measured easily, but that makes it no less valuable. It transcends politics and religion, and has deep roots in every region of our country.

As with improving individual lives, outdoor recreation propels our economy; through job creation, manufacturing, patronage of local businesses, and so much more. Fishing rods and rifles, backpacks and tents, not to mention the multitude of both functional and popular fashions in outerwear, all need to be manufactured somewhere. Whether it's parkas or swimsuits, there are tens of thousands of small manufacturers scattered around the world, including in rural or remote areas across the country. As any governor worth their salt knows, rural job creation is far more elusive and therefore more valuable than many other forms of economic development.

All of this we somewhat knew in Colorado's Governor's Office when Luis came in to discuss this novel idea we were considering: to start an official Office of Outdoor Recreation. Our neighboring state of Utah had just created such an office, and our total ignorance of what they were doing had whet our appetite to construct something new and our own. Luis made all of our wild ideas, our inclinations and intuitions, suddenly tangible. Within minutes we knew we had not only an idea of a new statewide office, but we'd also found our first director.

Luis helped evolve the concept of "topophilia," or love of place. There is a theory that we have a genetic inclination to love the places where we live, where we were born and raised. This affection for place would provide a preferential benefit to help humans survive famines and all manner of attacks and natural disasters. In times of extreme danger those who best knew and understood their local terrain and topography would have the highest probability of survival. While topophilia, this love of place, can apply to human-built cities as well as pristine wilderness, Luis saw how deeply rooted in our psyches the latter is.

I will leave the reader to discover in Luis' own words the story of how he weaved together the elements of the outdoor recreation industry to help build what is quickly becoming an international movement. The passion that led Luis to climb his first mountain continues to guide him to this day. He has first and foremost been a true servant-leader, and this book is a remarkable look at how one life, and by extension almost any life, can affect great change.

One thing is certain: the more people who use and experience our public lands, the more people who will want to protect these lands for future generations. If this book can engage more people in the mission to which Luis has dedicated his life, this world will be a better place!

—Sen. John W. Hickenlooper (D-CO), former Governor of Colorado and Mayor of Denver

COURAGE AND TRANSFORMATION

ERIK WEIHENMAYER

Back in 2000, there weren't too many people looking to partner up with a blind guy to climb Mt. Everest. One invitee responded, "I wouldn't touch that expedition with a ten-foot pole." I get it: Climbing with me can be a bit slower and take more work, but I like to think the rewards are richer, too. My friend Luis Benitez, who stood on the summit of Everest next to me after years of preparation and an undying belief in my abilities, would tend to agree. He could have easily written the famous Helen Keller Quote, "the best and most beautiful things in the world cannot be seen or even touched. They must be felt with the heart. " Luis saw possibilities when others saw limitations, and our achievement together has been the seed of our deep and lasting friendship. And what an honor it's been over the last twenty years watching his incredible trajectory, from our experience together to his advocacy fighting to protect the gift of America's wild spaces. Working for Colorado Governor John Hickenlooper, Luis set his sights on coalescing the growing community of outdoor enthusiasts, governmental agencies, and the thousands of outdoor businesses that only thrive through our healthy forests, deserts, mountains, and rivers.

The subjects within this book speak to who Luis is at his core: someone who believes that politics, policy, and the outdoors is inextricably connected, and that our impact as climbers on the global scale has vast capacity. In fact, politics and climbing were hurled together in the most violent way in the immediate aftermath of our Everest climb. Soon after submitting and getting down to base camp, we were celebrating our accomplishments and fielding calls from across the world, when the Nepali Minister's office contacted us to share some special news. The royal family of Nepal—the King, Queen, Prince, and Princess— would very much like to have an audience with us at the palace.

It would be a politically public meeting, so the American embassy asked to meet and brief us on royal family protocol. I remember Luis asking us in mild bewilderment, "Isn't it amazing that a group of dirtbags like us warrants an audience with a royal family and an ambassador? What should we press for? Insurance for Sherpas? More organized garbage removal on the big mountains? Better social services in Kathmandu? We cannot waste this chance to help."

While most of us were focused on the upcoming American style BBQ, Luis was able to see the unique role in which we had been placed, and realized if we didn't leverage the opportunity, then we were missing the boat. But above Namche Bazaar, we got the terrible news that the royal family had been assassinated by the Prince, who shot himself in the head after murdering his family. We flew into a chaotic Kathmandu. The government had declared Martial Law. The streets were on fire with flaming vehicles, tires, and trash. Loud, angry riots enveloped us. Police in riot gear barricaded themselves behind concrete bunkers with AK-47s pointing at the crowds. As we were trying to navigate to our hotel, one of my teammates shoved my head down as a flaming brick flew inches over my head. I shuttered, surviving Everest, and almost being killed on the streets of Kathmandu . . .

Luis and I both learned a lot from our Everest team leader, Pasquale "PV" Scaturro. As we descended and made it past the Khumbu Icefall, PV pulled me aside. At first, I assumed he was going to ask me to sign his baseball cap. But Instead, he said, "Erik, your life is about to change, in ways you probably can't imagine. But do me a favor: Don't make Everest the greatest thing you ever do!"

My first response was that this was the most poorly timed motivational advice in the history of the world. I'd lost almost 35 pounds; all I wanted to do was go home and drink Hazelnut lattes and eat chocolate croissants. However, after the initial shock wore off, I began to see the wisdom. He continued, "There's a tendency to put your trophies on the shelf and hang your honors on the wall, but those things can become your funeral. Always look forward. This experience isn't a resume builder. It's a catalyst to more growth, more learning, more impact. Don't waste it."

Each of our teams took PV's advice to heart. Luis went back and reached the top of the world six more times. PV rafted the entire Blue Nile from source to sea, thousands of miles and over a year—a first in history. With the help of my team, I founded No Barriers, a nonprofit organization with the mission to help those with challenges, both physical and emotional, rediscover themselves and reclaim their lives. Our work is predicated on our strong belief, "What's within you is stronger than what's in your way."

Through our outdoor programs, using the mountains and rivers as a laboratory to discover potential, we've helped our community make big and sometimes hard, changes. Folks have started businesses and founded their own nonprofits, have lost 50 pounds, gotten off painkillers and other drugs, written books, completed ultra-marathons, and so many more milestones. And some of our most successful programs have focused on injured veterans, and that's where Luis once again stepped into my life and elevated my path.

As the 10th anniversary of our Everest climb approached, my team and I sat around brainstorming how to celebrate the milestone. Lots of ideas were thrown around: a Disney cruise, a trip to Burning Man. But when we dug deeper, we knew the mountains had transformed our lives in profound ways, and we wanted to see if that held true for others. In the first decade of the millennium, we witnessed hundreds of news stories showing veterans returning from Iraq and Afghanistan suffering from the devastating wounds of war. So in 2010, We began reaching out to the VA and various vet organizations, to recruit a team of veterans for a Himalayan mountain expedition. We ultimately settled on Lobuche, a 6,000-meter peak in the Khumbu region, ten miles from Everest. We brought aboard service men and women with a mix of challenges: those missing limbs, a soldier blinded by a road-side bomb, a soldier who survived sexual trauma and a suicide attempt, those with traumatic brain injuries and those with post-traumatic stress who had watched best friends and loved-ones die next to them. Drawing on his experience leading Outward-Bound courses, Luis crafted a program equal part physically and emotionally strenuous, an experience that we hoped would tie the team together and help them move forward. Ironically, we were asking the vets to face adversity once again, but this time with the tools, the team, and the mindset to thrive. Afterwards, one veteran said that he'd been to five years of counseling, but this one-month expedition had done even more to affect positive changes in his life. We certainly didn't have it all figured out, but we knew we were on to something that could elevate people's lives.

One experience symbolized the entire trip for me. Steve Baskis was not only blind, but also hard-of-hearing and using a barely functioning hand – all suffered in a bomb blast. One morning, we prepared to cross a river on our approach to basecamp. Some of the team were able to hop from rock to rock, but we soon realized Steve was going to struggle. The river was swift and cold. In response, the team began to pile rocks in the water, building a bridge. We stacked and threw rocks in the rushing current, until the walkway was ready. Then, the vets stood in the water on both sides of the bridge, reaching up to support Steve as he wobbled unsteadily across. Sometimes, the river is just too wide, and we need a little help to make our way home or move forward into a new life. I owe Luis for teaching us many of these lessons.

Luis Benitez has been right at the heart of the outdoor industry through some of its most challenging times, leading important discourse about the balance of public access and preservation, and helping to shape the conversation surrounding consumerism and sustainability. His perspective provides a roadmap and clear guidance on the challenges that certainly lie ahead. The need to galvanize the political voice and force of our economy is clear, and this book is the first real effort to elevate that voice to power.

— Erik Weihenmayer
First blind man to summit Mt. Everest

The outdoor recreation industry is booming. It now employs more than 5 million people and delivers an annual economic impact of $1.1 trillion. That means more Americans than ever are enjoying the outdoors, which holds tremendous promise for our collective future. In his new book, "Higher Ground: How the Outdoor Recreation Industry Can Save the World," Luis Benitez explains how connecting people to nature addresses multiple societal ills at once.

At Trust for Public Land (TPL), where Luis serves as Chief Impact Officer, we believe access to the outdoors is a fundamental human need—essential to our health and well-being. Vibrant landscapes boost physical and mental health; bridge social divides; foster equitable communities, and help mitigate the climate crisis, both by storing greenhouse gases and defending towns and cities against weather extremes.

TPL is committed to the hard, but critical work of creating more places that bring us outside, whether parks, trails, playgrounds, or public lands. To that end, the conservation field and the outdoor recreation industry are natural partners. After all, the outdoor sector has flourished, in large part, because of the nation's bountiful public lands.

Today there is an opportunity for bold action in the outdoor realm, one that provides more communities with equitable access to the forests and rivers, grasslands and parks, that have fueled the outdoor industry's growth. Creating more accessible public spaces is a virtuous cycle for all of us, including the outdoor industry. The need is great. According to TPL's data scientists, more than 1 in 3 Americans—or 100 million people, including 28 million children—do not have access to a park within a 10-minute walk from home.

Despite these challenges, I am filled with hope for the future. In our first 50 years, TPL protected 4 million acres of land, created 5,420 parks and outdoor spaces, and connected nearly 10 million people to the outdoors. Over the next 50, we need to protect land and build parks and green spaces 10 times faster than we've done in the past, because that is what this moment requires. I am confident that, moving forward, conservationists and our outdoor recreation partners will work hand in hand to do just that--healing our environment and, in turn, letting it heal us.

—Diane Regas
Chief Executive Officer, Trust for Public Land

For KMJ my rock,
SGB my light,
and SAB my compass.

Chapter 1

LEFT SIDE, RIGHT SIDE, UNITED OUTSIDE

"Every man is tasked to make his life, even in its details, worthy of the contemplation of his most elevated and critical hour." —Henry David Thoreau

I was approaching the Hillary Step, arguably Mount Everest's most famous feature. This was my first time on the world's highest peak, and though the forty-foot wall of rock wasn't supposed to be hard by conventional climbing standards, its location at the oxygen-starved elevation of 28,839 feet would make it a considerable challenge. Tackling it blind is a whole other matter. Climbing just behind me as part of my ropeteam was Erik Weihenmayer, the first blind man to attempt to summit Everest.

The bright morning sun shone off the white snow of the Southeast Ridge, a knife edge half a sidewalk wide. On the right side was a snow cornice, overhanging a 10,000-foot vertical fall into Tibet. On the left was a 7,000-foot plunge into Nepal, where we'd started our journey and wound our way from Everest Basecamp through the notorious Khumbu Icefall, to camps I through IV, and finally onto the Summit Ridge. Our footsteps were the culmination of sixty-five days on the mountain, nine weeks total in Nepal, and more than two years of planning and preparation.

At a relatively young twenty-seven, and craving a shot at

Everest, I'd attached myself, for this 2001 attempt, to Erik's team through sheer will. A former middle-school teacher, Erik had summited Denali and Kilimanjaro, the highest mountains in North America and Africa respectively, but it wasn't until he ran into a swashbuckling expedition leader and Everest veteran from Denver named Pasquale Scaturro that the dream of Everest became a possibility.

Scaturro was my in. I hounded him in Denver, stopping by his office weekly to lobby for a spot on the team. Pasquale later said that because of the tenacity I'd shown, he felt he had no choice but to invite me. In preparing for Everest, we'd ice climbed all over Colorado, and been humbled by a failed shakedown expedition the autumn before to 22,349-foot Ama Dablam in Nepal.

Now, we were just 200 vertical feet from the top of the world. We'd started this final push at 10:30 p.m. the night before, climbing through the night. We were stepping in the postholes of the mountaineers ahead of us, moving in slow motion.

Not only was the air too thin to move at anything but half time, but we were bogged down by heavy gear. We wore down-filled suits, thick boots designed for the extreme conditions on Everest, and bulky mittens. Into our pockets we'd each tucked a radio and a headlamp with a hockey-puck-sized battery, and we each carried an ice axe, a backpack with an oxygen tank, and liters of water. The suit weighs 15 pounds alone, and by the time you've filled it with gear, it's an additional 20 pounds. At 27,000 feet, it feels like you're walking through wet concrete. We plodded along at about one step every three seconds.

Using a short cord, Erik had clipped his climbing harness into a fixed rope that ran along the ridge, set by teams of Sherpas and guides. The line is good in theory—it will keep a falling climber from plunging thousands of feet. But in the thin air, even with supplemental oxygen, it would be incredibly taxing to haul a person back up. I kept the rope between us really tight.

"Two questions, Luis," said Erik, moving his face mask aside. "How does it look, and are we there yet?"

"Buddy, it's a cakewalk," I said. "We're there." Internally, however, I was thinking, *I don't know how we are going to get up 40 feet of near-vertical rock known as the Hillary Step.*

We'd almost blown the whole thing just the night before. After leaving Camp IV, which is dug in on a high windswept plateau at 26,000 feet, at 10:30 p.m., by 11:30 p.m. and after climbing through a blizzard, we'd reached the Balcony—a semi-level snowfield the size of half a tennis court—of the Southeast Ridge/ South Col Route, at 27,500 feet, after climbing there from Camp IV through a blizzard. Exhausted and exasperated by the whiteout conditions, our team of nineteen people collapsed in a pile to preserve warmth in the wind and lashing snow. We lay there in the open for 45 minutes, debating whether to turn back because of the impossible conditions. Our headlamps were switched off, and our oxygen bottles were turned down as low as possible. We barely breathed. We knew we wouldn't get another shot.

I was mentally steeling myself to abort the mission, running the internal monologue of "live to climb another day," when from the radio came a broken transmission from far below at basecamp.

"Don't turn around, don't turn around," squawked our basecamp manager's voice from the radios tucked into our suits. Looking at the weather radar, he could see a break in the clouds approaching. The storm would clear.

We stood up, still in the howling whiteout, but within five minutes of trudging up the ridge, the clouds parted. Stars flickered in the black sky above us.

Now in the alpenglow of morning, nearing the Hillary Step—named after Sir Edmund Hillary, the first Westerner to summit Everest—I was having doubts about our ability to get to the summit and back down again safely: *What if Erik falls and I can't pull him back up? What if one of us suffers a sudden onset of pulmonary or cerebral edema?* It happens. Hundreds of people have died on the peak, many of them from causes—hypothermia, exposure, altitude sickness, exhaustion—other than falling. Their bodies just couldn't take the inhuman conditions.

Instead, I focused on believing in Erik as much as he'd believed in me. For the crux of the route, he'd trusted the youngest member of the team. One who'd never been to this altitude before. I'd taken over the guiding from the South Summit from Chris Morris, whose voice had been reduced to a whisper after needing to pull down his mask so much to share guidance with Erik. For some reason, my own voice was fine. We pressed onward—up the Summit Ridge and Hillary Step. Our team was spread out along the ridge. Never before had there been a more eclectic and varied bunch on the highest mountain on Earth. Many of us were unproven guides who at that point had nominal success at moderate altitudes. We were two full-time guides, one part-time guide who earned a living as a physician's assistant, an architect and his father, an expedition leader who was an oil and gas exploration expert, and an ER doctor.

Climbing above 26,000 ft, climbers typically utilize bottled oxygen to stay warm and focused. We always joked that we were doing a partial oxygenless ascent because the way we guided Erik up Everest was by talking him through it, which meant removing our oxygen masks from our faces. When we wanted him to take a step up, we'd indicate how high by telling him to step to "ankle," "shin," or "knee" height. We used the image of a clock, like the system pilots use, to indicate direction. So, if we wanted him to step high and to the right, it might be, "Erik: 2 o'clock, knee step." For hands, we used the clock plus "shoulder," "head," or "overhead" height. If there was a ladder, it might be, "Erik: 12 o'clock ladder, nine rungs." If the terrain was level or gently sloping, we'd lead him by ringing a bear bell, which is a little bell designed to make noise to scare off any bears close by.

Not everyone was cheering us and our innovative guiding techniques. Our expedition was controversial. Many other guides on the mountain that spring thought we were engaged in a reckless stunt, one that would get Erik, and maybe others, killed. Back in 2001, the relentless self-promotion practiced by today's social-media stars was barely on the horizon. Many feared we'd just continue a trail of carnage that had begun in 1996, when guided expeditions left a trail of eight bodies up and down the mountain in the wake of a massive storm. But we'd trained hard for more than a year, absorbing the tough lessons learned on our unsuccessful attempt at Ama Dablam in the fall of 2000. In what turned out to be one of the lowest snow years on record, with some of the warmest temps, we learned together how to sharpen our communication with Erik—instead of long, drawn-out explanations of what to do and why, we created our own shorthand code. We weren't reckless. We were committed and humble, and united by an ideological goal—to help Erik prove to the world that people with disabilities are capable of so much more than is expected of them.

When at last we arrived at the Hillary Step, I clipped Erik into the fixed rope running up the vertical wall and climbed above him, leaning down and verbally directing his hands and feet.

It took us 70 minutes to climb 40 vertical feet—one groping hand, then foot, at a time. At the top of the Step, all that was left was 160 feet of gently sloping ridgeline. Erik was clipped into the fixed line right to the summit. All he'd have to do was follow the rope.

"Go ahead, buddy," I said. "You are about to stand on top of the world."

Erik said, "You go first—you've been guiding your heart out for the last three hours."

"Let's go together," I said. We linked arms and strolled to the top at 10:25 a.m. on May 25, 2001.

The summit of Mount Everest is a surreal place. For the first time in your life, nothing is above you. Erik could sense that, too. "As long as I can remember," he later said, "I've been used to sound bouncing off of things from every direction. This time it only bounced from one direction—straight down."

From the summit, I could see every peak I'd ever dreamed of climbing—Lhotse, Nuptse, Makalu, Manaslu. I'd studied the entire Himalayan range on maps that folded out of *National Geographic* magazines and in the books I'd pored over as a sickly Midwestern kid suffering from asthma, dreaming of this day. I could see the glaciers fanning down the valleys, and climbers working their way up the Northeast Ridge route from Tibet, the mysterious kingdom.

I was overwhelmed with emotion, from today's effort and twenty-seven years of aspiration, and still scared out of my mind. I knelt in the snow and said a little prayer of gratitude. More of our expedition members arrived, one by one. We'd vowed that if Erik didn't summit, none of us would. I was proud of my own accomplishment, and to have fulfilled the dream I began as a child. But I was even prouder of the teamwork and indivisible spirit that had made our record-setting expedition possible. Even then, I understood that a group united in a common cause, one larger than themselves, is stronger than any individual. Eventually, nineteen of our team of twenty-one members would summit that day, and all of us returned home safely.

****

The best mountaineers are optimists, a mentor of mine once said. That mentor is Mark Udall, the former Colorado senator and a fine mountaineer in his own right, with first ascents to his name in Colorado and Nepal. He well understands that to reach a summit, it takes not only the optimism to strive for an audacious goal, but to set out on that uphill climb despite the obstacles of weather, gravity, and the mountains sending snow and rock tumbling down upon you. Similarly, Mark said that optimists make the best politicians. As a senator and scion of a famous family of politicians and conservationists, he understands the perseverance needed to build a political movement to make the world a better place.

I, too, have been a professional mountaineer. I've stood on top of Mount Everest six times. I've led dozens of expeditions to the highest summits on every continent—in South America, where my father is from, Africa, Alaska, and even Antarctica. I've reveled in the rosy glow of countless alpine sunrises and the satisfaction of fulfilling my childhood mountaineering dreams. I've also seen sunrises from duck blinds, growing up as a hunter in Missouri, my first exposure to outdoor adventure. I sat in those blinds alongside my grandfather, a WWII veteran and hunting and fishing guide who went on to own a St. Louis sporting-goods store. I worked in that store on weekends, helping stock shotgun shells and folding apparel and outerwear while ringing up customers.

My first exposure to high-altitude mountains was in Ecuador, visiting my father's family on their farm near the 19,000-foot glacier-capped volcanoes Cayambe and Cotopaxi when I was a boy in the 1980s. I hustled after my uncle Peppin on mountain trails and later cut my teeth as an assistant guide on Cotopaxi. In high school in the Midwestern United States, I discovered rock climbing and quickly became obsessed. Through the sport, I formed my first friendships and grew from a misfit to someone comfortable in his own skin and focused on his future goals of becoming an international mountain guide.

I often tell people who ask about my trajectory in this industry that everything good in my life has come from outdoor recreation, from the love and mentoring of my grandfather and my Ecuadorian uncles to the personal growth I gained rock climbing that helped me transcend the difficulties of adolescence. Early on, in my twenties, my career as an Outward Bound instructor in my twenties gave me not only experience teaching, but also in leading people with a moral compass that informs my decision-making to this day. That morality was why, when I witnessed an unconscionable massacre high on a Tibetan peak in 2006, I was unable to stay silent despite the peer pressure and had to largely forfeit a guiding career I'd worked a lifetime to build.

As I shifted gears, I instead looked for ways to make the world a better place by zeroing in on our society's power centers, leading executives through leadership workshops steeped in the moral training I'd received at Outward Bound. We trained in how to be more effective leaders, which usually means being more *humane* leaders. I eventually brought that mission to the VF Corporation, a Fortune 250 company comprising thirteen venerable outdoor adventure apparel and footwear brands like The North Face and Smartwool, working as the company's vice president of global impact and government affairs. My mission was to make sure the company was creating its products as ethically as possible, both in terms of human labor and in using less harmful materials. I also directed the corporation's charitable giving through the VF Foundation, helping fund projects in ninety-three countries with over seventy grant partners focusing on equitable access to the outdoors, education, and workforce development via the evolution of the trades and freedom of expression.

Between my time in the industry sectors of manufacturing, leadership development, guiding, and retail, dating back to my grandfather's shop, I noticed one unquestionably consistent thing about the outdoor industry: it unfailingly attracts good people. My theory is that the pastimes it supports require challenging skill building—from tying fishing flies to scaling sheer rock walls—and involve repeated failure and re-focused effort. That begets humility. That humility seems like an antidote we could all use in today's world. Make no mistake, like most other economies driven by larger industry segments in the United States we have our flaws, but my argument is simple, and it is clear. There is no other bi-partisan industry in our country that currently encourages rural and urban economic development, fosters in all of those places a deeper understanding of conservation and stewardship efforts, and elevates the national dialogue around public health via encouraging all that live in the US to spend time outside.

My gratitude for all that outdoor recreation has given me was behind the most unexpected turn of my life—government service. As the son of an immigrant and an indifferent student in my youth, I was shocked to find myself working directly with the governor of Colorado. In 2015, then-governor (now senator) John Hickenlooper asked me to lead the state's first Office of the Outdoor Recreation Industry. The idea was to be a government liaison and advocate for Colorado's outdoor-recreation businesses. I'd be working on behalf of Summit County's ski resorts and for hunting guides in the town of Rangely, as well as with growing gear manufacturers like Big Agnes and established retail giants like REI, who has a flagship store in Denver. Helping those businesses thrive meant improving access to outdoor recreation across the state by working with state parks and the national forests to build more trails, more bike paths, and even more whitewater rapids. In the same way the airline industry relies on the FAA and air-traffic controllers, and the transportation industry on highway departments, the outdoor industry needs government oversight of the places where we play.

Yet as honored as I was to be asked, the opportunity required sacrifice, a step back in pay, and a move from the mountain community of Eagle, where my wife and I had, beginning in 2014, made a home while we were still dating. We wrestled with the decision, but the chance to be of service to the industry and community won the day. I got to work.

In my four years—from 2015 to 2019—as the director of Colorado's Office of the Outdoor Recreation Industry, we grew that sector of the economy from $23 billion to $63 billion, recruiting businesses and individuals who saw the state as a great place to work, and more importantly, live. Promoting Colorado's recreational amenities to visitors and prospective businesses wasn't enough, though. I realized that ours was an industry that needed more support from academia, in the same way that the medical profession, the engineering professions and tech rely on universities to train and cultivate new talent. We needed to educate workers who could make the outdoor-recreation economy more resilient, and more importantly, sustainable. I urged Western Colorado University, in Gunnison, to create the nation's first MBA focused on outdoor rec in 2018, and had a hand in the creation of the University of Colorado Boulder's Master's of Economics of the Outdoor Recreation Economy, and University of Denver's Leadership in Outdoor Recreation Industry program. My industry was growing up.

I wasn't the only one realizing it. There was a national movement for the outdoor industry to be more involved in protecting and developing our playgrounds and natural play spaces for children in urban corridors and nurturing the essential conditions for our businesses. One tool was to establish the importance of our industry to the national economy. The numbers are huge.

In 2021, visits to national parks alone generated $20.5 billion in direct spending at hotels, restaurants, outfitters, and other amenities in nearby gateway communities, supporting over 322,600 jobs and generating over $42.5 billion in total economic output. The outdoor-recreation economy numbers for 2022 were just released by the Bureau of Economic Analysis (BEA). Turns out we are worth 1.1 trillion dollars in total gross output. Between the likes of gear manufacturers such as Columbia, whitewater-rafting outfitters in West Virginia, and bike shops in Moab, Utah. Again in 2022, we accounted for 5 million jobs, the majority of them in small businesses. We represent 2.2 percent of the GDP, and 3.2 percent of US employment.

In fact, the outdoor recreation industry is larger than the mineral-extraction industry, which only accounts for 1.8 percent of the country's GDP. This illustrates the stakes perfectly: Isn't a hiking trail just as important to our economy as an oil well? Why should our industry have to rely on a constellation of nonprofits like the Access Fund and the Trust for Public Land and the Appalachian Mountain Club to ensure that our businesses can continue to thrive by building and maintaining our recreation sites and our trails? Imagine just how different things would be if our industry's lobbying efforts were as sophisticated as the other economies in the United States. We need to treat recreational infrastructure the same way we treat transportation and the extractive-industries infrastructure—as vital to our national interests.

This type of investment works. According to the State of Virginia, in 2019, for every $1.00 of general tax revenue provided to state parks in Virginia, the parks brought in $17.68. That same year, the National Park System generated more than 30 times as much as the federal government invested. Look at Columbus, Ohio, which in 2023 converted an abandoned limestone quarry into a 180-acre park featuring mountain-bike trails, lakes for paddling, and a via ferrata rock-climbing course along the quarry's 150-foot-tall cliff face. That new park follows the city's 2009 investment in a climbing wall open to the public that is amongst the nation's largest. "Our goal with that park was to keep urban young professionals in Columbus," the city's park operations manager told *Outside* magazine.

Columbus is putting into play a trend that Salt Lake City has been benefiting from for years. In 2021, a University of Utah study looked at Utah's booming tech sector. The study found that 85 percent of tech workers working in the state chose to stay despite being offered a higher salary elsewhere, citing the outdoor-recreation opportunities as their motivation. For those workers who left and then returned, 62 percent said outdoor recreation was their primary reason, compared to 49 percent who said that family was the most important factor.

We aren't just talking about rock climbers and bird watchers. The outdoor-recreation economy encompasses motorsports fans too, featuring big-ticket items like Jet Skis, powerboats, and Quad-Runners. Dirt moto-bikers like me value long, challenging trails, where we can get away from suburbia and leave our problems behind, taking a mental-health break.

We are realizing that outdoor recreation has benefits beyond just fun. Studies are increasingly showing that time outside is a critical component of physical and mental health. Even just living near green space can provide a stunning array of advantages. In one Danish study, researchers used satellite data to assess children's exposure to green space, correlating each child's place of residence with nearby parks. Children who lived in neighborhoods with more green space had a reduced risk of depression, mood disorders, schizophrenia, eating disorders, and substance abuse later in life. Those with the lowest levels of green-space exposure during childhood had a 55 percent higher risk of developing mental illnesses than those who'd grown up with abundant green space. (Now imagine those same, city-bound kids with access to safe, green-lined pathways and a bicycle.) That was just one of the studies referenced in the Colorado Outdoor Rx Report my office produced illustrate to government departments the importance of allocating resources for better access for outdoor recreation, whether in the wild or in urban planning.

****

To get the word out about outdoor recreation's value for our health and our economy, I knew there needed to be more people like me working in state governments. With the governor's blessing, I personally met with delegations from a half dozen states including Montana and Michigan, urging them to create their own positions. The number of offices rose from two to eight in just three years and included states from both sides of the political spectrum, from Wyoming to Vermont. That felt significant in such a partisan political climate.

Realizing we'd be more effective all pulling in the same direction, we drafted the Confluence Accords. The document is an operational charter for state outdoor-recreation (ORec) offices and stands on four distinct pillars: economic development (keep this economy strong); conservation and stewardship (without the wild places, there would be no reason to buy that new fleece jacket); education and workforce development (where will the next generation of leadership for this industry come from and what will their education look like?); and, above all, public health (this was validated, for instance, by the returning-veteran community, which showed a significant decrease in traumatic brain injury [TBI] and post-traumatic stress disorder [PTSD] impacts by spending time outside, and has been codified by the handful of nations like Japan that can now formally—by a doctor— prescribe time outside instead of medication). The Accords are an agreement that each state agency signing on will work on behalf of each of those pillars.

Eleven states have signed the Confluence Accords, with more on the way. How many other industries have made a formal agreement to work for the greater good of society? None that I can think of.

That alignment across the industry and the states has led to some remarkable bipartisan political wins in recent years, at a time when such wins are nearly extinct. Armed with the GDP numbers and scientific studies, outdoor-recreation-industry leaders were major players in advocating for the John D. Dingell Jr. Conservation, Management, and Recreation Act in 2019, which created 1.3 million acres of Wilderness and ten new Wild and Scenic River segments, and increased the size of three national parks, amongst dozens of other conservation acts in dozens of states. The Senate passed it by a 92–8 vote, and it was signed into law by President Trump.

The following year saw similar bipartisan support for the Great American Outdoors Act, which permanently allocated $900 million annually to the Land and Water Conservation Fund, a source for recreational infrastructure created in 1965. The fund helped create some $18 billion in boat ramps, bike paths, and state parks over the years, but was allowed to lapse in 2018 amidst partisan bickering. The Great American Outdoors Act also allocated $9.5 billion to reduce the infamous National Park Service maintenance backlog. Some called it the most significant conservation legislation in a half century. The only thing both sides of the political aisle can agree on, seemingly, is funding and conservation for outdoor recreation.

Those successes have led us to start asking whether it is time to push Washington, D.C., to create a federal outdoor-recreation-industry office to continue the promotion and preservation of this unique and special economy and ecosystem. As we saw earlier, outdoor recreation comprises nearly 2 percent of our nation's economy and provides priceless quality-of-life and health benefits to our people, but there's no specific entity shepherding it in the federal government. Imagine how much more effective we could be with dedicated leadership?

What would such an agency do? Firstly, it would convene the state offices, which will hopefully eventually number 50, and help channel money their way. The Great American Outdoors Act shows there's an appetite for such spending across the political spectrum. We've also been able to educate D.C. about the value of such investments. The American Rescue Plan Act of 2021, for example, earmarks $750 million for investments in outdoor-recreation travel and tourism. The problem is, many local governments don't know how to access those funds. Furthermore, I believe the time has come for recreationists to ante up and pay into the system. Hunters and fishermen have, through special taxes on guns, ammunition, and fishing tackle approved decades ago, been helping pay for conservation and scientific management of wildlife habitat to the tune of $23 billion over the lifetime of the legislation that created the funding. Likewise, I think those of us using trails and boat ramps should help invest in their preservation. Similar taxes have been wildly successful in Minnesota, Missouri, and Georgia. It's time for us, too, to pay to play.

A national director of outdoor recreation would also help coordinate federal agencies like the United States Forest Service (USFS), National Park Service (NPS), Bureau of Land Management (BLM), and any other agency that managed land or resources of benefit to outdoor recreation. Right now, that's the job of the Federal Interagency Council on Outdoor Recreation (FICOR). It was created in 2011, and before it was dissolved by the Trump Administration, FICOR made significant strides on behalf of outdoor recreation, including combining most federal permits and reservations into the Recreation.gov website and helping the Bureau of Economic Analysis measure the economic impact of the ORec industry. Under the Biden Administration, FICOR is back, but the problem is that its leadership rotates annually between the agencies, so FICOR doesn't have the full attention of any of them.

It's an idea that already has a precedent. From 1962 until the late 1970s, there actually existed a federal Bureau of Outdoor Recreation, which worked on both the national and local levels to promote outdoor recreation. In addition to creating some of the foundational research on the health benefits of outdoor recreation, and on the importance of equity in getting Americans outside, the bureau was a prime driver behind some of the nation's seminal recreation and conservation legislation, including the Wilderness Act in 1964 and the creation of the Land and Water Conservation Fund that same year. The bureau was also the originator of the idea of rails to trails, converting abandoned railway lines into recreational pathways, and helped fund some of the earliest rail-to-trail projects in nine states including California, Maryland, and Pennsylvania.

The Bureau of Outdoor Recreation also set the precedent of cooperation between federal agencies to foster recreation. Even more prescient was its approach of establishing cooperation between such federal agencies and the states to create parks and trail systems. Ultimately, the Bureau of Outdoor Recreation was subsumed into the National Park Service in 1981. Because it had no real funding of its own, and couldn't make its own policy, it was easy prey for the anti-conservationists of the Reagan Administration.

Before you start thinking, "Uh oh, this smells like Big Government," I'd assure you that it doesn't need to be. I did my job with the State of Colorado with just my salary, a gas card, and a laptop. The outdoor industry is great at getting by with minimal resources—give us a roll of duct tape and some bailing wire, and we'll cobble something together. Furthermore, I would challenge you to ask yourself if you are comfortable with nonprofits and trade associations alone protecting and promoting our birthright, the public lands that Teddy Roosevelt called "America's best idea"?

In our frenetic, disconnected society, we need the outdoors now more than ever. The rise of virtual reality makes me shudder for my daughter's future; instead, I'm doing everything I can to introduce her to nature-based reality. I want to build her resilience with exposure to bug bites, wet, muddy shoes, and the ability to control panic when our whitewater raft gets off course in a rapid. Every kid—and every American of any age—should have that opportunity, no matter their race, creed, or gender identification.

That fact was never more apparent than during the Covid-19 pandemic. With facilities like bowling alleys, waterparks, and sports bars closed, our public parks, pathways, and national parks all saw record visitation. That was wonderful—people who seldom recreated outside were meeting up with their friends and family in the great outdoors. It became their emotional and spiritual salvation. We learned two things, though: not everyone had access to such opportunities because the communities where they live are underserved by public open space and mentors to get them into the outdoors. That needs to change. And secondly, that much of that public open space suffered. Trails were strewn with trash and human feces. Bonfire scars appeared in pristine meadows. We were loving nature to death. Not only for the next public health crisis, but for every American's well-being, we need more trails, paddle-able lakes, and pathways, and we need to take better care of the ones we already have. Most importantly, we need to see these resources as a vital part of our nation's infrastructure.

I come from a household of a Latino immigrant father who is a staunch Republican and an American mother who is a diehard Democrat. My American grandfather with the sporting-goods store? A Republican who married an Italian-American Democrat. Heck, I even went and married a Republican. (I am sensing a trend, now that I write all of this down!) However, there is one thing we all agree on: the importance of the great outdoors. It, and the industry that supports it, might be politicized from time to time from both sides, but it is truly overall the one remaining economy of its scale that knows no political stripe. At its core, it is bipartisan in nature. No side claims the outdoors as their own—they can't. It belongs to all of us. From the parent in a city who takes their child to see the falling leaves in their local park, to the family that hops in the car to visit a national monument, how we protect and promote the outdoors, I would argue, requires a different way of looking at government involvement and support.

You are about to read about the journey of my life, and about what led to the governor asking me to take on this role. People often comment that the arc and trajectory of their careers rarely intersect with who they are as a person. But if you *are* lucky enough to step into and find that rare moment when you can connect the magic of who you are with the impact of what you get to do every day, and you are willing to answer the call, magic happens. This is my story and my belief about how the great outdoors, and the industry that supports it, can impact our morality of hope.

Chapter 2

ASTHMA AND HEALTH

"Do not pray for easy times. Pray to be stronger men! Do not pray for tasks equal to your powers. Pray for powers equal to your tasks." —John F. Kennedy

"Breathe, honey. C'mon, Lucho, sweetheart, breathe . . ." I am eight years old, responding to Lucho, my family nickname, surrounded by darkness with an ever-growing monster pressing on my chest. I know this feeling, this terror; I am growing used to this fear of asthma rising from my lungs as the rest of the world sleeps. It is so severe that the dander raised from petting the neighbor's cat has sent me to the hospital not once, but three times.

If we mowed the lawn, grass clippings could send me to the emergency room. I'm that pale, wheezy kid, squinting at the bright sunshine, as often I am forced to stay inside and watch the world go by through the living room window.

"Mom? Mom, is that you?" I suspect we are off to the hospital, where I will play the role of human pincushion yet again for more allergy tests.

"Mom?"

"No, we aren't going to the emergency room. Dammit, you useless moron, wake the fuck up and stop calling me Mom!"

Fuzzy-headed, I am hearing the hiss of oxygen; it sounds like the hospital, but it's so cold. *Am I dreaming? Really cold now, hospitals are always so cold, but now I feel something cold on my face. Why would they put ice on my face?*

"Mom?"

"GODDAMIT, YOU IDIOT—WAKE UP!"

Okay, Mom doesn't talk like that. This realization snaps me back to reality. I focus my eyes and can just make out the little nylon coffin I am squeezed into with one of my best friends, the climber and photographer Didrik Johnck. As the wind screams around our tent like a banshee, I open my eyes to see Didrik looking like a space-age aardvark, with an oxygen mask, the sort that jet pilots use, strapped to his face. The only thing I see sticking out of his sleeping bag is the snout of his mask and his concerned eyes above it.

"Welcome back to Planet Earth, amigo," he says. "Glad you could join us."

"Dude, what the fuck happened?" I ask. "I really flipped out there."

"You were talking and thrashing in your sleep, so I leaned over to check your O2 bottle, and you were out. Basically, you were sucking on a mask attached to an empty bottle that was therefore suffocating you, dipshit."

What a good friend. We are at Camp IV on Mount Everest. It's May 2001, on the cusp of our summit day with Erik Weihenmayer. It's been a long time, and hundreds of grueling mountain summits, since I've felt the panic of being unable to breathe, but the memory of my disability is at the core of who I am.

****

Growing up as a kid just outside St. Louis, I suffered hundreds of asthma attacks. My chest would tighten up and my breathing would become shallow. (In Greek, *asthma* means panting.) Then I'd start to wheeze, high-pitched, an alarm, and if I could speak it was only in bursts—and then the fear began. In an asthma attack, I'm struggling to fill my lungs, raising my shoulders to my ears, extending my arms—anything to expand the chest cavity. It's the same feeling when you are out of air on a run, exhausted, but with asthma there's no slowing down to get relief. My speech is gone. I can't even call out for help.

My heart is pounding from my entire body straining to draw air. My eyes are popping out, and I'm turning pale. I can see the alarm on my mom's face as I'm slowly being strangled to death.

An asthma attack occurs when the bronchial tubes spasm and fill with fluid, restricting airflow to the alveoli. You lose this most essential survival function: respiration. Asthma isn't an infection, but the body reacts as if it's been attacked. It's terrifying, and unless the symptoms abate, it can result in death. Currently, there are 25 million Americans with asthma, and even now there's no one treatment or cure. Asthma is described as a syndrome with many different characteristics and causes, from genetics to environment.

In my case, it usually started when I was exposed to an allergen. Mold, pollen, ragweed, the neighbor's cat—all could put me into that terrifying, oxygen-less state. Even with my steroid inhalers to stave off many of the attacks, we still made hundreds of visits to the hospital. Our house was twenty minutes outside the city in farm country, which meant there were tons of particulates in the air, and that the trip to the ER was that much longer. We'd end up there as many as six times a month. I had two inhalers and a nebulizer at home. I felt deeply defective.

Part of the pressure was that my father had grown up in an Ecuadorian ranching family, in which time working outside in the fresh air was seen as a virtue. It was difficult for him to understand my limitations, especially as he was putting in very long hours working as an aerospace engineer. My mom, a primary-school art teacher, minded less, encouraging me on my inward journeys of self-expression when I was trapped indoors. My brother and sister didn't come along till much later, so all my years of physical struggle came mostly as an only child, much to my parents' relief.

I remember the visits to Dr. Boles's office for my weekly allergy tests when I was eight. They'd apply a board studded with pins to my back, each coated in some allergen. If the pinpricks caused a reaction—swelling and redness—then they'd circle the spot in Sharpie and add that allergen to the list. My mom called them "sad little Sharpie circles." As I sat on the white butcher paper on the examination table and they added another nine allergens to my list, Dr. Boles told my mom: "You are going to have to get used to the idea of Luis not being a very active kid. Consider him the boy in the bubble."

One problem with the steroid inhalers is that they caused hyperactivity. It was hard for me to sit still in school. After a couple blasts off the inhaler, my heart felt like it was going to pound out of my chest. Then, as with a sugar high, I'd crash and fall asleep in class. Recess was no help in blowing off steam because I was forced to stay inside. So there I was, the pale, wheezy, now-hyperactive kid stuck inside, alone when all the other kids were outside playing. It was involuntary introversion, torturous and lonely for a natural extrovert.

Reading became my everything. My parents had a wall of bookshelves in the living room. As a teacher, my mom loved books, and as an immigrant, my dad was motivated to learn English through reading. With so much time indoors avoiding allergens, I was reading at an eighth-grade level by second grade. Somewhat strangely, my favorite reading material was a set of Peanuts-branded encyclopedias, *Charlie Brown's Super Book of Questions and Answers*, volumes divided into animals, earth science, mechanical workings, and geography. Because I could rarely focus in school, most of my elementary education came from those books. (I recently bought the set from a rare bookseller on the internet for my daughter, Sofia.) Ultimately, too, it was reading that gave me the inspiration to move through asthma.

One day, deep into my father's collection of *National Geographics*, I came across the September 1963 issue with an article about the first American expedition to Mount Everest. On that climb was a man who had also been afflicted with asthma as a child. Jim Whittaker became the first American to summit Everest (and later, the first CEO of the outdoor-retail giant REI). I clearly remember dragging this magazine into my parents' bedroom and pointing to his picture and saying, "This guy has what I have, and if he can climb Everest, so can I. That's what I want to do—I want to be a mountain guide and climb Everest."

As a nine-year-old, I had no idea what it would take to climb the world's highest mountain, but I'm sure I realized I was going to have to get a lot stronger. I'd seen the *Rocky* movies, and knew that I needed to turn my life into a training montage. One of the first breakthroughs was competitive swimming. My mom had heard that the warm, humid environment of indoor swimming pools contained fewer allergens, and so we went. The pool didn't trigger me, and I was grateful for the chance to compete alongside other kids. More importantly, I finally got a chance to expand my lung capacity and strengthen my intercostal muscles and diaphragm, which helped offset constrictions in the bronchial tubes when an asthma attack set in.

As I aged, I became more adept at managing my asthma. I learned coping techniques like pressure breathing—forcefully exhaling from the belly, which helps improve gas exchange across the alveoli by increasing pressure in the lungs. I learned to better avoid allergens and to react more quickly with my inhaler when symptoms arose. Being able to improve my physical fitness, however, was the most important factor in beginning to live normally. Even today, when I go through periods of reduced exercise, like weeks of long work hours or intensive work travel, that old, familiar wheezing begins to return.

Reduced asthma attacks meant spending more time outside, which led to better fitness—a positive feedback loop. Of course, spending time outside was a balm in and of itself. I loved hunting and fishing with my grandfather, cherishing the peaceful, quiet (he wasn't a big talker) mornings in the Ozarks, watching sunrises and standing shin-deep in rivers flowing between verdant banks. I loved sitting outside on cool autumn days, letting the warm sun hit my face. At the most basic level, those were sensorially pleasurable experiences, but they were also improving my health, as science is starting to help us understand.

The first rigorous science on the healing power of time outside came from Japan. For decades, the Japanese have been using time in natural settings as a healing modality. It's known as *shirin-yoku*, a term coined in the 1980s and which translates roughly to "forest bathing." Between 2.5 million and 5 million people walk officially designated Forest Therapy trails in Japan each year. Starting in 2004, researchers began gathering data on hundreds of people before and after they went for leisurely forest walks and comparing these to strolls in urban environments. The walks in nature yielded a 12.4 percent decrease in the stress hormone cortisol, a 7 percent decrease in sympathetic nerve activity (the fight-or-flight response), a 1.4 percent decrease in blood pressure, and a 5.8 percent decrease in heart rate.

Those results helped kick off a host of other studies with some remarkable findings. One major study published in 2008 in *The Lancet* found that people in England living in greener areas had lower rates of death from circulatory diseases. A 2016 study from the Harvard T.H. Chan School of Public Health and Brigham and Women's Hospital compared the risk of death with the amount of plant life and vegetation near the homes of more than 100,000 women, finding that women who lived in the greenest areas had a 12 percent lower death rate than women living in the least green areas.

It has also been found that people who live in greener areas tend to have lower health-care costs. In a May 2022 study from the journal *Environment International*, researchers examined the total health-care costs of 5 million people in Northern California over a decade and compared those costs with the amount of green space around each subject's home. They found that the correlation persisted regardless of other health determinants like housing conditions, education, occupation, and income.

It's not just green spaces that help. From 2016 to 2020, researchers at the organization Blue Health Intelligence surveyed 18,000 people in 18 countries and collected information about their visits to blue spaces—adjacent to the ocean or lakes or rivers. The results suggest that not only are people living near blue spaces more physically active; they also experience higher well-being.

The evidence of the healing power of nature is overwhelming. In 2018, the journal *Environmental Research* found that a staggering 140 separate studies linked exposure to green space with health benefits ranging from lower blood pressure and cholesterol to lower rates of diabetes, stroke, heart disease, and asthma. In my case, it's possible that the time spent at my family's ranch in Ecuador each summer was helpful in curtailing my asthma.

Firstly, doctors told us that time spent at altitude would be helpful because breathing in the thinner air there—our Ecuadorian family split time between the ranch at 8,000 feet and the home in Quito at 10,000 feet—would strengthen my intercostal muscles and diaphragm. Secondly, working with the burros, horses, goats, and sheep at the ranch may have played a positive role. A 2001 study from *The Lancet* surveyed more than 3,500 Swiss, Austrian, and German parents with children aged 6 to 13. The survey showed that the children who were exposed to farm environments, such as stables, had lower frequencies of asthma, hay fever, and atopic sensitizations like eczema. The more exposure over time, the lower the frequency of the conditions. In my case, I loved helping my uncles pen the herd of over 100 sheep that grazed the ranch. I'd run around with the border collies, and when I started wheezing from all the dust being kicked up, I'd dash to the watering tank, wash off my face, and head back into the fray. I loved seeing the way the dogs steered the sheep this way and that, the animals flashing left and right like a school of fish.

Time outside in green spaces also improves brain function. In 2004, a study published in the *American Journal of Public Health* demonstrated that exposure to nature reduces children's ADHD symptoms. The study tracked 452 kids between the ages of 5 and 18, and found that time spent in the backyard or local green spaces reduced symptoms significantly more than the same activities done indoors or on playgrounds. The researchers' findings were consistent across severity of diagnosis as well as age, gender, geography, and income.

Then, in a 2019 study by University of Chicago researchers, experiments found that exposure to natural environments improves cognitive flexibility, attentional control, and working memory, while exposure to urban environments was linked to attention deficits. In another 2019 study, Danish researchers examined data from more than 900,000 residents and found that children who lived in neighborhoods with more green space had a reduced risk of psychiatric disorders later in life, including depression, mood disorders, schizophrenia, eating disorders, and substance-use disorder. For those with the lowest levels of green-space exposure during childhood, the risk of developing mental illness was 55 percent higher than for those who grew up with abundant green space.

Moreover, researchers believe that time outside can convey significant benefits whether you're exercising or simply sitting there. There are several theories about this. One idea is that natural stimuli like the sound of water rushing over stones or the rustling of leaves in the breeze activate the "rest and digest" functions of our bodies (the opposite of the "fight or flight" response). Conversely, when under stress, the body releases the hormone cortisol, which raises the blood pressure and heart rate. Chronically elevated levels of stress are connected to anxiety and depression, as well as obesity and heart disease.

Another theory holds that the feelings of awe commonly experienced in nature are a driver of these health benefits. We've all experienced wonder at a beautiful and vast vista like the Grand Canyon or a beach sunset, and can appreciate how it makes us feel small and gives perspective. In a 2018 study in the journal *Emotion,* researchers at the University of California, Berkeley detailed their investigations into the links between the feelings of awe experienced outdoors and improved health. They worked with the Sierra Club to send 124 military veterans and youth from underserved communities on whitewater raft trips on the American River, in California, and the Green River in Colorado. Participants' cortisol levels were measured before and after the expeditions, and they were asked to complete written surveys. Researchers found a 29 percent reduction in PTSD symptoms and a 21 percent decrease in general stress. They also noted that the more awe the participants reported experiencing, the higher their self-reported well-being levels were, and the lower their stress.

Yet another study has found that trees emit chemicals—called phytoncides—that boost our natural killer (NK) cells, which trap and consume viruses in the body. That's also without mentioning the health effects of increased vitamin-D levels from sunlight on skin, the way sunlight can reset your circadian system, and the fact that simply being in open spaces tends to increase movement, and therefore fitness.

Health professionals have been officially harnessing the healing power of nature since even before it had been extensively studied. In 2005, the Columbus, Ohio, cardiologist Dr. David Sagbir invited a few of his patients to meet him for a walk in a local park on a spring Saturday. Dozens showed up, and before long he formed the organization Walk with a Doc. Physicians with the organization now lead nature-based walks at more than 500 chapters around the world.

Soon, doctors began to prescribe time outside the same way they prescribe a course of antibiotics. Studies show that patients are much more likely to enact health practices if they are directed to by their physician—for example, they are four times as likely to adhere to a doctor-suggested weight-loss program. In 2017, the pioneering practitioner Dr. Robert Zarr launched the nonprofit

Park Rx America, to make it easier for health-care providers to prescribe time outside. The organization has created software to add nature prescriptions to a patient's electronic record and to help a physician map the nearest safe public open space in which to fulfill the prescription. More than 1,000 health-care professionals now use the system, and the standard recommendation is two hours of nature time per week, in no shorter than twenty-minute intervals.

These days, nature can be officially prescribed in thirty-five states and some fifteen nations, from New Zealand to Scotland. Through cooperation with their national park service, Canadian physicians can now issue free day and even annual passes to their patients. Similar programs exist in Vermont, where doctors can prescribe state-park passes, and in South Dakota, where patients can present a physician's park prescription for free entrance at a state park.

One form of outdoor health care I'm particularly excited about is climbing psychotherapy. A new treatment being pioneered in Germany and Austria, it combines rock climbing with talk therapy. According to practitioners, the sport's requirement of mindfulness and focus—if your attention wavers, you typically fall—is key to treating depression. Instead of thinking about your poor home life or alleged failures or body self-image, you are free to be in the moment. Climbing's well-known self-empowering metaphors are helpful too: "climbing out of your depression," "getting a hold on your emotions," and so on . . .

A 2021 study from *BMC Psychiatry* found that a climbing-based therapeutic program was as effective in treating depression as cognitive behavioral therapy and more effective than other exercise regimens that did not involve therapy. The trial followed 240 patients: one-third participated in bouldering therapy, another third did cognitive behavioral therapy, and the last third exercised at home. The climbing-treatment group improved significantly over those in just the exercise program and equivalently to the cognitive behavioral therapy group. In January 2021, about 200 people attended the first conference on climbing therapy in Germany, featuring workshops on anxiety, depression, PTSD, and addiction.

For me, some of the most dramatic results of the healing power of time outside have been in military veterans. My close friend Stacy Bare has been intimately involved with this process both personally and professionally. A veteran of the Iraq War, Stacy suffered a mild traumatic brain injury when his Humvee was hit by a roadside bomb. It wasn't until a few years later, though, that he hit rock bottom. Living in Boulder, Colorado, he was wracked by survivor's guilt, nightmares, and PTSD, thinking of the deaths he'd witnessed. He turned to drinking and cocaine, and spiraled further into suicidal ideation.

Fortunately, that's when an old Army friend invited him to climb in the Flatirons outside Boulder. Almost immediately, something shifted for Stacy. When he was climbing, he has said, "I could not feel guilty about the fact that I had a future when others, who I reasoned had far more to live for, came home dead in flag-draped boxes. I had to be focused on the moment to be successful, and that act of living in the moment saved me."

In 2014, Stacy was named a National Geographic Adventurer of the Year for his work as an advocate for the healing power of time spent outside. He has led expeditions and experiences for a half-dozen organizations, including the Sierra Club, with whom he teamed up to help researchers study nature's effect on combat veterans. In 2013, his work with the University of Michigan found that 50 of the 70 veterans participating in weeklong fly-fishing, kayaking, or backpacking experiences reported significant improvement in psychological well-being, increase in social functioning, and an enhanced outlook on life. Next, he worked with UC Berkeley scientists on the previously mentioned *Emotion* study on awe that found a 29 percent reduction in PTSD symptoms in veterans after rafting trips.

Through Stacy, I also learned about experiments at the Walter Reed National Military Medical Center incorporating time outside into healing military veterans. In 2016, the armed forces opened an eight-acre "wild healing garden" on the military medical base. Named the Green Road, the forested facility is designed to create quiet, contemplative spaces that allow for complete immersion in nature; it's also wheelchair accessible and includes clear and long sight lines to support a feeling of safety. "War is a wild thing, its damage is a wild thing, so we thought it should be healed by something wild," says Fred Foote, a neurologist with the Navy and one of the project's architects.

More than 12,000 service members so far have utilized the Green Road. It is also a research site. In 2021, Foote and his colleagues published a study that found walks in the Green Road elicited statistically more positive experiences for patients than walks in an adjacent urban environment. They also have plans to evaluate patient experiences through biomarkers of stress and changes in gene expression.

While I've long understood that time outside heals, both in my own life and through leading expeditions for Outward Bound, Soldiers to Summits, and other organizations, I find it incredibly compelling when an extremely conservative entity like the United States Military gets involved. They have begun focusing on what they call Total Force Fitness—keeping their soldiers healthy enough to fight—and are realizing that time in nature can be a huge boon. That was the eureka moment behind my push as the director of Colorado's Outdoor Recreation Industry Office to create our landmark Colorado Outdoor Rx Report in 2018. If time outside works as a healing modality for a bottom-line organization like the US Navy, I reasoned, it should work for the rest of us.

Over a year of work went into the seventy-four-page report. I wanted to collect the growing body of evidence in one place and help amplify it. I viewed my role as an advocate for all things outdoor recreation in Colorado, and for its remarkable ability to bolster individual and public health. I wanted to help normalize the idea of physicians prescribing time outside, to encourage the state's businesses, organizations, and government at all levels to make time for citizens to get outside, and to bolster the case for better funding for care and access to my state's public lands. I wanted every state agency to focus on the benefits of outdoor recreation.

We opened the report by noting that modern Americans spend a staggering 90 percent of their time indoors or in vehicles. We also pointed out that Colorado's obesity rate had risen from 6.9 percent in 1990 to 22 percent in 2018, and that our state had the eighth-highest rate of suicide and the seventh-highest recreational use of prescription pain relievers. We detailed work by governments to increase nature-based well-being, including in Finland, where government-funded researchers have recommended a minimum nature dosage per month and helped design "power trails" that encourage walking and mindfulness. In South Korea, the Korea Forest Service announced their plans to create 34 healing forests. The good news was that for our Colorado audience, we scarcely needed to point out that our remedies were near at hand—most every Coloradan knows firsthand the quality of our world-famous rivers, mountains, and open spaces.

For businesses, we highlighted companies that worked to reduce burnout and improve productivity by encouraging employee-led hikes and ski-days. Denver's GroundFloor Media and Aspen's Forum Phi Architecture + Interior Design were just two examples. My friendship with the CEO of GroundFloor was instrumental in allowing me to sell her on the program. We also noted that access to the benefits of outdoor recreation weren't necessarily equally available to all—many Colorado citizens lack the cultural tradition of outdoor recreation or the resources to buy expensive outdoor gear. By way of solutions, we highlighted programs like the "Walls Are Meant for Climbing" program, a $1 million partnership between The North Face and the Trust for Public Land (TPL) to build bouldering structures in public parks. The first installation in the nationwide project was in Montbello Open Space Park in Denver, a less affluent neighborhood with a low amount of green space. The North Face chose the site on the recommendation of Yessica Chavez, my youth ambassador, who grew up in the neighborhood. Today, the climbing wall is the centerpiece of a thriving 5.5-acre park built on a once-neglected, trash-strewn, and vacant lot.

Because we were using public money to create the report, I knew it had to be rigorous. I turned to Janette Heung, a Harvard-trained, Hong Kong–born public-health professional who'd fled her high-powered East Coast consulting gigs to be closer to rock climbing in Colorado. I'd met her rock climbing in Eldorado Canyon near Boulder, and when I started the Colorado Outdoor Rx project, she was the obvious choice as head. There was just one problem: I couldn't afford her; her consultant rate was at least twice what we had in the budget. My appeal to her was personal, as I, too, had taken a pay cut to serve the public good.[1] Furthermore, government and the outdoor community need more diverse leadership, I told her. Fortunately, Janette believed in the project strongly enough that she agreed to become a state employee— my deputy director of the Colorado Outdoor Recreation Industry Office—for the project's yearlong duration before returning to the more lucrative private sector.

For my appeals, Janette repaid me with the stubborn tenacity of someone who can climb the difficult grade of 5.12, as she could. She insisted that our office play more than a passive role in the movement—we'd need to do more than just report on the science behind the health benefits of time outside; we'd need to *contribute* to it, no matter the strains to our meager budget. We partnered with the University of Louisville and The Nature Conservancy in a study that used blood and urine samples to measure the effect of phytoncides, the chemicals emitted by green plants, on people spending time in green spaces. Janette and I sacrificed more than budget and political capital for the study; we both donated our urine and blood as control group subjects.

In a heartbreaking turn of events, Jeanette lost her life in a climbing accident in 2020 at the age of thirty-five. While she was rappelling from the summit of a climb in Wyoming's Wind River Range, a falling rock severed the webbing tethering her to the wall and she fell to her death. Rockfall accidents always feel random, as opposed to weather or avalanche conditions, which can be more easily predicted and therefore avoided. The only way to prevent a rockfall accident, seemingly, is not to go climbing at all. That would never have done for Jeanette. Climbing was

---

1. I strongly believe that in a functioning republic, we all have an obligation to serve in government. The pay is never as good as in the private sector, but as with storied Roman statesman Lucius Quinctius Cincinnatus who gave up the dictatorship of the fledgling Roman empire once the crisis he was recruited to solve was over, public service is meant to be temporary. The emphasis is on the word service.

not just an activity she was passionate about; it was a crucial component to her sense of self and well-being. It was, I believe, an indispensable aspect of her own health care.

I'm forever grateful to Jeanette for her work for the State of Colorado and for the greater good of our fellow humans and ecosystems. It is a small token, but a fitting one that the state honors her memory with the annual Janette Heung Get Outdoors Healthy Workplace Award. The award is given to the Colorado business that leads the way in promoting worker well-being by encouraging employees to participate in physical- and mental-health activities at the workplace, with a specific focus on spending time outdoors.

Chapter 3

HUNTING

"The earth has music for those who listen."
—William Shakespeare

It's before dawn on a December morning in 1984, and I'm walking with my grandfather and godfather, Mo Buder, along a levee toward a duck blind. I'm overdressed and sweating in my Duofold long underwear and insulated camo coveralls. My .410 shotgun rests unloaded in the crook of my arm, and I'm thinking about the .20 gauge I'm hoping to get for Christmas now that I'm twelve years old.

A thick fog has settled over the wetlands near the confluence of the Missouri and Mississippi Rivers. There's the crunch of our rubber boots on gravel and the jingle of the dog's tags, but my grandfather's flashlight isn't making much headway in the gloom. I can only see dried grass along the levee's banks and cottony fog above the water. Not that we need much illumination—this is my godfather's place, the Whistling Wings Duck Club, and he knows every foot of it. Even though I'm bursting with questions about where the ducks spent the summer, and where they'll nest in the spring, I stay quiet. It's important to keep talking and squirming to a minimum while hunting, I've been told a few times over the years, though around my grandfather is one of the few places I can find that stillness.

The blind is a metal box sunk into the ground beside the levee and camouflaged with reeds and cattails. The dog and I step inside, and I hand the decoys out to the men, who unfurl the anchor lines and spread them out in the water while the sky lightens in the east. Then the three of us sit side by side in the blind and watch the fog lift into a low white cloud layer. No eleven-year-old likes to get up before the sunrise, but I chose these hunting weekends winter after winter in order to spend time with my grandfather, and I'm content sitting quietly beside him, looking at the dawn. The clouds grow pink and then the sunrise streams in, casting a golden glow on the marsh. The mallards start winging in from the rivers, singly and in pairs, and suddenly I'm grateful to be there.

My grandfather was Bill Kelley, a machinist, World War II veteran, and Minor League catcher. He later became a hunting and fishing guide in the Ozarks and in places like Alaska's Kenai Peninsula for some of St. Louis's leading lights—people like Augie Busch, the beer magnate; and John Danforth, the US senator. Eventually, some of those same clients encouraged him to start a sporting-goods store. As my grandfather told it, he was fly-fishing with those gentlemen, standing beside the river, when they said, "Bill, we have to order our shotguns from Scotland and our fly reels from England, and we pay a lot of import duties. We think you should open a shop."

The problem was, he didn't have the capital to get started, so some of those wealthy clients wrote some big checks. The deal was, he wouldn't have to pay them back, but anytime they felt like it, they could stroll into the shop and pick out a waxed canvas coat or a McKay Brown 20-gauge free of charge. And, if they wanted my granddad to take them hunting, he'd need to get his manager to mind the shop for the week.

Kelley's Sporting Goods was in Clayton, Missouri, a quarter-mile from my school. When I'd stop by to say hello, I'd find those Missouri magnates hanging out by the woodstove, telling fishing stories and drinking highballs while my grandfather entertained them. Some of his best stories involved catching pitches from legendary players like Dizzy Dean and Babe Ruth on their 1930s barnstorming tours. The men taught me to mix the cocktails for them: "Use two fingers to my one finger, so that's four fingers of whiskey, put some soda water on it, and Bob's your uncle." I spent much of my young life at Kelley's, hanging out, stocking shelves, and getting to know the men who worked and shopped there. It was my place of peace.

PawPaw, as he was known to me, had forearms like Popeye, and when he spoke, retained the Southern twang of a kid who'd grown up playing baseball and hunting and fishing the Arkansas woods. He was a smoker, but quit when he realized that it exacerbated my asthma. He had an eighth-grade education, yet ran a successful business for forty years alongside his wife, Giaconda, whom everyone called Chic. I called her Nanni, and I spent almost as much time living with them as I did at home. They lived close enough that I could bike to their house, and when things weren't going well with my parents, I often did. My folks and I had what I've heard called "first-kid problems." I'm seven years older than my sister, Cristina, and fifteen years older than my brother, David, and it was hard for my parents and I to achieve the right balance of attention, discipline, and encouragement. Adding to that was the stress of instability with my dad's work. He lost his engineering job at McDonnell Douglas in the stagflation 1970s, and his subsequent absence from home had as much to do with a Latino father's grappling with profound emotions while striving to provide for his family, as it did with the susbsequent jobs that had him traveling almost full time to support us.

My best mentoring came from PawPaw, especially in his passion for the sporting life. My mother, for example, had simultaneously been a beauty queen and age-group skeet- and trap-shooting champion in the 1950s. I wasn't entering a lot of contests of either the popularity or sporting kind, but I did love learning to shoot clay pigeons with PawPaw—both for the bang-bang fireworks of it all, but also my grandfather's guidance. *Steady your breathing, clear your mind, keep both eyes open, and follow through on the target*—I cherished PawPaw's attention then, and value the life lessons still.

A little less wholesome was the time I spent at the Whistling Wings clubhouse. The former plantation mansion had bunks stacked dorm-style in the rooms upstairs. In the basement, floor drains helped clean the dog kennels as well as blood from the game cleaning and de-feathering station. In the kitchen, Mo Buder cooked piles of bacon, eggs, and potatoes while he told tall tales of country-club dudes and "skybusters," hunters who shot at birds far out of range. The great room had tall windows, booze stacked on tables, and unshaven men lounging in La-Z-Boys drinking coffee or cocktails. I pilfered the Coke mixers and leafed through the *Playboy* magazines as casually as possible while storing away the profanity I overheard to impress my classmates on Monday. There was shit talk and shenanigans, including one prank of people shooting pistols at each other with blanks, sending me diving outside because I was sure someone must have loaded a live round by accident. I was usually the only kid there, essentially the mascot thanks to Mo being my godfather. They couldn't make sense of the name Luis, so he told them just to call me Lou. My mom hated me being there, but spending time at Whistling Wings was its own kind of education.

Even more valuable was the hunting education. As boisterous

as the men could be, at base the experience was about spending time outside, quietly observing. I did learn that the mallards spend their summers nesting in Manitoba and their spring nesting in Mexico, traveling the Mississippi flyway in between. I learned that they typically cruise at 10,000 feet, have been known to live for twenty years in the wild, and will mate with other duck species, producing hybrids like the mallard X northern pintail. I learned to imitate the female's decrescendo call to lure the ducks down to our corner of the marsh. I learned to be an active participant in the ecosystem, not just an observer glancing at random birds through a car windshield. You love what you know, and to hunt well, it helps to understand the species and how they relate to their habitat.

I also learned the value of a life. Naturally, it was upsetting to watch the first duck I shot struggle to its last. But it was also upsetting to think that the chicken cutlets in the freezer represented lives that had never flown free, or really even walked. The lives of the birds we shot—duck, quail, pheasant—weren't wasted. We shared them, gratefully, in recipes like my grandfather's pheasant with orange sauce alongside rice and asparagus. Or pulled duck-breast sandwiches, soaked in Maull's BBQ Sauce. Hunting those birds and catching trout on the Current River were a celebration of the facts that that wildlife still existed and that much of the habitat it lived in had been preserved thanks to hunters and anglers.

****

One thing that has been lost in the outdoors during the culture wars of the last decade has been the understanding of the link between hunting and angling and conservation. We fundamentally agree on needing clean air, clean water, and public land preservation. The most obvious link in this conversation goes back to President Teddy Roosevelt.

Our nation's twenty-sixth president was our first conservation president. He established some fifty-one federal bird reserves and four national game preserves, and worked with Congress to create five national parks, including Oregon's Crater Lake and South Dakota's Wind Cave. It was under his administration that the USFS was formed and had hundreds of thousands of acres assigned to it.

Roosevelt also urged the creation of the national monument system, partly thanks to a tug-of-war at the Grand Canyon. He'd first visited the canyon in 1903, and when he learned that there were interests who preferred to mine it or to line the rim with homes and hotels, he was dismayed. "Leave it as it is," he urged in a speech at the site. "Man cannot improve on it; not a bit. The ages have been at work on it and man can only mar it. What you can do is to keep it for your children and your children's children and for all who come after you."

Congress wasn't willing to designate the canyon a national park, however, fearful of angering local mining interests. (The local Arizona newspaper *The Williams Sun* editorialized that whoever proposed Grand Canyon for a national park must have been "suckled by a cow and raised by an idiot.") So, Roosevelt turned to the Antiquities Act of 1906, which he'd helped lobby for, and which allows the President to solely designate a national monument. After first wielding it to create Devils Tower National Monument in Wyoming, he applied it to the Grand Canyon in 1908, along with sixteen other monuments by the end of his second term. Congress finally made the Grand Canyon into a national park in 1919.

In all, a stunning 230 million acres were placed into federal protection with Roosevelt's blessing—an area larger than California, Oregon, and Washington combined. It's safe to say that without Roosevelt's foresight, we wouldn't be talking about the outdoor-recreation economy at all. Those lands would have been privatized, and we'd all be financially and spiritually the poorer for it. Grand Canyon National Park, after all, contributes some $1.2 billion to the economies of its gateway communities and may be the most majestic place on Earth.

Before I spend more pages lauding Roosevelt's accomplishments, let me first say that he was also deeply flawed. He was known to be racist toward Native Americans, supporting their removal from the lands he federally protected. He embraced the concept of Manifest Destiny in the United States and abroad, and he supported crackpot and plainly racist eugenics theories. He was, however, a supporter of Black leaders, including famously inviting Booker T. Washington to dine with him at the White House in 1901. As Roosevelt himself noted in 1907, "Men must be judged with reference to the age in which they dwell." It's obvious that Teddy was dead wrong on issues of race, but for his time he was a true progressive, working hard against his party's base to improve conditions for the everyday laborer.

I should also say that my reverence for Roosevelt goes beyond politics. He has been one of my life's heroes because, like me, he suffered from childhood asthma, and through my eyes, I can see that it defined his life.

Teddy Roosevelt wrote forty-one books in his life and kept journals from the age of eight (some of which I was lucky enough to peruse a few years ago, while wearing library-issue white cotton gloves, when I was a student at the Harvard Kennedy School). Yet he wrote remarkably little about his childhood asthma, likely because, as more than one biographer has theorized, it was just too painful a memory to dwell upon. One of its only mentions in his autobiography was, "I was a sickly, delicate boy, suffered much from chronic asthma, and frequently had to be taken away on trips to find a place where I could breathe." In another he wrote that "no one seemed to think I would live."

The stunning line "I sat up for four successive hours and Papa made me smoke a cigar" does appear in one of his childhood diaries. Treatments for asthmatics in the 1860s included remedies like smoking cigarettes, drinking coffee, and inhaling chloroform. Parents and physicians would seemingly try anything, desperate to ease their children's terrible strangulation and wide-eyed panic. My heart goes out to young Teedie, as his family called him. He never had the benefit of remedies like bottled oxygen and inhalers like I did. He had to just endure the terror of his attacks, never knowing if they'd subside.

Eventually, Teedie's father hit upon the correct treatment—exercise. He took his son walking and horseback riding, and when Teedie turned twelve converted a room in the family's Manhattan brownstone into a home gym and hired a boxer to train him. The point was to improve the boy's strength and stamina so he could at least endure his sufferings, but the exercise also improved his lung capacity, which was ultimately what let him rise above the debilitation. My experience was much the same, beginning with those blessed chlorine-soaked breaststroke laps for the Little Debbie Swim Team and progressing through play with cousins and hiking at altitude in Ecuador. Through increased fitness, both his and my asthma began to wane.

In Teedie, his fitness regimes also ignited a passion for activity. He was famous, even while serving as president, for his daily rounds of rowing, tennis, horseback riding, hiking, and wrestling. As governor of New York, he had a wrestling mat installed in the governor's mansion, and at one meeting with Gifford Pinchot, whom he later appointed head of the newly formed USFS, Roosevelt required that the younger man engage him in both a boxing match and a wrestling bout. Roosevelt bested Pinchot in wrestling but lost in boxing. "I had the honor of knocking the future President of the United States off his very solid pins," Pinchot later wrote. Undoubtedly, Roosevelt loved it—the friends continued their boxing and wrestling contests over subsequent years.[2]

He was also a genuine adventurer. In 1881, during his honeymoon in Europe at the young age of twenty-three, Roosevelt hired a guide and became an early summiteer of the Matterhorn. In April of 1903, he spent sixteen days camping out in Yellowstone during a stump-speech tour of the West. Then, starting in 1913, he spent five months on a first-descent expedition of the River of Doubt in the Amazon Basin. It was pretty hairball—most of the exploratory party contracted malaria, the expedition ran out of food, one man drowned, another was murdered, and the murderer was left behind. Roosevelt himself had a severe case of malaria and nearly lost his leg from an infected wound. "The Brazilian wilderness stole ten years of my life," he later wrote. "But, I am always willing to pay the piper when I have a good dance . . ."

That gung-ho philosophy, I believe, stemmed from the remedy he found to his debilitating asthma—vigorous activity. I also

---

2. I actually got interested in boxing for fitness as an adult after reading a few Roosevelt biographies. Grandpa Bill had boxed in the Navy, I remembered, and it seemed like a fun way to vary my training routines. I have a heavy bag in my basement to this day, which has come in particularly handy after certain more frustrating Zoom meetings on days I work from home.

believe that when you so frequently face your demise, as he did from his earliest days, you aren't apt to let any opportunity pass. It's been my guiding philosophy, too.

My experience with Teddy Roosevelt has been one of continuously unfolding awe. Every time I read this famous quote on conservation from *A Book-Lovers Holidays in the Open* (1916), I'm stunned anew by his prescience: "We treasure pictures and sculpture. We regard Attic temples and Roman triumphal arches and Gothic cathedrals as of priceless value. But we are,

as a whole, still in that low state of civilization where we do not understand that it is also vandalism wantonly to destroy or permit the destruction of what is beautiful in nature, whether it be a cliff, a forest, or a species of mammal or bird. Here in the United States, we turn our rivers and streams into sewers and dumping-grounds, we pollute the air, we destroy forests and exterminate fishes, birds, and mammals, not to speak of vulgarizing charming landscapes with hideous advertisements." If I didn't know better, I'd think Edward Abbey had written it.

Roosevelt also wrote several books about hunting, his lifelong passion, beginning in childhood trips to the Maine woods with his father. His feelings about it were probably best summed up in this passage from *The Wilderness Hunter,* in which he described hunting as: "the free, self-reliant, adventurous life, with its rugged and stalwart democracy; the wild surroundings, the grand beauty of the scenery, the chance to study the ways and habits of the woodland creatures—all these unite to give to the career of the wilderness hunter its peculiar charm."

Maybe best known of his hunting exploits was his post-presidential eleven-month African safari, during which he and his son Kermit shot and preserved 512 animals from what is now Kenya, South Sudan, and Uganda in the name of science—the expedition was sponsored by the Smithsonian and brought back more than 25,000 specimens of animals, insects, and plants. Roosevelt's love of the rugged sportsman's life was intertwined with a passion for naturalism. As a child confined to his room, he'd become a prodigious reader (another thing we share), notably of naturalists like James Audubon, Alexander Wilson, and William Bartram. Encouraged by his father, a co-founder of the American Museum of Natural History[3], he began collecting specimens and practicing taxidermy at an early age. He shot and preserved several birds as a child on a family trip to Egypt, his boarding house room at Harvard was full of live turtles and insects for study, and as an undergraduate there he published his first ornithological work, "The Summer Birds of the Adirondacks in Franklin County, N.Y."

It was also in hunting that he sought solace when his life took an unimaginably tragic turn. In 1883, in a quest to hunt bison before the species disappeared, Roosevelt took a train to North Dakota. He loved it so much that he bought a ranch nestled deep in the Dakota Badlands, and it was there that he retreated after his mother and young wife died on the same day—the former of typhoid, the latter of Bright's disease—in February of 1884. He remained in the Badlands for two years, ranching and hunting. To me, it's no surprise that he was drawn here in his darkest hour. The wilderness has been a place of healing for countless people through time, as it certainly has been for me. As my friend Land Tawney, president of Backcountry Hunters & Anglers, points out, it is significant that Roosevelt did his healing with a rifle in his hand. Through hunting, he was connected to the land in a very

3. The same museum that rightly removed Teddy Roosevelt's statue from its entrance in 2020 over concerns of colonialist iconography. While Roosevelt was mounted on horseback, a Native American man and an African man flanked him on foot, connoting their subservience.

direct and focused way.

His experience there would have consequences for the larger world, too. Roosevelt wrote a book about his time in the Badlands, *Hunting Trips of a Ranchman*. When George Bird Grinnell, an influential naturalist and the editor of *Forest and Stream* magazine, mildly panned it by, Roosevelt burst into Grinnell's office to complain. The two parted the meeting as lifelong friends, however, and that friendship led directly to the birth of the modern conservation movement.

In 1887, the pair founded the Boone and Crockett Club to "promote manly sport with the rifle," but also to advocate for wildlife preservation, spread the ideals of ethical hunting, and promote scientific understanding and management of game. Their first task was to fight market hunting—the mass harvesting and sale of game meat. In the absence of legal limits, duck hunters routinely laid waste to hundreds of birds a day with cannon-like guns mounted on boats. The harvest was also often ethically deplorable. Water-killing deer, for example, involved driving them with dogs into lakes or rivers, where market hunters waited in boats to shoot them or cut their throats. In response, the Boone and Crockett Club lobbied for "fair chase" laws at the state and federal level, including ethical treatment of game animals as well as harvesting limits.

The club's work led directly to a spate of some of the earliest science-based wildlife management legislation, including the Yellowstone National Park Protection Act, the Timberland Reserve Bill, the Lacey Act, and the Migratory Bird Treaty Act. At the same time, club members realized that habitat loss was a problem, and pushed for the creation of wildlife refuges, an idea that reached its optimal fruition under Roosevelt's presidency.

Many have forgotten that hunting and fishing organizations

like the Boone and Crockett Club and Ducks Unlimited were amongst our first environmental groups. My American grandfather PawPaw was a member of both Ducks Unlimited and Trout Unlimited, had their stickers on his Chevy, and took me to their annual banquets—one of the auction items was always a day out hunting at Whistling Wings with Bill Kelley. Eventually, Mo donated all 780 acres of Whistling Wings to Ducks Unlimited.

Altogether, the wildlife-management reforms and system championed by Roosevelt and the Boone and Crockett Club came to be known as the "North American model." They stand in direct contrast to the way game had been managed in Europe, where hunting had been the sole provenance. Commoners had long been prohibited from hunting the nobleman's game—just look at the legend of Robin Hood, a character who was wanted for execution for poaching the king's deer. By contrast, in the United States we hold that, in the words of the U.S. Fish and Wildlife Service, "wildlife is a public resource, independent of the land and water where wildlife may live. Government at various levels have a role in managing that resource on behalf of all citizens and to ensure the long-term sustainability of wildlife populations." In our nation, wildlife is, like our government, for the people.

****

Also democratic is the way that the North American model supports wildlife management—through participant funding via licenses and taxes. Once I was old enough to run the register at Kelley's, I sold countless deer licenses and duck stamps. When I asked my grandfather where the money went, he told me it was to "protect the resource."

What I wasn't aware of at the time was the taxes on guns and ammo and fishing gear that also went directly to the agencies who manage wildlife. The 1937 Pittman-Robertson Wildlife Restoration Act set an 11 percent tax on the sale of any gun or ammunition, and the Dingell-Johnson Sport Fish Restoration Act of 1950 has a similar provision for fishing and boating gear. The two laws have funneled more than $23 billion into wildlife research and habitat restoration, and currently pull in well over a billion dollars a year. Together, they are the definition of a pay-to-play model.

Those taxes, plus hunting and fishing licenses, make up nearly 60 percent of wildlife service funding at the state and federal levels. The work funded is not just about increasing elk-herd size and catching poachers, though; these agencies are also tasked with protecting threatened and endangered species. Furthermore, these agencies are employers, providing fulfilling and important work—state wildlife agencies alone employ 50,000 people in America.

I love to celebrate the contributions to conversation, both historically and currently, of the hook-and-bullet crowd. I think it can help build bridges between groups frequently separated by the culture wars—the hunters and anglers versus the bird watchers and tourists vying to spy wildlife in our national parks. Without the former, it's unlikely we'd have the latter. I cannot stress enough that for decades, the hunting and fishing community has literally and figuratively been "carrying the water" when it came to paying for a lion's share of conservation and stewardship efforts in the United States.

It's also important to recognize that the rest of the outdoor community hasn't equally shared in the burden of caring for our wildlands and wildlife. Certain companies do their part and more—the Planet members like Patagonia, Kleen Kanteen, and Jones Snowboards donate 1 percent of their gross sales to approved environmental organizations. Companies like the North Face, REI, and again, Patagonia fund the work of The Conservation Alliance in doing great conservation work. But those efforts pale in comparison to the billions that sportsmen and women have anteed up over almost a century. It's time for the rest of us to pitch in.

It's no secret that our national parks, wildlife refuges, and national forests are underfunded, even with recent legislative victories like the 2020 Dingell Act and the 2021 Great American Outdoors Act. In my home state of Colorado, it has been estimated that it'll take $24 million to repair trails on its Fourteeners—the fifty-plus peaks above 14,000 feet—alone. That estimate was made in 2017, well before our state's trails received record use during the pandemic. Wildlife, too, needs more help than ever. State wildlife agencies have identified 12,000 species in need of protection, including bats, butterflies, and bees, pollinators who may just be the keystones of our ecosystems.

I believe that it is time for all outdoorists to chip in through a sales tax on items like tents, hiking boots, and teardrop camping trailers. Not only do our nation's open spaces and trails need the help, but we should all be invested in their upkeep. In many states, motorcycle dirt bikers and ATV drivers buy a mandatory sticker whose proceeds help maintain trail networks. Why aren't mountain bikers required to as well? We should all be paying to play.

I've heard the arguments against it—that manufacturers like the one I worked for already pay high import taxes (14–37.5 percent) on the goods they manufacture overseas. Manufacturers don't want to pass any more costs on to the consumer than they already do when the point is to encourage more people to get outside. What of the tax on a backpack that serves as a child's book bag—what does that have to do with maintaining trails? These are the arguments made by the Outdoor Industry Association (OIA), founded in 1989 by a group of fourteen visionary outdoor-industry leaders and which has provided great leadership for the outdoor community in the past, but whose prime directive off and on through the years remains to fight excise taxes on outdoor gear.

My counter is this: a $3 tax on a $300 sleeping bag isn't going to dissuade the customer from making the purchase, but it might markedly improve their camping experience if there were more USFS staff to clear the forty trees that have fallen across their trail after an autumn wind event, or if there's a well-maintained pit toilet at the trailhead instead of feces scattered in the bushes.

What of that young mother paying a few extra dollars for her child's North Face school pack? Why can't retailers like The North Face tell the story that money from the sale of their packs will help maintain trails everywhere, including the one through the local park? People always value more highly something they're financially invested in. Like at a garage sale, an item priced at even just $5 will invariably be more coveted than the same item placed in the free bin. What Tawney of Backcountry Hunters & Anglers proposes we call an Outdoor Legacy Fund is simply us putting a nominal price on our public lands and wildlife.

Some states are already raising money for wildlands and parks with sales tax. In 2010, Minnesota passed a three-eighths of one percent general sales tax earmarked specifically for conservation, recreation, and the arts. It has generated $1.765 billion to fund science and buy land, and for projects like a 100-mile interconnected mountain-bike trail system within the city limits of Duluth. That's a tourist draw and will raise the fortunes of the state not only with economic prosperity, but in terms of better wellness for citizens. My home state of Missouri has a similar sales tax on sporting goods, and has raised $100 million for projects like removing feral hogs and renting private land to provide public access for hunting and fishing.

In 2018, an overwhelming 83 percent of Georgia voters approved the Georgia Outdoor Stewardship Act, which dedicates 40 percent of state sales-tax revenue from purchases at outdoor recreation stores to fund land conservation, trail improvements, and restoration. In 2022, $28 million from the act went to fund projects like a new visitor center at Vogel State Park, and trail improvements at Sweetwater Creek State Park. Texas voters passed a similar amendment in 2019—with 88 percent voting to send 100 percent of the state's sporting-goods sales tax to the Texas Parks & Wildlife Department and Texas Historical Commission. These two laws don't create new sales taxes, but their overwhelming popularity at the ballot box shows that citizens aren't afraid of using sales taxes to fund ORec infrastructure.

If the outdoor-recreation boom of the pandemic showed us anything, it's that our outdoor infrastructure is under serious strain and needs an upgrade. We need to maintain our trails to better withstand heavier use. We need more trails to disperse users. We need more rangers to prevent abuse of our wild places and help when accidents occur. We need more scientists to help us figure out the best way to preserve what we still have. We've taken the public good of our open spaces for granted ever since Teddy Roosevelt secured them for us. We can't afford to do so any longer. Our public lands are the privilege of the public—but they are also our shared responsibility, regardless of where we stand politically.

****

My favorite example of building consensus around wildlands in recent times took place in northern Maine, in what some called the state's "woodbasket" for its long history of lumbering and sawmilling. In 2011, the region was in an uproar over one philanthropist's attempt to donate 87,500 acres to create what would eventually become Katahdin Woods and Waters National Monument. Roxanne Quimby is the founder of Burt's Bees, the lip-balm and lotion company. She'd been amassing the land for more than a decade, buying it for sometimes just $200 an acre as lumbering corporations like International Paper phased out operations in the area. (The area's sawmills primarily made paper for phone books. As Lucas St. Clair, Quimby's son, likes to joke, "I don't think my kids have ever even seen a phone book.")

When the last of the region's paper mills closed in the town of Millinocket in 2008, unemployment shot to 22 percent and the town's population eventually shrank by two-thirds. When Quimby unveiled her plan to donate her lands to the NPS, the local public was largely against it. They saw it as another step away from the region's heritage as a lumbering region—locking those lands out of timber production forever. Probably more importantly, Quimby had unapologetically closed off access to hunting, fishing, and snowmobiling on her holdings, a 180-degree turn from the policies of the lumber companies, who'd freely allowed such pastimes. "Ban Roxanne" bumper stickers appeared across northern Maine.

After fighting with locals for years, Quimby asked her son Lucas to help create better PR for the project. Lucas is a natural-born politician, an extremely patient extrovert who will talk to anyone anywhere. (We serve together on the TPL's board of directors.) In 2011, as Lucas likes to say, he set out to create a national monument "one cup of coffee at a time."

Over the next five years, Lucas met with a majority of the 10,000-or so residents of Millinocket and other towns surrounding the proposed park, often over coffee, but ultimately wherever he could. He met one grocery-store owner in the walk-in freezer because the man didn't want to be seen talking to Lucas. When people insulted his family or the proposed monument on social media, he knocked on their doors and asked to have a face-to-face discussion instead. The message was almost always that the new monument could revitalize the region's sagging, post-paper-mill economy. He was armed with economic studies that showed that economies adjacent to seventeen different national monuments had all expanded in the years after designation, per capita income rising by as much as 17 percent and personal income by 32 percent. One study predicted that Katahdin Woods and Waters could spur "the ability to attract people, retirees, and businesses across a range of sectors; economic growth including higher-wage jobs; and increases in non-labor sources of income."

Mostly though, he did a lot of listening. Lucas listened to the concerns of his critics, showing them that he wasn't out to erase their community's culture, but rather augment it. With face-to-face discussions between people of different viewpoints—something missing in our era of us-vs-them social-media silos—the two sides realized they had more in common than they thought. That built trust, the precursor to consensus.

Furthermore, Lucas convinced his mother to reverse her stance on the hunting[4] and snowmobiling ban. That compromise showed that Lucas, his mother, and other national-monument proponents really were listening. By 2016, President Obama was satisfied enough in local support to use Teddy Roosevelt's

---

4. There is precedent for hunting in national parks and monuments. There are 41 that allow it in some form, including Grand Teton National Park and Denali National Park and Preserve.

favorite lever, the Antiquities Act, to designate the parcel as Katahdin Woods and Waters National Monument. Hunting and snowmobiling is allowed in designated areas of the monument.

Lucas' predictions are starting to come true. In 2020, there were 41,000 visitors to the monument, driving $3.3 million in economic activity and supporting thirty-eight local jobs. The grocery store whose owners wouldn't be seen talking to Lucas in person recently expanded, buoyed by an influx of business. Dozens of bike trails have been built in the area, too, and the resulting upswing in recreation is not just from tourists. As Lucas likes to say, "The outdoor-recreation economy isn't just making burritos and renting bicycles"; it's attracting high-end businesses whose employees want to live in northern Maine for the ORec lifestyle. "Recreation is our industrial park," he says.

What I love about this story is that the national-monument campaign served as the rare instance in modern America of people actually changing their minds and building agreement. It's no coincidence, in my opinion, that outdoor recreation was the thing that could be agreed upon. It's notable, however, that it took

an extraordinary amount of effort and patience—primarily on the part of a single person—to build that consensus. It's fashionable to say, "Work smarter, not harder," but sometimes you just have to work harder, which in this case meant putting in more time connecting with people.

Lucas St. Clair's success in changing minds reminds me of another such instance in Maine. In 2022, Chloe Maxmin and Canyon Woodward published their book, *Dirt Road Revival*, which tells the story of how a twenty-five-year-old climate activist, Maxmin, was able to win a pair of elections in the Maine legislature in traditionally conservative districts. In 2018, Maxmin became the first Democrat to win rural Maine House District 88, erasing a 16 percent Republican advantage from the previous election. Then, in 2020, she defeated the state's highest-ranking Republican to win Senate District 13. What's important to me in this story isn't that a Democrat won an election; rather it's that minds were changed. How'd Maxmin and her campaign manager, Woodward, do it? They bothered to contact *all* the voters in their districts, not just those who'd voted for Democrats in the past. In other words, they talked to people.

Maxmin and Woodward describe how the Maine Senate Democratic Campaign Committee told them it didn't believe in talking to Republicans; instead, they focused on motivating their base-registered Democrats. Maxmin and Woodward rejected that idea, preferring to roll up their sleeves and knock on every door. Then they listened to what those people had to say.

Maxmin describes a conversation with a man who opposed Medicaid expansion in Maine. At first, he told her to get off his property, but she persisted in asking him for his perspective. He'd grown up, he said, without electricity or running water, and had worked hard to build a life, including buying his own healthcare. Maxmin thanked him for explaining. She said her support of Medicaid was not to take anything away from his hard work; it was about supporting others who remained in need. At the end of the conversation, the guy said he would vote for her.

They talked to voters who had literally never been contacted before by a Democratic candidate or canvasser. "There were Chloe signs going up next to Trump signs all over the district," they wrote. Maxmin and her canvassers never hid their progressive positions, but they put in face time and did a lot of listening. As with Lucas St. Clair's campaign for Katahdin Woods and Waters, showing up and listening was what ultimately built agreement. "We focused on what could unify us," Maxmin and Woodward wrote.

The approach bore similar results in 2022 for Pennsylvania Senator John Fetterman. Before his stroke limited his campaigning, he waged a famously vigorous ground game, meeting with voters everywhere in the state, particularly in rural areas that felt they were no longer part of the conversation. His mantra was "every county, every vote," and he repeatedly showed up in places that Democrats rarely visited.

What can unify us is clean air, clean water, and access to open spaces, but as the campaigns in Maine and Pennsylvania have shown, you must have conversations person-to-person. I used the same approach when I got the job as director of the Colorado Outdoor Recreation Industry Office. I spent my first months on a statewide listening tour, traveling to the obvious outdoor-rec hotspots like Steamboat and Durango, but also to places like La Junta, out on the pool-table-flat eastern plains. The agricultural community had been one of the hubs for Governor Hickenlooper's beloved Pedal the Plains bike tour, which he launched in 2012 to champion outdoor-recreation travel to the non-mountainous parts of Colorado.

I had a lot of conversations out there with local officials that went something like, "Well, you are working for a Democrat." But he wants you to thrive, too, I'd say, and one way to do that is to promote the outdoor spaces that you love.

I loved Hick's bottom-line, economics-first approach. As governor, he famously championed all of Colorado's industries, from the mineral industry to aerospace to tourism. He realized that the best way to improve his citizens' well-being was to ensure their prosperity. In my own job, I followed his lead. When I convened my advisory board, I was sure it included representatives from all the ORec factions, from conservationists to hunters, and from hikers to off-road-vehicle enthusiasts.

It wasn't just that it was prudent to include the many, diverse user groups; I also did so because I'm a constituent of each. I ski, I climb, I ride motorcycles, and I shoot guns. Not just shotguns—I also own an AR-15. The gun was a gift of sorts from my friend Rob, who had just returned from serving in the Marines in the second Gulf War in Iraq when I met him at CrossFit in Eagle, Colorado. He was crashing at his parent's second home there, decompressing from some very heavy experiences—he'd seen action in Fallujah. I liked him right away, but I also knew how resort towns can be lonely for newcomers. Well-adjusted locals can be cliquey, while others party so much that it can seem like everyone is having a great time except you, even when that partying is fairly self-destructive. Rob and I spent time at the shooting range, a practice I'd kept up since childhood. I took him climbing and skiing, loaning him gear from my basement—working as a guide and ski instructor, I had spares of everything.

A few years later, he'd settled in beautifully. He was working at the newspaper and had met his future wife at the CrossFit gym. One day, over beers, he told me, "I want to help you build a rifle." Assembling and using guns was the thing he did best; it was where he could most easily quiet his mind and feel competent. I understood that. I had the same relationship to climbing. I never imagined personally owning an AR-15, but I felt honored to be invited into Rob's world, and will forever be grateful to him for being such an amazing friend and teacher in this space.

We built the gun together from specialized parts we ordered from the local shop. We registered it. He had me practice taking it apart and putting it back together again blindfolded, the way he'd been taught in the Marines. He taught me how to shoot tactically. Just as with a lot of the outdoor sports I practice, I loved learning a new skill. I've kept those skills up. I annually spend weekend retreats with self-defense groups I've gotten to know over the years while guiding veteran groups for therapy, and while practicing shooting and martial arts.

That said, my relationship to guns is not uncomplicated, and like so many of us I'm horrified by the epidemic of gun violence in our country—too many of us get shot, or almost get shot, just going about our daily lives. One of my childhood's most formative experiences was a close call with my grandfather and a shotgun. I was eleven, we were in the duck blind, and PawPaw was standing next to me, calling the ducks in. I was resting my shotgun on the bench, pointing upward. I thought the safety was on. It wasn't, and the gun went off, sending the blast up toward my grandfather. It was the most fear I've ever felt, and there wasn't much consolation in the near-miss—the blast was inches from his face. It gnaws at the pit of my stomach to this day.

The consequences were that PawPaw made me take a hunter-safety course with the National Rifle Association. In those days, the organization was primarily a hunter-safety and -advocacy organization. I don't see them that way now, but at the time I felt ushered into a culture I loved and recognized, one that was built on feelings of responsibility and respect for wildlife and wild places. This segment of the industry will always be my first and forever home.

Chapter 4

ROCK CLIMBING

"If I were to wish for anything, I should not wish for wealth and power, but for the passionate sense of the potential, for the eye, which ever young and ardent, sees the possible." —Søren Kierkegaard

I've made my livelihood in outdoor adventures across the globe, and more recently working in government and in manufacturing supporting outdoor adventuring. My most important friendships were forged in the outdoors, and my young family was created in the outdoor-adventure town of Eagle, Colorado. I fell in love with the beauty of nature, watching ducks fly at sunrise with my grandfather, and grew to crave the clear air of high altitude from spending summers with my Ecuadorian family. My dream of the guiding life was that of a young, bookish boy who spotted a way out of his physical misery in the pages of *National Geographic*. But no factor was as important in my life's course as my pursuit of rock climbing as a dopey, uncoordinated teenager in the heartland state of Missouri.

It all began in 1987, one morning early in my freshman year. I was walking through the parking lot on my way to first-period class, my backpack slung as casually over my shoulder as I could make it look, when I spotted an older kid hopping down from a metallic blue Jeep CJ-7. I was obsessed with Jeeps in the way teenage boys, at least in that era, became obsessed with a certain model of car. It was the final, maximum craving for the toys of childhood, but also a symbol of the identity they aspired to, whether it was a Porsche for slick urbanity or a pickup for country masculinity. For young Lou, as I was known to my American friends, it was the Jeep and my belief in the access it provided to the outdoors.

On that morning, my soon-to-be friend Hartley Comfort spun out of his jacked-up, tricked-out 4x4 as I stood and stared. He'd left the doors and the top at home, and the open-air Jeep looked like pure freedom to me.

"Nice Jeep," I'm sure I said. "Do you take it off-road?"

"Hell yeah," he said, full of pride—and that was enough to start a friendship.

Hartley was a junior, an exceptionally kind, easygoing kid with curly blond hair who followed his own lights. He'd grown up going to summer camp, and like me, was finding he just felt more like himself when he was adventuring outdoors.

Hartley was delighted to find another kid in the suburbs of St. Louis who was excited to go camping, even if he was with a hyperactive freshman. I'd spent the previous summer in Ecuador, hanging out on our family's ranch and idolizing my uncle Peppin, who was a member of the small but passionate Ecuadorian mountaineering community. My recollection is that Hartley and I met on a Tuesday, and then headed out in his Jeep to the Ozarks that very weekend. My parents were pleased to see me go—undoubtedly relieved that I'd found a friend.

Our goal that year was to camp in every state park in Missouri. We probably went twice a month, slinging our $5 hammocks between dogwood trees and cooking canned ravioli and instant oatmeal over a campfire. We bought backpacks and knocked off the twelve-mile Bell Mountain Loop and sections of the Ozark Trail, eating MREs from the Army-surplus store. Hartley had used topographic maps at summer camp, and we got them on a discount from my grandfather's shop and pieced together weekend overland routes. I remember the pride of feeling that I was doing something more unique than lining up at the cineplex or cramming into the arcade with all the other bored kids.

Then we got into rappelling, which was a common gateway drug for climbers in the 1980s and 1990s, before the proliferation of climbing gyms. Even without much instruction, it was easy for us to sling a rope around a tree, slide into a harness, and then revel in the thrill of backing over a cliff edge—we loved the buzz of defying that primordial survival instinct. We even got into the Aussie rappel, in which you descend the rope facing down toward the ground (think SWAT teams bounding down skyscrapers in action movies), and we'd time each other to see who could descend the fastest. Hartley bought us larger, rescue-style figure-8 devices that let us go as fast as possible, screaming our heads off the whole way down.

Over the next few years, Hartley's generosity is what enabled us to procure all the expensive climbing gear that would change my life, and I'm forever grateful, and deeply aware that not everyone is so fortunate to be able to afford the often-costly equipment you need for adventure sports.

Climbing, of course, was the obvious progression after rappelling, and I came back from Ecuador the summer I turned fifteen with a pair of stiff, hand-me-down 1970s-era EB rock shoes from Peppin. Hartley and I went from toproping anchored to trees to trying our hand at trad climbing on the chunky, conglomerate, old-school, mid-grade climbs at Missouri's Elephant Rocks and Johnson Shut-Ins state parks. Elephant Rocks, as the name implies, is a collection of enormous boulders sitting atop glacial plains that we loved to scramble around on, getting strong and working out sequences of moves. The Shut-Ins are something else entirely. The cliffs overlook the East Fork of the Black River. The cliffs are about 75 feet high, with the water rushing below. The routes were steep and dirty. As much time was spent cleaning holds and brushing away lichen as doing the actual climbs. Apart from our smudged and dog-eared copies of the classic climber's bible, *Mountaineering: The Freedom of the Hills,* we were self-taught.

We were lucky to have survived it. There was one day at the Shut-Ins when another climber, a complete stranger, started yelling at us, afraid we were going to kill ourselves. We didn't realize that each piece of removable protection—the passive pro known as nuts and the active protection known as cams, or Friends—we crammed into the cliff's cracks to arrest a fall needed two carabiners: one to attach it to a nylon sling, and another to attach the sling to the rope. Instead, we had been threading our slings directly through the wire cable loop on the nut or cam, not really understanding that in a hard leader fall, the wire cable could easily slice through the nylon sling, landing us on the ground. That old-timer sure knew it, though, and when he wandered by and got a look at our setup, with Hartley three-quarters of the way up the cliff and me belaying from the ground, he started screaming, "STOP! STOP! STOP! Freeze right there!"

The climber promptly sprinted around to the top of the cliff, slung his rope around a tree, and rappelled down to Hartley. He clipped Hartley to his own harness, and then continued rappelling to the bottom of the cliff with Hartley in tow. When we were all safely on the ground, the climber started berating us again: "You cannot have webbing on cable. Ever! You're going to kill yourselves!" Were we stupid, he asked, or just too cheap to buy enough carabiners? The answer was both. I think I may have cried.

Apart from that learning experience, though, we were jamming. We climbed every weekend, and because Hartley was now a senior, he started skipping school to climb, which means that as his climbing partner, I started skipping school to climb. We visited every climbing destination within a ten-hour drive: Devil's Thumb in Carbondale, Illinois, the Tennessee Wall in Chattanooga, West Virginia's New River Gorge, and Kentucky's Red River Gorge. We built a climbing wall of sorts in Hartley's basement—two sheets of plywood with some of the first artificial climbing holds you could buy bolted to them—and spent hours down there clambering around.

That winter, David Lee Roth's solo album *Skyscraper* came out, the one with the cover featuring him rock climbing high above Yosemite Valley wearing a freaking black beret for some reason. (The photo, it turns out, was shot by the legendary photographer Galen Rowell, as was the video for the song "Just Like Paradise," which featured Roth aid climbing in Yosemite and doing the famous Tyrolean traverse—a rope rigged horizontally between two points—to the airy Lost Arrow Spire.) We listened to the album nonstop that year, mirroring Roth's hyperactive enthusiasm, not to mention his spandex tights and tank tops. In our minds' eyes, whenever we high-fived each other, there was a dramatic puff of climbing chalk.

As it happened, climbing was the perfect sport to cure the ills of a small, awkward, and anxious teenager. Because climbing is so difficult, and potentially perilous, I had to quiet down all the adolescent noise in my head in order to succeed. Instead of dwelling on my failures in school, in my social life, and at home, I had to focus on my fingertips and my feet on the rock, and on getting to the next foothold or handhold. I couldn't daydream my way up the cliff—I had to climb it. It was the first time I was truly living in the moment, right there with myself, not escaping reality with my nose in a book.

Rock climbing gives you grit. You fall often, and then keep on trying, literally climbing through adversity. You get banged up, scraped to hell. I was used to physical suffering from asthma, and social suffering because of, well, everything, but climbing gave me the resilience to rise above the suffering. I was pretty fragile until I started climbing. Even without access to today's formal climbing-therapy programs, climbing was extremely therapeutic for me. I was succeeding at something for the first time in my life, and that thing was cool and dangerous. No one else we knew back home was climbing, and we felt special for that.

While I was an unmotivated student in school, I was more than happy to study *Mountaineering: The Freedom of the Hills,* and to practice the rope systems diagrammed there. Hartley and I would climb a few hours until our forearms were shot, and then spend the rest of the day at the cliff base using applied trigonometry and physics to set up equalized anchors. We spent time hoisting ourselves up the trees in Hartley's backyard with our climbing gear, practicing systems. We were dedicated to the craft of getting better.

Just as importantly, I finally had a real friend to do all of that with. Before climbing, I'd been a wheezy, pale, and anonymous kid, but finally someone valued my friendship. In fact, my friend needed me—as his belayer and climbing partner—to do the thing we both loved. We were literally tethered together.

Not that my friendship instantly cured me of dorkdum. There was that one time Hartley and I were lying in our hammocks at camp, goofing around with knives. Hartley had a Crocodile Dundee–sized survival knife he'd picked up somewhere, and I had a machete I'd brought back from Ecuador—the universal tool of my family's ranch life. The next thing I knew, I'd managed to slice through the cord that anchored my hammock to the tree and I landed flat on the ground. Hartley and I laughed about that for months.

By my junior year, climbing had helped me evolve enough to achieve what is for teenage boys the highest honor: an actual girlfriend. I'd grown four inches, and thanks to climbing, put on ten pounds of muscle. Hartley was off to Utah for college, but I'd interested another guy I knew, David Von Alman, in climbing. He was a hockey player and a cool kid, and one weekend he invited me to tag along to a house party, where he introduced me to people as his "climbing buddy." I could see in their eyes that they were impressed. Rock climbing—*that sounds cool.* Finally, I wasn't invisible. I also wasn't intimidated. I'd been hanging off a cliff by my fingertips—leaning against a kitchen counter at some high school party chatting with other kids wasn't about to scare me.

To my surprise, even girls wanted to talk to me. Holly White was tall and pretty, even while rocking that 1980s Midwestern hairdo. She wanted to know about rock climbing and wanted to go camping sometime. "I could take you," I said, and before long, we were spending time together in the outdoors, her seeming to be really interested in this aspect of my life when, at the time, no one else but Hartley was. My head was swimming at this swift turn of events.

Holly was my first real girlfriend, and we dated for a year. True to my word, I took her camping and backpacking. Most memorable was the snowstorm we were caught in one October weekend. The snowstorm was fine—it hit after we set up our camp along the Taum Sauk Trail, and we spent a comfortable night in the tent, marveling at the silence that snowfall brings into the woods, laughing whenever we peeked out the door at the inches of snow accumulating. In the morning, we lined our boots with trash bags to keep our socks dry and took our time hiking out, careful not to slip on the snow. What we didn't know was that Holly's dad had been worried about us, which is natural when your child is out in the backcountry and the weather turns severe. What most dads didn't have, however, was a regionally famous nighttime talk show on KMOX, the St. Louis based news and talk-radio station that could be heard across multiple states. While he was urging his listeners to stay off the roads unless absolutely necessary, he also told them that his daughter was out camping with her boyfriend in the storm. "I haven't heard from them," he told listeners across the Midwest. "It seems like they should give us a call to let us know they are okay. Listeners, what do you think?"

Of course, we didn't hear any of it and didn't call in (the cell-phone era had not yet dawned), but plenty of other people did, and agreed with Mr. White that, yes, it was foolish to be out camping in such a storm, and yes, it was irresponsible not to give your parents a call. Years later, once Mr. White heard I'd made it to the top of Everest, he sent along a tape of that show via Holly with a nice note: "Well, Lou, looks like you figured it out."

And yet, I'm far from the only person who has used climbing to figure things out. In fact, these days climbing is experiencing its largest-ever growth period. Formerly a fairly niche activity—not every place has mountains or places suitable for outdoor rock climbing, after all—the sport has seen a huge influx in participants thanks to gyms. Sales of climbing shoes have skyrocketed as the number of climbing gyms has tripled since 2009. There are more than 700 climbing gyms in North America now, with 53 of them opening in 2021.[5] That last bump was achieved, likely, thanks to that year's debut of climbing as an Olympic sport.

It's no wonder. The cost of a day pass is typically less than $30, and much less per session if you buy a monthly or annual pass—compare that with $100-plus a day for a lift ticket at most ski resorts or the $60 median price for 18 holes of golf. Unlike those two sports, or most any sport outside of hiking or running, it's intuitive: you simply climb, as you would a ladder or a tree. Even first-timers can have fun and feel accomplished. Most gyms are at least partially indoors, meaning climbing is something you can do any time of day in any weather, and it's extremely social. Because there are a mix of hard and easy routes, often side-by-side, people of different abilities can all climb together, their belayers chatting away with each other.

Furthermore, climbing gyms are great for the differently abled, with easier access than outdoor climbing spots, and are perfect for kids. A lot of gyms cater specifically to children, with special rooms for birthday parties. My daughter, Sofia, loves going to the Movement gym in Golden, Colorado, for birthday parties or just for a family outing. Some days she'll boulder around, and other days she'll just hang out with friends. To me, it's the adventure sport in which multi-generational growth is most core to the activity. You can make an argument for skiing, where ski school is a core part of the culture, but again, skiing isn't common everywhere—and it's seasonal.

Climbing gyms like Brooklyn Boulders, BlocHaven in Greenville, South Carolina, El Cap in Chicago, and The Strongold

---

5. Climbing gyms were more resilient than traditional gyms during the pandemic, too. Only 3 percent of climbing gyms went out of business during the Covid-19 pandemic, whereas some 20 percent of traditional gyms permanently or temporarily went out of business.

in Los Angeles are typical of the climbing business—mixing climbing and yoga with espresso and co-working spaces. Again, I can go to Movement with Sofia and log onto a work Zoom while she boulders around by herself or with friends. Probably coolest of all the climbing gyms is the nonprofit Memphis Rox, right in the heart of the predominantly Black South Memphis. It offers passes in exchange for volunteering to those for whom money is tight, and free lunches and after-school programs. It's a come-as-you-are haven, offering a safe, climate-controlled place to exercise and grow in a challenged community.

One quirk of the climbing industry is that indoor climbing is currently more popular than outdoor climbing, primarily for reasons of geography—there is only so much exposed rock around, but you can open a climbing gym anywhere—although at hotspots like Red Rock outside Las Vegas, Eldorado Canyon near Boulder, and Joshua Tree National Park in Southern California, the rock is more populated than ever. What I love about climbing, though, is that it can bring economic development to less affluent areas.

I first visited Kentucky's Red River Gorge, in the state's east-central portion, in the 1980s with Hartley, flailing my way up obscure crack climbs with suitably gloomy names like *Boilerplate, Nobody Wins,* and *Darkside of the Flume.* I shudder thinking of groveling up *Darkside's* terrifying offwidth crack, greasy from moss and filled with spider webs—yes, I've grown a little soft living under Colorado's blue skies. When I next returned in the mid-2000s, the Red, as climbers call it, had exploded. There were thousands of new outstanding routes, most of them safely bolted sport climbs. No surprise—the beautiful orange- and brown-splotched cliffs in the Red River Gorge are made of grippy sandstone rife with good pockets and crimper edges, the perfect features for climbing on dead-vertical and overhanging walls, which remains the ultimate climbing thrill. The cliffs are cool in their own right, too, featuring natural amphitheaters and small towers, not to mention hundreds of natural stone arches—the ideal place to fire the imagination of adventuresome climbers.

My first time in the Red, I don't think we stopped at Miguel's, then a little-visited ice-cream shop along a two-lane mountain byway, but I didn't miss it in 2005. Miguel's is a family-owned pizza place and now climber campground that is widely credited for putting rock climbing, and therefore outdoor recreation, on the map in the Red. The Red River Gorge runs through the Daniel Boone National Forest and lies at the intersection of six of the nation's poorest counties. While coal mining supported the economies of Estill, Lee, Menifee, Owsley, Powell, and Wolfe counties starting from the turn of the last century, that industry has been in decline for the last three decades as cheaper, cleaner energy sources power our cities and factories. The region is rich in natural beauty, though—the aforementioned cliffs rise above a rich hardwood canopy, famed for its bright foliage come fall, and mist drifts through the valleys year-round.

The Portuguese immigrant Miguel Ventura and his wife moved to the Red in 1984 and opened their ice-cream shop alongside Natural Bridge Road, which is below a state park of the same name—and is today the route to many of the popular crags. A year later, the climber Martin Hackworth opened a tiny climbing-gear shop in a corner of the store, and Miguel's primary customers became climbers. To feed them something more substantial, he began making pizza, and an institution was born. These days, Miguel's empire includes seven rental cabins, a standalone gear shop, and a field for tent camping. It hosts parties at the pavilion, and employs climbers, giving them a place to live. Since its days as the so-called "dirtbag salon" in the 1980s, it has given climbers and visitors a place for community to coalesce, encouraging yet more visitation.

Today, the Red River Gorge sees about 102,000 climber visits a year according to a 2020 Eastern Kentucky University study, and climbers bring in an estimated $8.7 million to the six counties around the Red. The study found that typically climbers spend $74 per person per trip, and an additional $5 to $40 for lodging (the $5 figure is most likely tent camping at Miguel's). That may not sound like a lot of money overall, but it goes a long way in rural Kentucky—the median household income in the Red River Gorge region is $30,064.

Importantly, climbers were the first to visit the Red for recreation. Hikers followed them, and these days the region is home to a remarkable cornucopia of ORec options, from ziplining to mini golf to horseback riding to, somewhat bizarrely, kayak tours in a flooded underground mine.

The report also makes the point that climbers tend to be well educated, with 44 percent holding a bachelor's and 40 percent holding an advanced degree. Not to stereotype too much, but tourists with master's degrees tend to be a little easier on the communities they visit—they aren't the ones typically starting bar fights at the local watering hole.

In another community whose coal-mining prospects are dimming, Orangeville, Utah, residents are starting to understand the same thing: rock climbers who seem to dress like homeless vagrants usually, in fact, aren't. Orangeville is a very quiet, predominantly Mormon ranching and coal community well off the beaten path from Utah's recreation hotspots like Moab, Park City, and Kanab. It just so happens to be the site of one of rock climbing's emerging hotspots, the sandstone boulders of Joe's

Valley. Climbers have been visiting the house-sized rocks in a valley near a pair of recently closed coal mines for almost thirty years, but visitation has skyrocketed in the last decade.

At first, Orangeville locals were perplexed by the crowds of youngsters wandering along the road with what seemed to be small mattresses (their bouldering crashpads) strapped to their backs and paying $5 to shower at the town rec center. Then, about a decade ago, a group of Salt Lake City climbers saw a flier at the grocery store for a community cleanup and decided to pitch in. When they showed up, though, the women running the event told them the free food wouldn't be available for several hours, assuming the climbers were just looking for a handout. Climber Steven Jefferey laughed, grabbed a garbage bag, and said that they really were there to help with the cleanup. "I swear I thought you guys were just taking naps up there amongst the rocks with those mattresses," one of the Orangeville residents said that day.

The local chamber of commerce brought Jeffery in to give a presentation to members about rock climbers. He cited a 2017 version of the University of Eastern Kentucky study about the economic impact of climbers in the Red River Gorge—$3.8 million annually at the time—and he showed them a slide of a Sprinter van. "You've all seen these, right?" he asked, and they all laughed because of course they'd seen dozens of them streaming through town, driven by climbers, and parked at the grocery store. "Fully outfitted, those things run $60,000 to $100,000. This isn't the old Volkswagen Bus." That got their attention.

Eventually, Jeffery and a few locals started a climbing festival with the express interest of integrating climbers with residents. They brought in local vendors like the pizza shop and the butcher to sell their wares, and raffled off donated apparel and gear to climbers and locals alike in order to build a public kid's climbing wall. Unique to the Joe's Valley Fest is the climber's rodeo, where all are invited to try their hand at bronc riding and a chicken chase.

The Orangeville grocery began stocking microbrews, kombucha, and even climbing chalk. Bed and breakfasts with names like Boulder Haus and the Hangout have appeared. One local Mormon couple opened a coffee shop in the front room of their house—Cup of Joe's—even though their faith prohibits them from drinking the stuff. Cammie Stilson needed to work from home in order to take care of her son with special needs, and they liked the climbers they'd met in town. Cammie learned to pull an espresso shot with good crema from YouTube, and five years later, their business is booming and the couple is delighted that the world map they hung in the café is bristling with pins from more than fifty nations. Cammie and Doug Stilson count Jeffery and other climbers who've moved to town as close friends, and are grateful that Cammie was able to create a fulfilling career without having to leave her hometown.

In my home state of Colorado, the most dramatic story of recreation transforming a community in recent times is that of Fruita[6]. The town of 4,000 was traditionally a ranching town and bedroom community for neighboring Grand Junction, Colorado's

---

6. I'm largely setting aside name-brand ski towns in this book, apart from addressing concerns in the last chapter of ski resort communities being impacted by the exorbitant prices and overcrowding brought by the pandemic Zoom boom. While many ski resorts were founded for community fun in the 1930s through the 1960s, many of the major modern resorts established since that time were designed by the rich for the rich, often as development ventures to sell second homes. That boom largely ended in the 1970s. In Colorado, for example, before Silverton Mountain opened in 2002, the most recently opened resort had been Beaver Creek, in 1980. Given the changing climate, virtually no one is considering opening new ski resorts. Rather, ski resort operators are more concerned with developing summertime recreation—mountain biking, hiking, rock climbing, and zip lines—in order to increase revenue and hedge against diminishing snowpacks.

mineral-extraction capital. Then, in the 1980s, a historic shale bust leveled the local economy. Homes and storefronts in both Grand Junction and Fruita lay vacant as more than 10,000 residents migrated away for better economic opportunity. Then, in the early 1990s, as mountain biking began flourishing, locals began riding their bikes on the cow trails threading federal BLM range surrounding town. Soon, they began improving those trails and building new ones, hosting weekend-long dig parties to create interesting routes through the desert. By 1995, there was enough demand for a local bike shop, and Over the Edge opened downtown and helped launch their now-famous Fruita Fat Tire Festival, drawing thousands from across the nation to ride and camp in the desert.

By 2017, Fruita boasted 250 miles of serpentine, swooping trail and new residents were moving to town to take advantage of the trail system and bike culture. The population had nearly tripled to 13,000, and derelict homes were being bid up to a median home price of $235,000, an increase of 147 percent over 1995. What critics of outdoor recreation often misunderstand is that recreation amenities don't just bring tourists; they also bring new residents and businesses. Bike shops, breweries, and restaurants had revitalized the once-foundering community. In an echo of Miguel's in the Red River Gorge, Fruita's cycling community centered on a pizza place—The Hot Tomato. The pizza shop was founded by an openly gay couple, Jen Zeuner and Anne Keller, a heartening thing to see in a rural town.

Former mayor Lori Buck estimates that mountain biking brings $14.5 million annually to the community. I met Buck on a trip to Fruita in 2017, when I was working as the Colorado ORec director. I was there with Governor Hickenlooper to celebrate a state grant of $2 million to help complete the Colorado Riverfront Trail, a hugely popular, paved twenty-two-mile pathway stretching from Fruita through Grand Junction along the Colorado River.

As the governor's delegation cycled the path, Lori told me how much more vital Fruita has become. She mentioned driving downtown with her twelve-year-old daughter one busy fall day, with all the parking spaces occupied by cars draped in mountain bikes, and pedestrians crossing from one shop to another. Spontaneously, her daughter said, "I love living here!" That's not something I would ever have said about Fruita when I was twelve," Lori told me. "It was just a decaying, dull town when I was a kid."

The resurgence continues. In 2020, the manufacturer Canfield Bikes moved to Fruita from Bellingham, Washington, drawn by the warm, dry weather and thriving outdoor culture. Helping that decision was the $60,000 grant from the Colorado Office of Economic Development and International Trade and a second, $62,500 grant from the Grand Junction Economic Partnership awarded to Canfield for bringing twenty year-round, good-paying jobs to the region. The grants stipulate that the added jobs pay 111 percent of the average Mesa County wage ($24.77/hour in 2020). Then, in 2021, the city implemented a 3 percent lodging tax for short-term rentals and hotels to help fund parks and trails, amongst other things. Fruita expects to collect $64,000 annually and plans to keep expanding the local trail system, with thirty more miles of trail on tap paid for with tax revenue and grants from the State of Colorado.

The former logging town of Oakridge, Oregon, has been similarly transformed by mountain-bike trails. The town of 3,200 about 40 miles east of Eugene fell on hard times when their sawmill closed in the 1990s. In 2004, the city received a grant to develop a trail plan and subsequently built 380 miles of trails. A

2014 University of Oregon study estimated that mountain-bike tourism generates as much as $5 million in direct spending a year. New businesses like the bike-tour company Cog Wild, the Deep Woods Distillery, a coffee shop, and a microbrewery have opened in town to serve visitors and locals alike. Lucas St. Clair likes to joke that you can really tell the ORec economy has taken hold in a place when someone opens a microbrewery there.

More surprising has been the case of the Cuyuna Lakes region of Minnesota, where mountain bikers have built trails atop century-old mine tailings and around the lakes formed in abandoned mine pits. The Cuyuna region's iron mines had supplied the girders that built the first Chicago and New York skyscrapers, and tanks and aircraft carriers for world wars I and II. By the 1970s, however, the most valuable ore had been mined and the companies had moved on, leaving piles of red tailings, rusting old mining equipment, and toxic, turquoise-tinged lakes in the ore pits. People dumped trash and broken appliances at the site, and the surrounding communities of Cuyuna, Crosby, and Ironton lost population and businesses.

In 1993, old-timers worked to declare the 5,000-acre site a state recreation area to honor the region's mining heritage (and help dissuade illegal dumping). Birch trees and ferns returned, even if few people paid the protected land much mind. Then, in the mid-2000s, mountain bikers from Minneapolis, 125 miles to the south, decided that Cuyuna Country State Recreation Area would make a perfect place to ride. They liked the rolling hills (200-foot-tall tailings piles) and grip of the ground-up bedrock (bikers there have deemed this "Cayuna Gold" the perfect mountain-biking surface). With the help of the International Mountain Bicycling Association (IMBA), the Minneapolis cyclists successfully lobbied Minnesota to create the state's first mountain-biking state park, within the state recreation area.

The locals were perplexed, or worse—many had used the recreation area for dirt biking and ATV riding, and realized the new trails would ruin their fun. Moreover, they figured the $700,000 the state spent on twenty-five miles of trails wouldn't yield much economic return. According to the Minnesota Public Radio reporter Dan Kraker, the joke around Crosby was that the spandex-clad mountain bikers "don't have pockets on their pants, so how can they bring any money to town?"

Those jokes, while funny, became quickly obsolete. When the trails opened in 2011, visitation began immediately. That first year, 18,000 riders hit the trails. By 2020, that number was up to 180,000, an amazing tenfold increase. The trail system has expanded to more than fifty miles, and twenty new businesses have opened in neighboring communities, including bike shops, two wood-fired pizza restaurants, a yoga studio, a tiny-house hotel that caters to cyclists, and yes, a microbrewery—the Cuyuna Brewing Company. "It's unbelievable—eighteen months ago, probably 50 percent of the buildings in town were vacant," the Crosby realtor Joel Hartman told Kraker in 2016. "But now, today, there are very few opportunities for investors to buy buildings because they have been purchased."

According to the Minnesota Department of Employment and Economic Development, Crosby, Ironton and Irondale Township added 132 jobs between 2011 and 2016—a 7.7 percent growth rate that was about twice that of the rest of the region. Even the longtime owner of the Dairy Queen changed his mind. The former dirt biker had originally opposed the trails, but once he rode them on his circa-1985 mountain bike, he threw down $3,200 on a brand-new modern rig the following week.

Inspired by Cuyuna's success, just a few years later Minnesota's

Iron Range Resources and Rehabilitation (IRRR) development agency plunked $2 million into yet another twenty-five-mile trail system built atop mine tailings, this time in Chisholm, 108 miles to the north. Within a year of their 2021 opening, 25,000 people had ridden the newly christened Redhead Mountain Bike Park. The city of Chisolm has also opened a kayak- and paddleboard-rental operation on the lake the trail system circumnavigates.

Critics had charged that the IRRR funds could be better spent investing in industries with higher-paying jobs than retail and food service, but IRRR Commissioner Mark Phillips told Minnesota Public Radio's Dan Kraker that improving quality of life is an equally important goal, because people want to live and work in places with outdoor-recreation amenities. "I want to create a higher-, a better-quality life on the Iron Range," said Phillips. "So that people want to live here, and then they'll start businesses . . . and I think the mountain-biking thing is just one component of that."

Also chipping in funds to develop Redhead and expand Cuyuna is the three-eighths of 1 percent sales tax that Minnesota voters approved in 2008—the Clean Water, Land, and Legacy Amendment. The program has helped fund more than $2 billion in work for projects like rehabbing abandoned mine sites into mountain-bike parks, building 100 miles of trail within Duluth, and supporting game- and fish-habitat restoration. There's no doubt that Minnesota understands that recreation needs to be funded for both its citizens' quality of life and to keep the wheels of commerce moving.

****

It's not just communities where extractive industries have

moved on—one of my favorite stories of outdoor recreation transforming unlikely places is in Bentonville, Arkansas. Famously the home of the Walmart headquarters, Bentonville is also the site of an experiment led by the Walmart heirs—the brothers and cycling fanatics Tom and Steuart Walton—to transform Bentonville via bicycle trails. In 2007, Bentonville began building bike trails in city parks and open spaces, largely paid for via $74 million in Walton Family Foundation grants. Today, there are 142 miles of linked trail in Bentonville, part of a trail network of 500 miles in the Northwest Arkansas region, virtually all of it built in the last fifteen years.

The results have been dramatic, so much so that IMBA picked Bentonville for their world summit in 2016. Bentonville also now calls itself the Mountain Biking Capital of the World, and thousands visit annually to see if the audacious claim holds up. For my money, the town is certainly in the running. The system features trails for all levels, from pump tracks for kids to dramatic jump lines for fearless teens to rolling cross-country for Gen-Xers like me. I saw the network firsthand in 2016, while representing the State of Colorado for the IMBA summit, and zipped around berms and over artful wooden structures on an e-bike.[7] A 2017 study by the nonprofit PeopleForBikes showed that bicycling brought $137 million in economic benefits to the region in the previous year, including $27 million from out-of-state visitors.

What has made Bentonville most successful in the eyes of many, however, is that trail-building efforts focused first and foremost on the needs of residents. The first batch of trails was built in and around neighborhoods and connected to the paved

---

7. I borrowed an e-bike to ride the trails, because I wanted to demonstrate that e-bikes aren't out of place on the trails. Some have a tendency to criticize e-bikes as cheating, but I've long been a proponent of them as a way to increase access for the differently abled—outdoor recreation is a benefit that should be open to all, regardless of age or health status.

Razorback Regional Greenway. Not only is the ideal trailhead your home's garage, as the saying goes, but the trails make great connectors between different parts of the city—for kids riding to school, for adults commuting to work, and for residents cycling to dinner. A 2021 PeopleForBikes survey found that 26 percent of Benton County residents reported riding more than 35 days a year, landing them in the organization's "enthusiastic rider" category. The study also found that 79 percent of residents agree or strongly agree that bicycling is good for the community. That puts Bentonville at the number-one spot in the organization's Community Score rankings.

Additional smart community support came from the Walton Family Foundation: in 2022, it gave the City of Bentonville a $725,943 grant to help pay for six new fire-department employees, recognizing that increased cycling has led to a rise in cycling accidents, to which firefighters typically respond.

What is so great to me is that one of the hidden motivations for the Waltons' investment was to help attract and retain talent for Walmart itself. I saw firsthand working at the VF Corp that money isn't enough for Gen X, Millennials, and Gen Z—they demand amenities for a high quality of life, and in the rocky, rolling woodlands of northwest Arkansas, cycling was the quickest way to stamp Bentonville as exceptional. Along with the trails came hip bike shops, and the sort of tony restaurants and coffee shops that cyclists love to frequent (many established by Tom Walton himself). According to Bentonville city staff, in 2005, there were one retailer and two restaurants downtown. Now, there are eight retailers and sixteen restaurants. It is of course the great irony that a company that has been charged with hollowing out the downtown business core of countless communities has reinvested in the core of their own hometown.

The agenda to attract and retain young talent with trails is working, Tom Walton told me in 2016 at the conference. The company's new recruits have seemingly begun to change the corporation's culture. In recent years, the famously bottom-line-above-all-company has added benefits such as parental leave, and, in 2015, it sided against legislation that created the potential for hiring discrimination among LGBTQIA+ applicants. Then, in 2018, Walmart raised the minimum age for buying guns from 18 to 21, following a school shooting in Florida.

The Waltons aren't just building trails to attract new workers; they actually paid people to move to Bentonville. In 2020, the Walton Family Foundation-funded Northwest Arkansas Council launched a program to offer people $10,000 and a bicycle to relocate to the region. (Those who aren't interested in the bike could swap it out for a free annual membership to a local arts-and-culture institution like Bentonville's famous Crystal Bridges Museum of American Art.) The incentive program attracted more than 66,000 applicants, from whom 100 winners were selected. The incentive program is currently paused, but their website still serves as an advertisement for the region's low cost of living and cultural and outdoor amenities, featuring several photos of cyclists.

Such incentive programs to entice remote workers to relocate exist in other places like Tulsa, Oklahoma, but programs in Vermont and in West Virginia tout outdoor recreation as a primary draw along with a lower cost of living. The Ascend West Virginia website goes particularly hard on outdoor rec, flashing up-top a reel of people paddleboarding, rock climbing, and mountain biking in atmospheric 4K resolution. That's above a headline that offers $12,000 in cash plus free outdoor recreation for a year. The details: $10K in payments over your first year, an additional $2K at the end of your second year of residency, and coupons for free lift tickets and rentals at ski areas, whitewater rafting companies, and guided rock climbing, among other things. The coupons are good for two years. Beneath that is a list of the state's ORec bona fides: 4,000 climbing routes, 98,000 miles of rivers and streams, thirty-five state parks, etc. The program aspires to recruit 1,000 new residents to West Virginia by 2025. It's pretty tempting to apply, even as a Colorado resident.

West Virginia is interesting, too, in that they are also angling for the motorized crowd. One of the outdoor amenities that the Ascend West Virginia website touts is the Hatfield-McCoy Trails. Purpose-built for ATVs, the trail network first opened in 2000, and now comprises some 1,000 miles of trail across nine counties. Like the mountain-bike trail systems in Fruita, Oregon, and Minnesota, the Hatfield-McCoy Trails were envisioned as both a tourism draw and an amenity for locals. They are administered by a quasi-governmental agency that collects revenue from trail permits, 95,000 of which were sold in 2021. Most interesting to me is that the trails are largely built on private land, with agreements forged between landowners and the agency. It's all possible because landowners in the system are protected from liability by state law. It's a great model for trails in states where there aren't vast swaths of publicly owned land.

States like Utah and Colorado hardly need to advertise themselves to remote workers as great places to live if you like to ski or climb—just watch the fleets of tricked-out Sprinter vans inching through bumper-to-bumper traffic in Moab, Utah, and Aspen, Colorado. Those two states are in a constant cold war to recruit employers, however, often touting outdoor rec as an employee benefit. Salt Lake City, famously, landed a huge staff expansion from Goldman Sachs and Adobe based partly on the world-class skiing above town. Salt Lake's Lucid Software has made outdoor recreation a cornerstone of its recruiting efforts, competing with tech giants like Apple and Google in hiring more than 1,000 software engineers. As the outdoor-recreation czar for Colorado, part of my job was to help lure industry to the state. Outdoor recreation (not legalized weed) was the first bullet point on our sales pitch—the twenty-six ski resorts, the eleven national forests, the dozens of wild rivers. On my watch, at least five companies, including the medical-equipment manufacturer DaVita Kidney Care and the multi-billion-dollar VF Corp, for whom I later worked, relocated to Colorado.

Outdoor recreation isn't the perfect panacea. There can be negative side effects to growth, as any Moab resident will tell you—things like traffic, overcrowding, trash, erosion on local trails, and higher grocery costs and property taxes. For a relatively low cost, however, outdoor-rec infrastructure like new trails, or parking and restrooms at climber's trailheads, can have a remarkable return on investment. For example, the Silver Comet Trail, a multiuse path thirteen miles northwest of Atlanta, draws an estimated 1.9 million users per year. According to studies, the $59 million trail system generates $4.64 in direct and indirect benefits for every $1 spent on its construction and maintenance. Communities unfailingly see an economic uptick when they invest in outdoor recreation, not only in home values and tax base, but in allowing opportunities for rural communities to retain residents—as in the case of the Stilsons in Orangeville, Utah.

Even more important, however, is the quality-of-life benefit. The newly avid local riders of Bentonville would agree, as would the Dairy Queen owner in Cayuna, Minnesota. I want the outdoor-recreation lifestyle for *every* resident of *every* community, because I've lived a life in which it made all the difference for me. After I found climbing, even though I was the kid with the weird last name who might still get called "spic" or "wetback," it just didn't bother me much because I had an identity: I was a climber, and I was on my way to the top of the highest mountain in the world.

Chapter 5

ECUADOR AND EQUITY

"You can discover more about an individual in an hour of play than in a year of conversation."
—Quote attributed to Plato

In June 2001, a few weeks after Erik Weihenmayer and the rest of our team returned from Everest, we were making the rounds of the television talk shows. I accompanied Erik to the *Today* show. We were hanging out in the green room, along with Erik's wife, Ellie, and their one-year-old daughter, Emma, when the producer appeared to brief us. She said they just wanted Erik for the segment—no other team members. I was a little disappointed, but had been prepared for the vagaries of such shows. I was holding Emma, making faces, trying to coax her to laugh. I may even have had her diaper bag over my shoulder.

"How long have you been with the Weihenmayers?" the producer asked me, taking a seat. I looked at her with a quizzical expression, so she followed up with, "Do you like being an au pair?"

Before I could correct her, Erik, with a chuckle, said, "We are so happy to have Luis here. We really want Emma to learn Spanish." Busting your Everest guide down to the level of exchange-student baby wrangler was precisely the kind of good-spirited hazing our team had perfected over the past three months, and I thought it was hilarious. (I'm no Paul Rudd, but what adult doesn't enjoy being teased for appearing to be younger than they actually are?) Before I could set the record straight, though, Erik was called to the set, and he and the producer left the green room.

During his appearance, Erik did give me a shout out, saying that the Everest team had remained close and were far from fame-seeking mercenaries. "In fact, the guy I walked to the very summit with is backstage right now, holding my toddler," said Erik. The producer was mortified, but I thought it was great. I saw it for the innocuous misunderstanding that it was, predicated on my race, yes, but mostly on my baby-faced looks. The mix-up was indicative, though, of how few people of color were outdoor professionals or even participants in 2001. Though the situation has improved today, we've still got a long way to go.

My grandmother Blanca Marina Vasconez de Benítez was Quechua, the people native to the Andes. In my grandfather, she married an Ecuadorian of Spanish descent, and much of their time was spent in the city so their children could attend school. As often as she could, though, she spent time on the family's ranch near Cayambe, where she loved to be outside gardening or tending to the animals, or walking the highlands, fishing, or gathering wild herbs.

Abuelita, as my cousins and I called her, grew up without a pharmacy, so her remedies were of the land. To help clear my lungs, she made me sit over bowls of steaming, acrid liquid, medicine she'd concocted from herbs she'd picked herself. I inhaled the vapors with a warm, wet towel over my head. For the soup she served me, she dug the potatoes herself and killed the chickens. I remember chicken feet floating in my bowl. She was dark-skinned and spoke both Quechua and Spanish. Even now, my Spanish is peppered with Quechua—terms like *nyana* and *nyano* standing in for *hermana* and *hermano,* Spanish for "sister" and "brother," or *jua jua* for "baby," in lieu of the Spanish *bebe*.

The first time I saw an animal butchered was by Abuelita's hand. When I was nine, she told me that we were going to have lamb for dinner. She handed me a machete and told me to collect firewood. We didn't use axes in Ecuador—all of the cutting and chopping was done with a machete. By the time I returned from the brush with an armload of wood, the animal was hanging in the courtyard, dripping blood from its neck into a bowl, and Abuelita was skinning its fleece. She cooked the lamb over the fire on a spit that we took turns spinning for hours.

The family ranch was two hours northeast of Quito, in the high desert at 8,000 feet. The snow-capped volcano Cayambe loomed just north of the ranch, rising to 18,996 feet. When our family came from St. Louis in the summers to visit, Abuelita would point to the cement basin in the courtyard where the laundry was scrubbed and tell me, "That's where I used to give you a bath, Lucho." She wasn't trying to embarrass me, but to help me remember.

My Ecuadorian family's ambition all resided in my father, Ramiro, the eldest of their five children. He'd been sent to the best schools in Quito, and then to Saint Louis University in the United States to study aerospace engineering. There, he met a smart and sophisticated Irish-Italian art student named Rosanna Kelley at a party (my mom likes to tell stories that she was the only one in her circle of friends growing up who was both a skeet shooting champion and a beauty queen at the same time), and it wasn't long before he and my mother were married. After college, he went to work for the aerospace giant McDonnell Douglas as an engineer working on the NASA Mercury and Gemini projects as well as fighter-jet cockpits. Though he'd planned on returning to Ecuador to live, the severity of my asthma made it more practical to stay in the United States, closer to better medical care.

We visited Ecuador once when I was six months old, but then not again until I was ten. By then, we'd started to get the asthma under control thanks to better application of medicines and my hard work on the Little Debbie Swim Team. The real breakthrough came when our doctor said that the high altitudes of Ecuador might be just the thing to help strengthen my lungs. The Barrio San Juan neighborhood where my father's family lived was at an altitude of 9,300 feet and had hills as steep as those in San Francisco; we started spending summers there, getting to know my aunts and uncles and the dozens of cousins.

Apart from my Abuelita, of my family in Ecuador, I was closest to my uncles. My uncle Alfonso was six-foot-four and looked like a Latino Abraham Lincoln—lean and with thick, tousled black hair and eyebrows. He took charge of the family ranch, working to diversify its operations. He eschewed the roses that were the popular cash crop in the 1990s—all exported to the United States via the Quito airport—and decided to plant watermelon and avocado instead. Rather than deplete the soils with the frivolous roses, he wanted to plant things that would help feed the Ecuadorian population. He also experimented with a trout farm, working to create a more natural riverine environment for the fish rather than the typical concrete ponds.

The ranch was a passion project for him. His day job was helping his wife run her successful line of boutique clothing stores. In fact, profits from the products she designed and the shops they ran actually subsidized the ranch and Alfonso's efforts to make its operations more sustainable. I'm sure he enjoyed the clothing business, but he always looked more comfortable to me in his ranchwear than in his business suit. He was a man far ahead of his time, and has been an ongoing inspiration to me in my conservation, recreation, and sustainability work for the State of Colorado and for the VF corp.

As a teenager, I had a real *Lion King* moment with Alfonso. We were taking in the vista from the ranch's high point, overlooking the watermelon fields and the trout ponds, the broad cone of Cayambe looming over it all, its glaciers reflecting the sun. "Wherever you go, whatever you do, however long you stay away, this is who you are," he said. "This land is who you are."

From my uncle Peppin, I got a love of the mountains. Peppin was an engineer by trade, but a mountaineer by passion. He was a member of one of Ecuador's avid mountaineering clubs, spending weekends scaling any of the nation's dozen glaciated volcanoes, from Cayambe to 16,480-foot Tungurahua, 17,218-foot Illinaza, Chimborazo at 20,564 feet, and of course Ecuador's crown jewel, the perfect cone of 19,347-foot Cotopaxi. Peppin was of medium height, slight of build, and a very swift hiker, as I learned trying to keep up with him. My family says that if I were to grow a mustache, I'd look exactly like he did. It's a poignant reminder—both Peppin and Alfonso passed away from cancer in the early 2000s. Losing Peppin and Alfonso, not to mention Grandfather Kelley, set me emotionally adrift for a long time. No one has had a bigger influence on my life than these three men. Not a day goes by that I don't wish I had their council.

I spent as much time hiking in the mountains with Peppin as I could. I remember rumbling up the dirt roads to the trailheads in his sky-blue Land Rover Defender 110. He was quiet, though with a deep, full-body laugh, and my Spanish wasn't as good as it should have been in those early summers, so a lot of the two-hour drives were spent in silence, listening to the radio. Sometimes, I'd point to different things out the windshield and he'd tell me the names: a pine tree (*pino*), the tall bunch grass (*paramo*). On the trail, he taught me how to change my pace depending on the terrain, conserving my energy with rest steps heading uphill in the thin air. In later summers, he also taught me to drive in his Land Rover on the steep streets of the Barrio San Juan in Quito.

It must have been Peppin's idea when I was twelve to bring us all to the Cotopaxi mountaineer's *refugio* for a picnic—my first of literally hundreds of visits to the fabled mountain. Many of Ecuador's volcanoes feature stone-walled lodges that serve as basecamps for climbers, generally just a kilometer from the trailhead. Perhaps Peppin reasoned that if the 9,300-foot altitude of the Bario San Juan was good for sickly little Lucho, the 15,000-foot altitude of the Cotopaxi refugio would be even better. Peppin, I, and a few aunts and cousins all piled into my aunt's pickup for the Sunday outing. I should say that the adults piled in—the kids were made to sit in the bed of the pickup truck as we roared down the Pan-American Highway in the brisk air at 11,000 feet. I remember fighting off the cold by huddling against the cab under the wool blankets they'd thrown into the back with us, thrilled by the wind creasing my hair and the new landscape unfurling around me.

The picnic tradition is a strong one in Latino culture. In the United States, it's one of Latinos' most common forms of outdoor recreation, a model less of "individualistic adventurer" and more of "collective sustenance." All over Colorado, I see Latino families gathered around picnic tables at municipal parks and USFS day-use areas. It's not just day use either. At state parks, the group campsites are often booked by multigenerational families; you seldom see them occupying single-family sites. I continue to call on USFS, NPS, and BLM park planners nationwide to create more group campsites with the Latino population in mind. These small acts can provide more inclusivity to families who believe in the strength and experience of doing things together.

On Cotopaxi, though, we didn't have the mouthwatering barbacoa beef or tamales of those gatherings—we'd packed just baloney sandwiches for the hourlong hike. Furthermore, once we arrived at the orange-roofed stone refuge, it was snowing and the glaciated peak above was obscured by clouds. We quickly hustled inside.

Peppin greeted the hut keeper, whom he knew well, and we sat at the wooden tables in the living room to eat our sandwiches. Soon, the front door opened, and a team of mountaineers stumbled in from the pelting snow. The men, their beards clad in ice, and women clomped across the wooden floor in thick, heavy boots, dropping packs that clanked and jangled with metal axes and crampons. They all had the sort of determined presence of people fully engaged in a mission. It was like they'd walked right out of the pages of the mountaineering books and magazines I'd been reading back home. I instantly recognized them as the community that I wanted to belong to. Pepin laughed and told me to stop staring.

A few years later, I got a summer position working as a hut boy at the Cotopaxi refugio. My job was to get up in the dark to melt ice to fill water bottles, to help make breakfast, and to sweep the floors once the mountaineers had all left to head up the peak in the pre-dawn hours. I'd step outside in the dark and look uphill to see the pinpoints of light from the climbers' headlamps winding up the glacier, seemingly right into the stars.

When the climbers returned from the peak, I'd make friends. There were always people who turned back early from the summit attempt, because of fatigue, fear, or most commonly, altitude sickness—when your headache sharpens with every upward step, and every other thought you have is, "If I just head down now, this pain will subside."

I'd find the turnarounders hunched over the tables in the living room and strike up a conversation. The Ecuadorian volcanoes are a training ground for the stratosphere of the Himalaya and were always packed with climbers from around the world. I'd ask them about their nations: the politics, the economics, the climbing culture. It often got deep, as climbers who have come up against failure can be very vulnerable and honest. Turning back on a climb is a raw moment, and that appealed to me as a teenager navigating the superficial world of American high school. One young man was about to become a father for the first time. One woman said she felt bad about leaving her kids at home. "Climbing is in my blood," she said. "I can't seem to help it." Everyone seemed to be searching for a way to test themselves. I began to realize that adventure in these mountains involved more than just the physical challenge of reaching the top.

One day, while sitting at a table with a Swiss, a Russian, a Czech, and a Dutch woman, all from different climbing parties, discussing economics and politics in English, I felt as happy as I'd ever been. I was an Ecuadorian-American kid, hanging out having real discussions with adults about the world, all at 15,000 feet on the side of a mountain. I felt like this was where I was meant to be, that I'd taken my first steps toward my Everest dream.

I also felt physically stronger than ever. Despite the oxygen-thin air at altitude, mountaineering helped me breathe more easily. Pressure breathing is a common technique for mountaineers at high altitude: you inhale as fully as possible, and then forcefully exhale from the belly. It helps improve gas exchange across the alveoli by increasing pressure in the lungs. It was also the technique a nurse had taught me as a young kid when I was having an asthma attack.

"Pretend you are sitting across the table from a birthday cake," she'd said. "Now purse your lips and try to blow out the candles." I took as big a breath as I could and then exhaled slowly, imagining the cake, the flickering candles, the gifts. Almost immediately, it worked. I felt better, more oxygenated, and less panicky. I used pressure breathing as a kid whenever I felt short of breath. When I arrived on Ecuador's high peaks, I was ahead of the curve physically for the first time in my life.

My first break into the guiding ranks happened on Cotopaxi. One of the international mountain guides wandered into the refugio kitchen one evening when I was working. "Luis, we have a problem," he said. "Our assistant guide didn't come up from Quito this afternoon. We don't have a turnaround guide for if anyone gets sick and needs to be escorted back to the hut."

I still had to do the job I'd been hired to do—clean up dinner, sweep the floors, make sure all the water bottles were filled—but what I heard was, "You just got your first job as a mountain guide."

He handed me a radio. If any of their clients turned back, he said, he'd radio for me to hike to the bottom of the glacier and lead them back to the hut, over the talus field in the dark. As I lay in my bunk that night, I remember thinking, "Please, let somebody get altitude sickness." I was desperate to prove myself to these guides, my heroes.

At 3:00 a.m., the radio crackled to life.

"Luis, I have two clients who aren't feeling well. I'm going to leave them at the edge of the glacier. Can you come up and help them down?"

I jumped out of bed and raced downstairs. I chopped up cheese and salami, and filled a thermos with tea, wanting to impress the ailing clients with the royal treatment I assumed they were accustomed to. I raced up to the glacier, about a mile through the red, volcanic talus. At 4:00 a.m., still in the dark, I laid out my beautiful picnic.

"Good morning—my name is Luis," I said to the two guys zombie-stepping toward me down the slope, pale, sweaty, and queasy from the altitude. "Would you like some cheese and crackers and salami?" Instead, one of them threw up all over my spread.

The next summer, when I was fifteen, I transitioned into being a junior guide for a local company called Safari Tours. I was the turnaround kid. If anyone got sick, I turned around with them and headed back down to the hut. If someone had read *Outside* magazine, liked the glossy pictures, and bought all the gear at REI, but then took one step onto the glacier and thought, "This isn't for me," I turned around with them. I climbed on Cotopaxi twenty-two times before I ever summited.

When I finally did summit late that summer, it was worth the wait. I crawled out of my sleeping bag at midnight and stumbled downstairs to shovel down porridge even though I wasn't the least bit hungry yet. I herded the group along through coffee and breakfast, and trips to the bathroom, and waited patiently on the concrete pad outside for the ropeteam to assemble. Once the team was all there, we switched on our headlamps and started the slow, hour-long trudge toward the glacier, wobbly on the loose rocks in the stiff plastic boots we required of our clients—boots suited to taking crampons for glacier travel.

At the glacier's edge, we sat down and pulled the crampons on, threaded the rope through our harness loops, and started upward, ice axes in hand. The crunch of the metal on ice always seems louder in the dark.

In the lead, I marked crevasses with a bamboo wand. Walking slowly to preserve breath in the thin air, I had plenty of time to look at the view. I could see the glow of the Quito's lights to the north. To the east, clouds covering the oceanic and dark Amazon Basin, occasionally illuminated by heat lightning, floated well below us.

The sunrise on the equatorial volcanoes is like nowhere else on Earth. Sunlight streaming through the moist tropical air makes colors somehow denser and richer. The snow surface blazing, almost rosy, the blue and red jackets of my climbers incandescent, their faces glowing with the swell of mood after hours of trudging through the dark. Finally, around 8:00 a.m., we made our final small steps to the summit.

What I'd always heard about but hadn't been prepared for was Cotopaxi's smoking volcanic crater. Just beyond the summit, it plunges malevolently to 800 feet deep, with its gray and red walls and floor. Steam issued from several vents. I couldn't help but think of the mountain's violent potential power. Stratovolcanoes like it had blown with devastating force, as Mount Saint Helen's had in my youth—and indeed, Cotopaxi is currently closed to climbing because of frequent small eruptions. Just being near that force was an additional thrill. I couldn't help but feel tiny and humble. I hoped that these clients, high-fiving one another, their fatigue replaced for the moment by triumph, felt it too.

I'm grateful for my time on Cotopaxi, for the foundation it gave me in the mountaineering profession. I'm also grateful to have gotten my start in a place where the industry was populated by people who looked and sounded like me—people like Iván Vallejo, who worked with Peppin and was the first Ecuadorian to climb Everest and was one of the first ten people to climb all fourteen of the 8,000-meter peaks without supplemental oxygen. No matter how few people of color I encountered in the outdoor industry in the United States, I knew that in South America the mountains and rivers were full of people who looked and sounded like me.

Not everyone is so lucky.

In the United States, only 20–30 percent of outdoorists are people of color. It's similar in the outdoor industry itself. Of the 20,000 or so NPS employees, for example, 83 percent are white. In certain sports—skiing, mountain biking, surfing—it's worse. Only 3 percent of hunters are people of color.

To me, that's a tragedy. The awe I've felt watching the sun rise from the flank of a mountain, or when ducks set their wings to land as the first rays of light break through the trees, should be available to everyone. Every American should be able to challenge their minds and bodies rock climbing, or shooting tumultuous whitewater, as I was able to.

I want everyone to experience the satisfying simplicity of living for days out of the pack on your back as you walk the spine of a mountain range. The health benefits of letting your mind unspool in a desert canyon far from the incessant honking of cars and screeching of tires should not be reserved for the most privileged amongst us. The open spaces that Grinnell, Roosevelt, and thousands of others before and after them fought to preserve is the birthright of every American. How do we bring more people of color to those experiences?

My friend José González, an immigrant from Mexico, founded Latino Outdoors in 2013 to do just that. Jose was born in Amatlán de Cañas in the Mexican state of Nayarit. As a kid, he loved playing in the foothills and the river near home, but shortly before he turned nine, his family moved to the United States. With his dad qualifying under the Immigration Reform and Control Act of 1986, they settled in Turlock, California, where his father worked in a poultry-processing plant and his mother worked in agriculture and later an industrial laundry. José was a brilliant student, and ended up at UC Davis, studying to become a history teacher.

When as part of his teacher training, however, he did a stint teaching environmental education to migrant schoolkids, he fell in love with it. He pivoted to a master's program at the University of Michigan's School for Environment and Sustainability.

At one point, José Googled "Latino" and "outdoors," wondering which Latino organizations were doing outdoor and environmental-education work. He was surprised when the search brought back nothing, and he decided to buy the domain name for $10. In 2013, working with the Tuolumne River Trust on Latino outreach, he turned the site into a blog, writing posts to elucidate the Latino outdoor culture. That same year, he began taking Latino groups camping, hiking, and kayaking free of charge to Point Reyes National Seashore northwest of San Francisco. Later, in 2014, funded by a grant from the conservation organization Resources Legacy Fund, the first official launch of Latino Outdoors outings was born.

On the outings, José was thrilled to break down participants' preconceived notions about recreating in nature. Some people connoted sleeping on the ground with the poverty they were working to rise above, or even traumatic migrations to the United States. Service projects to build trails or restore wetlands sounded a lot like free labor. More often than not, however, people found value in the experiences. Sometimes hiking and kayaking were new to them, or for others, it was the first time they'd been able to do outdoor activities in community with other Latinos. That sense of belonging was integral to the Latino Outdoors mission. "We wanted to connect people to a place so that they felt they weren't trespassing," José likes to say. "These are public lands. If you are a member of the public, then you should be here."

Quickly, José worked to form Latino Outdoors chapters across the country. As of 2021, there were 27 chapters in 13 states. That same year, volunteers led 115 outings serving more than 1,600 people, ranging from camping to fishing to sailing to gravel riding. The chapters vary widely—in California, participants are often recent immigrants being introduced to activities like kayaking and snowshoeing. The groups often comprise entire families, and there are partnerships with organizations that have caches of equipment to loan. In Washington, D.C., Latino Outdoors participants may be young professionals with plenty of gear and experience but who are looking for camaraderie. Sometimes the outings are happy-hour meetups at the REI beer garden.

Latino Outdoors is also a thought and culture leader. Its Yo Cuento division is the communication arm of the organization, starting with a blog detailing Latinos' experiences in the outdoors. In Spanish, *Yo cuento* means "I tell a story," but also "I matter" or "I count." It also sponsors films about the Latino Outdoors experience and hosts panels and events in person and online— some nineteen separate gatherings in 2021. Through sharing stories and ideas, Latino Outdoors is creating an outdoor culture in the same way that British mountaineering and exploring clubs created the recreational outdoor culture for white Europeans and Americans in the nineteenth century. Culture requires the underpinning of story.

Similar to Latino Outdoors, there has been a flowering of organizations aiming to get African Americans outside, groups like GirlTrek, Outdoorsy Black Women, and Blackpackers, which is based in Colorado and has hiking trips as well as rock climbing and skiing. (The National Brotherhood of Skiers, of course, has been putting on their famously fun and inclusive gatherings since 1973.) As with participants in Latino Outdoors outings who feel that hiking and camping smacks too much of the fieldwork they are hoping to rise above, African American outdoorists often point out that, for them, the outdoors can connote violence. The long history of lynching isn't that far in the past, and continues to some extent today with incidents like the 2020 murder of Ahmaud Arbery, killed while out for a jog in rural Georgia.

Groups like GirlTrek are taking back that narrative with outings that provide a safe, supportive community to venture outdoors with, and mentors to teach what gear to bring and how to use it. There's a lot to learn if you don't have a family history of outdoor adventuring. There's also reclaiming history. Harriet Tubman, as some point out, is a legendary outdoorswoman: How else could she have led people to freedom through the woods under the cover of night?

Blackpackers, amongst other orgs, also provides swimming lessons for kids. Black children are drowning at five times the rate of white children the same age, a legacy of segregation. For generations, Black Americans weren't allowed at public beaches or pools, and were subjected to violence for even trying, so they lost the practice of swimming.

I also love the gear libraries of the Outdoor Empowered Network, a coalition of nineteen nonprofits helping train outdoor leaders in minority communities ranging from New York City to Detroit. Each operates gear-lending libraries full of tents, sleeping bags, cooking kits, and even base layers and other apparel. Network member Bay Area Wilderness Training has more than 10,000 items in their three separate branches. From the Chicago Park District gear library, people can borrow fishing rods and kayaks. At Get Outdoors Leadville!, in Colorado, members can borrow snow bikes. We know that the cost of gear and complications accessing it present a huge barrier to entry for new outdoorists—gear libraries are a great fix.[8]

These efforts are making a difference. According to the Outdoor Foundation, over the last seven years, the number of Latino and African Americans participating in outdoor activities has increased. In total, Latino participation rose from 34 percent of the Latino community in the United States in 2015 to 56 percent in 2022, while participation for African Americans has risen by about 5 percent altogether to 40 percent. (While 57 percent of Asian Americans report that they participate in outdoor

recreation, including running outdoors, that figure has fallen from a high of 70 percent in 2017.) The LGBTQIA+ community is a bright spot—with 61 percent of folks identifying as a part of that community participating in outdoor recreation.

I'm pleased with the growth in leadership and awareness. On a personal note, in May 2022, I was so happy to help support, through the North Face and a VF Foundation grant, an all-Black expedition led by my friend Phil Henderson to Everest. I was ecstatic when they put seven African Americans on the summit.

Beyond that, how can we encourage more people of color to make their careers in the outdoors? How do we get more National Park Service rangers of color? More raft guides and ski instructors? I want this for representational purposes—when people encounter others who look like them, they naturally feel more comfortable in a space—but I also feel that the outdoor

---

8. In Millinocket, Maine, in addition to books and video games, the public library also loans out gear. Anyone with a library card can borrow mountain bikes, ice skates, tents, or hundreds of other items. In 2015, the library closed briefly, the victim of a shrinking municipal budget brought on by the collapse of the timber industry. When locals hired Matt Delaney the next year to revive the library, he realized that despite a growing network of singletrack trails and the addition of Katahdin Woods and Waters National Monument, locals would have a hard time taking advantage. Even if they could afford the gear, Millinocket lacked a bike shop or any other outdoor specialty retailer. The library began loaning gear as a way to bridge that gap and to foster learning and healthy recreation.

industry offers great careers with a terrific work-life-time-outside balance. It's something I worked to foster in my time with the state and afterward, helping set up educational programs at Colorado's Western State University, University of Colorado, and University of Denver that train students for executive careers in the outdoor industry. I know that people of color are more likely to enter the industry once they are equipped with the training and tools to excel. We can't in good conscience recruit anyone, but especially people of color, if there is no hope of advancement.

As much as I love the efforts by José and other leaders to bring people of color to America's wild spaces, it may be even more important to ensure that people of color have open space where they live. A 2020 study by the Trust for Public Land (TPL) found that in the country's 100 most populated cities, neighborhoods where most residents identify as people of color have access to 44 percent less park space than predominantly white neighborhoods. The parks that serve those neighborhoods are, on average, half as large—45 acres compared to 87 acres—and serve nearly five times more people.

Given what we are learning about the health benefits of time outside—lowered stress, lowered depression, reduced blood pressure, and greater longevity, you'll recall—the lack of access to parks for people of color is a public health emergency as well as a tragedy. Other studies have found that formerly redlined areas—neighborhoods once designated for segregation—tend to be as much as 12.6 degrees Fahrenheit hotter because of a lack of greenery along streets and in parks. I think of the way so many people looked to outdoor spaces for solace and social distancing during the Covid-19 lockdowns, and the opportunities lost for residents of those neighborhoods. Furthermore, experiences in local green and open spaces, from parks to beaches, are gateways to more extensive outdoor experiences in state parks, national parks, and national forests.

I joined the TPL's board of directors in 2021 because of the work they are doing to correct those injustices. One of the organization's primary missions is ensuring that every American has a park within a ten-minute walk of their house. (Their studies show that currently, 1 in 3 US citizens do not. That includes, for example, 70 percent of Los Angeles residents.) One of their solutions is to open public schoolyards to communities during non-school hours, which would solve the problem of access to park space for nearly 20 million Americans.

For the effort to be successful, many of those public schoolyards need improvement, which is where the Community Schoolyards project comes in. Too often in the communities that need them most, the yards are marred by cracked asphalt, broken play equipment, and a lack of greenery and shade. TPL has worked with more than 280 schools across the country from Tacoma, Washington, to New York City, to Dallas to renovate school playgrounds with more green space and new play equipment and to staff them with volunteers to ensure safety outside of school hours. The results have been impressive in places. At the Sussex Avenue School in Newark, for example, attendance rose by 6 percent, disciplinary actions declined, and test scores rose after a 2015 schoolyard renovation. The school was also removed from the state's list of at-risk schools.

At a 2022 board meeting, we visited three of the transformed schools in Dallas—Guzick, Salazar, and Ireland elementaries. At each, the first goal has been to plant 80 to 100 trees to help with the heat-island effect and to get the kids to help steward the trees. In 2021, each of the schools also received new playground equipment, a loop trail, and murals.

At Salazar, I visited with about fifteen Latino and Hispanic fourth-graders in the renovated schoolyard. In the center, they've built a twenty-five-foot-high hill sided with AstroTurf. Naturally, that's where most of the kids were, climbing up it, rolling down, and just hanging out on top. During a break in our tour, I walked over, climbed the hill, and started talking to the kids. One was wearing Vans shoes, which is owned by VF corp. "I work for Vans," I said, in Spanish. The kid's eyes got all big.

"Do you like this hill?" I asked the kids. They did indeed.

"This is the highest I've ever been," said one kid. "I can see the roof of my house from up here," said another, pointing off in the distance. Getting a taller vantage opens a child's mind.

I told them I had been a climber for a job. "I thought you worked for Vans," said a kid.

"This was before," I said, and pulled out my phone, showing them pictures from Everest. I hoped that I was providing some inspiration, firing dreams that a Latino man in America can do all kinds of things.

I love innovative thinking and results like the Community Schoolyards project, but even more I love TPL's community-involvement model, especially in places where the government doesn't always best represent the community. In South Wenatchee, Washington, the organization facilitated the renewal of Kiwanis Methow Park primarily by involving local residents. The 1.26-acre park in a predominantly Latino community had been sterilized by town managers to discourage gang activity—trees had been cut down and bathrooms removed, and the park was floodlit all night. In 2016, however, TPL sent a staffer to organize local citizens to help re-imagine the park, signing up more than 120 Parque Padrinos, or park godparents. The first thing the Padrinos agreed on was that Methow Park needed a *kiosko*, a covered pavilion like the ones so common across Latin America.

Steered by the Parque Padrinos, Methow reopened in 2020 sporting a bathroom, a new turf field, and new shade trees. The kiosko hosts performances by the Wenatchee High School's mariachi band and the town's Mexican folk-dance troupe. One amazing side effect of the park-renewal process was that once the Padrinos began showing up at city-council meetings to advocate for the park, they stayed involved in community politics: South Wenatchee's Latino-voter turnout tripled in the 2018 elections.

José Gonzáles has stepped away from the day-to-day running of Latino Outdoors to focus on being an educator and thought leader. He serves on the boards of several prominent outdoor-recreation entities, amongst them the National Outdoor Leadership School and the California State Parks Foundation, and with the state's boating and waterways commission. He also works as a diversity and equity consultant. His mission is to help make outdoor institutions and spaces safe and welcoming for all people.

When José's work with Latino Outdoors began, he was interested in getting more people of color outdoors to help them "get their stoke on." That's still a very valuable goal, he says, but now he also sees the outdoors as a portal to heal the wounds of our society at large. Pointing to the growing mountains of evidence of the health benefits of time outside, José says the outdoors can be a healing space where we are better and more receptive listeners, where we can be more open and vulnerable. It's easier to heal severed connections while convening outdoors than in, say, a conference room.

I love his warrior-poet's mind. In his writing and speaking, José encourages his audience to embrace more nature-centric language, to move from "egocentric" to "ecocentric." Instead of an organization being a "well-oiled machine," why not model it on a "healthy habitat"? How does leadership change, he asks, if we envision leaders not as directors, but as keystones? He touts the model of the river to think about our efforts to improve equity and inclusivity in the outdoors. Rivers are formed of diverging and converging channels. That is like the work of bringing change—"[We] are bringing in diversity and difference (Divergence) into a space and work on what inclusion means (Convergence)," he writes. "It is Emergence from Divergence and Convergence." The river, he writes, "does not flow in a straight line, but it is not scattered."

Chapter 6

OUTWARD BOUND TO EVEREST

"I regard it as the foremost task of education to ensure survival of these qualities; an enterprising curiosity, an undefeatable spirit, tenacity in pursuit, readiness for sensible self-denial, and above all, compassion." —Kurt Hahn

It was a classic Outward Bound day. My co-instructor and I were following our teenage students as they tromped ahead of us in high spirits, taking big strides with light backpacks. They had no idea they were going in the wrong direction, and when they found out, they were going to be very, very disappointed.

That morning, all twelve of us had been standing triumphantly on the summit of Colorado's Hagerman Peak, hugging, high-fiving, and admiring the view of the famous Maroon Bells spread out before us, green valleys descending from the towering red-rock peaks. Now the group was headed for resupply—a truck meeting us with fresh food, and possibly ice-cream bars courtesy of our logistics coordinator. The problem was, descending from the peak this afternoon, the students had dropped into the wrong drainage and were now officially four miles off course. To make it right this late in the day, we'd probably need to hike into the night. Some sixteen days into a twenty-three-day course, the students were now doing their own navigation with map and compass, and we instructors were following behind, offering assistance when asked. In this case, they hadn't asked.

When it was safe to do so, we always liked to let our students make mistakes. We wanted them to learn skills like navigation, rock climbing, and how to cook rice over a camp stove, but we also wanted them to experience the consequences of errors, both physical and social. How would they respond to their mistakes? Could they rebound emotionally? Could they forgive each other? Around 6:00 p.m., one of the kids called for a water break and everyone dropped their packs, pulled out water bottles, and sat down.

"How much farther, Steve?" one of the kids asked.

Steve looked down at the map, and then up at the surrounding peaks, trying to read the contour lines to see exactly where we were. I could see the doubt creep into his face. The map wasn't reflecting what he was seeing. Steve conferred with Brad (not their real names), his co-navigator, and then the other eight students started getting antsy, gathering that something was amiss.

"Uh, Luis," said Steve, getting up and walking toward me, map in hand. "I'm a little confused on where we are . . ." I helped him work out some of the obvious landmarks of the valley we were in, and he finally saw how far we'd detoured. "Oh crap," he said.

There was an uproar, of course, roughly following the seven stages of grief: shock, denial, anger, bargaining, etc. There was some finger-pointing at Steve and Brad, but we pointed out to the students that while they'd been happily hiking downhill singing songs, any one of them could have called a break to check the maps. They knew it was the entire group's responsibility, and that we instructors would be happy to let them err. This was all in preparation for finals, when they'd travel without instructors for three days.

My favorite of the stages of grief is always bargaining. "Can't we just camp here and go in in the morning?" someone asked.

"No way," I said. "Our logistics coordinator is waiting for us and has somewhere to be midmorning. He can't be the one paying for our mistake. Everybody grab your headlamps. We need to be there tonight."

On the trail, the students moved through depression, reconstruction, and acceptance pretty quickly, especially when my co-instructor and I filtered into the line to help keep morale up. We wanted them to experience the recovery from a mistake as a positive. The day that had started before dawn stretched to midnight, pushed the students to exhaustion, and ended in high spirits at the resupply truck at midnight, when we cracked open a cooler of ice cream. It was a day fondly remembered as a highlight at the course end.

The summer I turned twenty, I was accepted into the new-staff training program at the Colorado Outward Bound School (COBS). Outward Bound is the single largest outdoor-education and adventure organization in the world, and offers dozens of positions each year to younger, aspiring outdoor professionals. Even so, I was the youngest person in my program, a hyperactive kid who thought that his experience guiding adults on two-day jaunts up Cotopaxi made him ready for anything the relatively low-altitude mountains of Colorado could throw his way. I didn't know just how little I knew.

Outward Bound has more than thirty individual schools across the globe, including six in the United States, and runs courses ranging from five-day whitewater-rafting trips to semester-long programs that include ski mountaineering, sea kayaking, and desert-canyon travel. Generally, a pair of instructors trained in expedition travel and group dynamics leads each group of between six and ten students. The curriculum is based on the technical skills, but those are really just a vehicle for personal growth like the sort experienced by Steve and Brad, who had to swallow their pride and ask for forgiveness from the group for neglecting their navigation that day. Or for any of the dozens of students I taught who learned that they could overcome their fear of heights and summit a peak, or some who stretched their comfort zone simply by sleeping under the stars for their very first time.

Outward Bound was founded in 1941 in the United Kingdom as a partnership between the German-Jewish educator Kurt Hahn and the British shipping magnate Sir Lawrence Durning Holt. Hahn was a pioneer in the experiential-education movement, emphasizing hands-on learning and physical fitness over didactic classroom lectures. Jailed by the Nazis when he publicly criticized Hitler's policies in 1933, Hahn was able to flee soon after to the United Kingdom, where he founded the Gordonstoun School in Scotland. At Gordonstoun, Hahn refined his educational ideas even further, developing a curriculum that placed equal emphasis on the development of character, leadership, and service alongside intellectual studies that were particularly hands-on in nature. Students took silent, contemplative walks around the school, and every day began with a run before breakfast. The curriculum also included hiking and climbing expeditions.[9]

When WWII broke out in Europe in 1939, the father of a Gordonstoun student approached Hahn with an idea. Sir Lawrence Durning Holt was a partner and manager in the shipping company Blue Funnel Line, many of whose ships were being torpedoed by German U-boats. Holt was dismayed that many of his younger sailors weren't surviving in the water long enough to be rescued, whereas paradoxically, the older, presumably less hearty sailors were. He believed that the younger men lacked

9. Both Prince Philip and King Charles of England attended Gordonstoun. In the second season of The Crown, Hahn appears as a character.

the grit that comes from experience, and wondered if the sort of rigorous training his son was experiencing at Gordonstoun could be the solution. In 1941, Hahn and Holt devised a one-month course that immersed the sailors in outdoor expeditions to help them discover they were far more capable and resilient than they realized, with an eye toward surviving a shipwreck. They named the course Outward Bound after the nautical term describing a ship leaving the safety of its harbor for open seas.

Outward Bound's logo remains the compass rose—the face of a compass showing the cardinal directions. Each student who completes a course receives a lapel pin with the design. During the pin ceremony at course end, I would celebrate the students' successes, but would also remind them that the biggest challenge hadn't been surviving the physical rigors of the course or finding your true voice in a group of strangers, but rather translating those successes to life back home. "You guys have righted your ships on this course," I'd say. "But my favorite saying about ships is this: 'A ship is safe at harbor, but that is not what it was built for.'"

Of course, when I signed on with Outward Bound to become an assistant instructor in 1991, I didn't know any of the history or philosophy; I was just looking for a climbing job. Always with an eye on the Himalaya, I'd figured out that most of the United States' best high-altitude mountaineers had been COBS instructors, starting with the legendary Willi Unsoeld and progressing through Wally Berg, Kitty Calhoun, Dan Jenkins, and the great Pete Athans.

To me, climbing had always been an individual pursuit. It was the struggle against nature or against the self. Most of the climbing I'd done, whether in the Midwest with Hartley or on Cotopaxi, I could either do the climb or I couldn't. It was a skill or endurance problem. Wilderness mountaineering problems, on the other hand, feel more existential. They are fraught with choices that seem to call your judgment and character into question: about the length of the approach and the incoming weather, not to mention the variables of your climbing team's behavior. Outward Bound mountaineering was all about the human variable.

This was the variable I was particularly ill-prepared for. I got some hard feedback from my New Staff program trainer, Paul Duba, as we sat in the middle of the Collegiate Peaks in Colorado high above Leadville. Duba said, "Luis, you are a good climber, and you can lead a ropeteam" (thanks to my experience with clients on Cotopaxi). But then he added, "But your people skills kind of suck."

That stung. I'd been thinking I hadn't been fitting into the group on our two-week expedition because the program wasn't a good fit. What was this sit-in-a-circle-and-share-our-feelings stuff? Why all the talk about "experiential education"? I thought we were there to get people to the top of things and high-five each other on the summit. "I think that if you'd let your guard down a little, you'd do better," said Duba.

I felt suddenly hollow. Of course, I'd had my guard up. I'd grown up isolated as a kid, and social settings didn't yet come easily for me. Building trust was a slow process. I wasn't particularly mature. Yet here was a guy I was looking up to telling me that I should loosen up a little and be myself. Could it be that easy?

I gave it a shot. I started opening up during the nightly debrief, telling my story about how traditional education had been a struggle and that climbing had saved me. On the trail, I cracked terrible jokes—and was overjoyed when people indulgently laughed with me. Just like that, I was outward bound myself.

I worked at COBS for a decade straight, and have returned to it continually throughout my adult life, leading courses for populations ranging from fourteen-year-olds to college kids to specially designed courses for business leaders or military veterans. My own interpersonal journey with the school gave me the compassion to understand and aid in my students' struggles. I loved watching the overachieving Harvard undergrad develop empathy for those less capable than herself. I loved watching as a proud but suffering student gave up weight from his pack so the entire group could move more quickly (and as the whole group started figuring out equity vs. equality). I loved getting a letter from a student years later telling me that his course was the reason he had joined the Army to fight the Taliban in Afghanistan—he'd "always had a problem with bullies," but before Outward Bound would never have believed himself strong enough to do anything about it.

Everything I stand for that didn't come from my family came from Outward Bound. The basic formula of the program—a group of strangers working together to overcome challenges in an unpredictable location far from their normal circumstances—does most of the work, but I always appreciated the school's codification of its values. Those are found in the school's five pillars: an enterprising curiosity, an indefatigable spirit, tenacity in pursuit, a readiness for sensible self-denial, and above all, compassion.

Compassion is the crowning pillar because it is the most noble value. It's the value that goes beyond the self. It's also effectively the byproduct of the other pillars. If you have curiosity, an indefatigable spirit, tenacity, and self-discipline, you are more likely to be a success. In my experience, success leads to healthy self-esteem, which often breeds compassion. (It's easy to recognize the opposite—those who aren't succeeding are often jealous and petty, rather than openhearted and generous.) I don't think there's any debate that compassion feels like it's in short supply lately.

In the Outward Bound model, the output of compassion is service. If you have compassion for others, you will naturally want to help them. Nothing is more beautiful to me than a culture of people who go out of their way to be helpful to each other, whether sharing loads on an Outward Bound course, pitching in during a disaster, or just being patient and courteous while moving around society on an average day—practicing random acts of kindness. Beyond the spontaneous service elements of group travel, Outward Bound courses also have a scheduled service component. Students pitch in on USFS trail-maintenance or invasive-species-removal projects, or spend a day mentoring at-risk kids in rock climbing. The idea goes all the way back to Kurt Hahn's Gordonstoun School, where students have always helped build and repair facilities and for a time were also required to join a rescue squad. Students had three choices—a mountain rescue service, a coastal rescue service (the school is on Scotland's north coast), or a fire rescue brigade—and could be called to duty at any time of day or night.

Service work has been intertwined with the outdoors since the 1930s in this country too, most famously with Franklin Delano Roosevelt's Civilian Conservation Corps. While his cousin Teddy is widely considered the father of American political conservationism, FDR may have been even more important. His conservation tally stands at a whopping 118 million acres, including the creation of 140 national wildlife refuges, 29 national forests, and the first national seashore, North Carolina's Cape Hatteras. He pushed for the creation of dozens of national parks, including Olympic, Isle Royale, Big Bend, Kings Canyon, and the Everglades. FDR personally designated five national monuments:

Joshua Tree, the Dry Tortugas, Capitol Reef, the Channel Islands, and Jackson Hole National Monument, which later became Grand Teton National Park.

Crucially, however, FDR wasn't just drawing lines on maps. "Heretofore our conservation policy has been merely to preserve as much as possible of the existing forests," he said in 1931 while still governor of New York. "Our new policy goes a step further. It will not only preserve the existing forests, but create new ones." FDR's policies as a governor and as a president worked to improve the health of public and private lands with scientifically oriented work on the ground.

Like his cousin Teddy, FDR was interested in ecology from an early age. His childhood was spent roaming the fields and forests at Hyde Park, his family's estate fifty miles north of New York City. According to Douglas Brinkley's book *Rightful Heritage,* FDR's interest in the natural world may have crystalized as an eleven-year-old at the 1893 World's Columbian Exposition in Chicago, where he pored over the naturalists' specimens that would go on to form the nucleus of Chicago's Field Museum. He marveled at life-sized models of a giant octopus spanning eighteen feet and a reproduction of a wooly mammoth. Others have theorized that his time spent swimming in the pools of Warm Springs, Georgia, after his polio diagnosis in 1921 opened his mind to the pleasures of public outdoor recreation.

Whatever the genesis, what's undeniable is that FDR was interested in restoring natural landscapes. At Hyde Park, he planted some half a million trees over his lifetime, enlisting the most current silviculture practices. When he was governor of New York, he displayed a solid ecological understanding of the benefits of healthy forests. "They protect the headwaters of our rivers and streams, they prevent the too rapid run-off of rain and melting snow and tend to equalize the flow of streams," he said in a 1930 radio address. "They return to the land more than they take from it and maintain its fertility."

FDR championed the 1931 Hewitt Reforestation Amendment to the New York Constitution. The act authorized the purchase of blocks of abandoned farmland greater than 500 acres, most of it sandy and eroded or otherwise unsuitable for agriculture. Then, in August 1931, FDR used the Temporary Emergency Relief Administration to create a forerunner to the Civilian Conservation Corps, putting unemployed men to work planting trees and battling erosion. More than 10,000 men planted trees and built fire roads on the lands purchased through the Hewitt Amendment.

As president, FDR spearheaded more than a handful of landmark, scientifically driven federal laws, from the Taylor Grazing Act of 1934, which worked to reduce overgrazing on public lands, to the Soil Conservation Act he signed in 1935, which subsidized farmers to plant native grasses and trees or to plant subsistence gardens in lieu of the commercial crops that were creating the Dust Bowl. I feel most connected to the Migratory Bird Hunting and Conservation Stamp Act of 1934, which required duck and geese hunters to buy a license to hunt the animals, the proceeds of which went to waterfowl conservation. I've already written about how important the 1937 Pittman-Robertson Wildlife Restoration Act, which funnels tax revenue from guns and ammo toward wildlife, has been to conservation.

Of course, in my opinion, FDR's masterpiece was the CCC, which he established in 1933, just a month into his presidency. The service famously employed 3.4 million men over its nine years of existence, a mind-boggling 5 percent of the US population at the time. CCC staff worked to rehabilitate wildlife habitat and establish erosion control on 40 million acres of farmland. The service planted 3 billion trees, and built 13,000 miles of trail, including large swaths of the Appalachian Trail. Much of the 125,000 miles of road they built created access to national forests and national parks like Yellowstone, Yosemite, and the Grand Canyon. You can still see stonework done by the CCC today in Great Smoky Mountains and Glacier national parks. It wasn't just national parks either—the corps built trails, roads, campgrounds, and visitors centers in more than 800 state parks in 22 states, places like Minnesota's Gooseberry Falls State Park and California's Mount Diablo State Park. Mount Hood, Oregon's famous Timberline Lodge is a log-and-stone masterpiece still used today by skiers and mountaineers.

For FDR, conservation and ecological restoration were an engine for economic growth—a crucial tool for a president faced with our nation's largest economic crisis, the Great Depression. The nation's economy, he argued, would never recover if its natural resources continued to suffer. He sold the CCC as a jobs program, but its work to repair the Dust Bowl was also a way to save America's struggling farms. The CCC's projects drove tourism to national parks and landmarks like Mount Hood. During his administration, visitation to national parks increased fivefold, increasing economic activity and, undoubtedly, awe at our nation's natural wonders.

I also love what the CCC did for its participants. Many recruits were unskilled and unemployed, but then left the program with work skills and experience. It's estimated that some 57,000 men were taught to read and write in CCC camps. Additionally, millions of CCC participants recruited from Eastern cities received the benefit of time outside, working and living in some of our nation's most beautiful mountain ranges and valleys. They were banded together in teams, living in wilderness camps, and the work increased their physical fitness, grit, and morale during a dark time in our nation's history. It was almost like a national Outward Bound program. Many of the CCC alumni went on to form the backbone of our nation's armed forces for WWII, but even if they hadn't, it's impossible to think that millions receiving the benefit of the fitness, camaraderie, connectivity to nature, and a service practice wouldn't have lifted the nation.

I've always believed that our nation needs more such programs for young people. I'd be in favor of a system like those of Switzerland and Finland, which have mandatory military service for all eighteen-year-old men—or, for those who prefer, paid civilian service. Women can also volunteer to join either branch. In my experience, those who have done military service or a service program like Teach for America or AmeriCorps are more engaged members of society. Often they are happier people, too. Studies have shown that acts of service increase feel-good chemicals like serotonin, dopamine, and oxytocin, the same hormone that floods a mother's brain when she breastfeeds her child. Studies have also shown that those who volunteer live longer than those who don't. Furthermore, there is plenty of evidence that military veterans and participants in yearlong service programs like AmeriCorps have better education and employment outcomes.

As on an Outward Bound course, national service programs bring together participants from across all walks of life, uniting them in common cause. Isn't that sort of common ground exactly what our divided society is missing right now? As Jonathan Holloway, president of Rutgers University, wrote in 2021, "A sensible system of compulsory national service would build bridges between people and turn them into citizens," shoring up our fragile communities and strengthening us as individuals and as a nation as we all became more self-reliant yet also interdependent.

When Biden first took office, one of his most popular proposals was for a Civilian Climate Corps modeled after FDR's CCC. The program would pay as many as 20,000 people to work to help improve our nation's resilience in the face of climate change. They'd work in national parks and national forests and on other federal public lands doing habitat restoration, invasive-species removal, and wildfire mitigation. The proposal found little-to-no support from the GOP, whose adherents largely oppose anything that aims to mitigate climate change. However, I believe that if Biden had marketed the proposal differently, calling it Civilian Conservation Corps 2.0 or the like, it would have found conservative supporters. I've seen land-conservation laws proposals and laws win big in both blue states and red ones, so long as they sidestep political buzzwords.

In 2023, the Biden Administration ultimately pushed their proposal through, and I think it is a win-win-win for young people and state and federal wildlands. The corps will join a network of 130-such organizations, including Volunteers in Service to America (VISTA), which was established in 1964 as a domestic equivalent to the Peace Corps. The work of the various service corps ranges from building trails in national parks to performing disaster relief to daily educational support in schools. I think they could play an even larger role in our society, and the federal Outdoor Recreation Office would be a great facilitator for that, especially supporting outdoor recreation both in wildlands and in our communities. Imagine a yearlong service program for young Americans that also works on behalf of the great outdoors and facilitates getting people outside. You would be creating a whole new generation focused on conservation and stewardship.

According to a February 2023 survey of more than 1,000 Gen-Z and Millennial-aged people conducted by the workwear brand Carhartt, 74 percent of respondents said that climate change and/ or the environment are a top concern for their generation and future generations. On top of that, 92 percent of respondents agreed that preserving America's national parks for future generations is important. Of those surveyed, 85 percent said they are at least somewhat open to a job in nature conservation or the outdoors.

In addition to providing me some of the most fulfilling work of my life, COBS also introduced me to one of my personal heroes. I met Mark Udall on my New Staff Training course. The future senator was then the school's director and cut an almost mythic figure with his height of six-foot-six, his booming voice, and his family history. He was, of course, the son of Representative Mo Udall of Arizona and the nephew of former Secretary of the Interior Stewart Udall, two seminal figures in the conservation movement. It was hard not to be starstruck around Mark.

Even at age twenty, I was a wonk about land-use politics. My uncles Peppin and Alfonso talked to me all the time about land use and conservation. Our family's ranch is adjacent to Cayambe Coca National Park in Ecuador, and they were interested in the question of whether tourism was a higher and better use of the land than agriculture. As a young climber, I was always keenly aware of who managed the land where I loved to climb, from Cotopaxi National Park in Ecuador to Johnson's Shut-Ins State Park in Missouri. I was always grateful that these inspiring places had been set aside.

When I met him, I was sitting on a boulder in the meadow having that conversation with my trainer Paul Duba, the one during which he told me that my interpersonal skills needed work. Up the trail came a giant man carrying a pack with a pair of skis strapped to it. He walked right up to us, and Paul introduced us. This man said he'd probably do a little spring skiing once he'd had a chance to meet the new staff. He oozed competence.

When he had gone, Paul mentioned that Mark had just returned from the Himalaya. Once I heard that, I was a goner, and Mark Udall has been a role model ever since, especially when he finally retired from the school and got into politics. Mark made three separate attempts at Everest including via the notorious *White Limbo* route on the north side, each unsuccessful, though he never had a regret. He always told me it was about the climbing, not the summit.

****

By the mid-1990s, I was still leading courses for Outward Bound but had gotten my foot in the door at the mountain-guiding company Alpine Ascents International (AAI). Because of my fluency in Spanish and personal and professional history in Ecuador, I was fortunate to land coveted slots guiding on the Ecuadorian high peaks and on 22,837-foot Aconcagua, the highest peak in the Americas and one of the fabled Seven Summits—the highest point on each of the seven continents. Fair or not, I never had to grind my way up Mount Rainier or Baker all summer long alongside the other new guides aspiring to the plum international assignments.

At AAI, I fell in with some of the biggest legends in American mountaineering, old-school characters like Willi Prittie and Vern Tejas. Vern, a lifetime guide, is famous for being the first to make ten separate ascents of each of the Seven Summits and for his winter solos of both Denali (20,310 feet) and Mount Logan (17,224 feet), amongst other incredibly rugged undertakings. These days, Willi is famous for competing on the *Ultimate Survival Alaska* reality TV show, but before that he established himself as one of the most respected and experienced guides in history. They were amazing mentors to learn from.

All the while, I was still dreaming of the Himalaya and knew I needed to get some of my own experience there. In 1999, I teamed up with a group of other Colorado mountaineers for an ambitious, self-funded attempt at a new route on Gangapurna, a 24,459-foot peak in Nepal. We were in way over our heads.

To start with, the terminus of the glacier where our route began was so hideously broken that ferrying loads through it to our higher camps took more than twice the time and energy we'd anticipated. I lost twenty-eight pounds on the trip. Next, our team doctor was hit in the eye by falling rock and had to leave the expedition. Then, one of our gear caches on the glacier we'd worked so hard to establish was lost—tens of thousands of dollars' worth of gear was swallowed up when a new crevasse opened overnight. Finally, the storms started rolling in, driving up the avalanche danger until our expedition leader pulled the plug and we headed home, our tails tucked between our legs.

Even though we weren't successful, it helped open a door in a different way. When one of the Sherpas on our Gangapurna trip discovered that I lived in Colorado, he asked if I would bring a gift to his friend Pasquale "PV" Scaturro in Denver.

When I met PV back in Colorado that July of 1999, he told me that he was working on a project with a blind teacher from Colorado who wanted to climb Everest. That teacher, of course, was Erik Weihenmayer. The project sounded like exactly what I wanted to spend my time doing. "How can I get involved?" I asked.

Though my Himalayan experience was less than others who were vying for spots on the team, I think my Outward Bound experience helped sway PV. In the outdoor community, Outward Bound instructors are known for their patience and willingness to subvert the ego for a common goal, both qualities that would be essential for the project.

"Erik and I are going climbing this weekend," PV said. "Why don't you come along?" So began a yearlong process of building trust on rock- and ice-climbing outings. Erik had been proficient at both mediums for years. Climbing rock for him was like reading braille, patiently feeling his way around for the next hold. That slow approach requires incredible endurance, hanging onto tiny hand- and footholds for two or three times longer than a sighted climber would need to. Ice climbing, he'd learned to test the quality and thickness of the ice by listening to the sound it made when he tapped it with his ice tools. He learned to avoid the clink of brittle or thin ice; a solid thunk meant it was good to go. In either medium, when speed was of the essence, Erik relied on his belayer for direction on the best holds or sequence to use. From the start, I was blown away with Erik's tenacity, and was grateful for his trust in me.

In addition, I was a pest to PV. I stopped by his office weekly to lobby for a spot on the team. PV later said that because of my persistence, he felt he had no choice but to invite me.

The team's first big test was a shakedown trip in 2000 to Nepal's 22,349-foot Ama Dablam, to test out our systems. It went terribly. The first problem was that we'd arrived in a low-snow year, which meant that the route was much more rock than snow and ice, which in turn meant slower going, especially for Erik. Then a huge storm rolled in, and we all retreated to basecamp to wait it out, except Erik. He felt too fatigued to descend safely from 20,000 feet all the way to basecamp at 15,000 feet, so opted to pitch a tent on a rock ledge and ride it out with teammate Eric Alexander. Seven days later, with Eric and Erik still bunkered up at 20,000 feet, conditions hadn't improved, and PV called the expedition off. Which is when it took a serious turn.

During the retreat, Eric Alexander suffered a brutal 150-foot fall. What followed was an arduous, Sherpa-assisted descent that lasted long into the night through awful weather. Once at basecamp, we realized that he'd also developed a pulmonary edema. He spent three days in a Gamow Bag, a claustrophobic, coffin-sized tube that allows air to be pumped in, increasing pressure and helping relieve conditions like high-altitude cerebral and pulmonary edemas (HACE and HAPE, respectively). It was incredibly tense, taking turns pumping air into the bag and keeping our fingers crossed that Eric would survive. Finally, after three days, the weather cleared enough to helivac him out to a hospital. We were grateful and relieved when Eric improved there, but we felt the sting of defeat.

For me, I was zero for two on Himalayan expeditions. Erik Weihenmayer, however, was undaunted. In fact, he was inspired, feeling that the successful rescue had catalyzed us into a real team, one capable of not only achieving the objective, but doing so with a higher degree of safety. So it was that one year later, in the spring of 2001, we found ourselves at the base of Everest, a team of twenty-one, including a documentary film crew.

If we were sure of our capabilities, we were likely the only ones at Everest Basecamp who felt so. The guiding community was still stinging from the negative publicity generated by the 1997 book *Into Thin Air*, which graphically detailed the eight deaths during a single storm in May 1996, including several guides and their clients. I heard comments accusing us of being a circus stunt and predicting that we were sure to get Erik killed.

A few days into the climb, we encountered so much difficulty that even we thought the naysayers might be right. The Khumbu Icefall is one of Everest's most notorious obstacles, three miles of shattered glacier with house-sized blocks of ice toppling and crevasses widening and narrowing overnight. To make passage easier, the Nepali government hires a crew of Sherpas each season to build a route through the icefall—the so-called Icefall Doctors—fixing ropes for self-belay and laying aluminum ladders up vertical walls and across crevasses. Even with all that, the Khumbu is a huge and potentially deadly obstacle course at such a high altitude (18,000 feet). It was hell for Erik—verbal cues about the terrain were so ineffectual because almost every single step was unique, with a peculiar stride length or foot angle, and crampons catching on ladder rungs. We'd set out and turned back twice due to Erik's exhaustion, each time returning to a louder chorus of doubters at basecamp.

Finally, we decided that Erik would start out from basecamp at 1:00 a.m., switching out climbing partners as he went. At hour twelve, I was the one climbing with Erik, giving him verbal direction as best I could. We were within sight of Camp I, nearly through the maze of ice, when Erik stumbled as he tried to hop across a narrow crevasse. I should have let the fixed rope he was attached to arrest his fall, but in my own exhaustion I reflexively reached out to catch him, and the handle of trekking pole that was dangling from my wrist clocked him on the nose. In the thin air, his nose exploded like he'd been punched by Mike Tyson. There was blood everywhere, and a sickly green bruise spreading into his eye sockets. I hauled him up, cringing at the sight of his battered face, and as we drew closer to the rest of the team cheering us on from Camp I, everyone fell silent. I couldn't stop apologizing, but instead of doubting me, and saying, "I can't trust you," he put his effort into cheering me, and the rest of us up. Erik offered me compassion by simply turning to me and saying, "Well, that was fun—better than a strong cup of coffee, that's for sure."

As Erik slept off the effort in his tent, even PV was having doubts. That night at dinner, though, Erik wouldn't hear of our proposal to leave him at Camp I while the rest of us ferried our remaining supplies up through the Khumbu Icefall. He was resolute that he, too, would make the trip up and down carrying his full share of loads. "You guys aren't going to carry me up there and spike me like a football," he said. Over the next days and weeks, Erik made ten round trips, cutting his time down to five hours.

The next six days were anything but easy. We made our way to camps II, III, and IV in succession, climbing higher to acclimate, and then returning to basecamp to recover. On a low-snow year, there was more falling ice than usual, and we often found ourselves tucked into the lee of a wall, or simply hiding under our packs while being pelted from above. By the time we reached the Balcony (~27,600 feet) above Camp IV, though, we knew our biggest obstacle was no longer the mountain itself, but the weather. Our teamwork was dialed, and when the weather cleared for us that auspicious morning, we knew it would carry us to the summit of the world.

Chapter 7

THE GUIDE LIFE

"On the mountain of truth, you never climb in vain. You either reach a higher step today or you exercise your strength in order to climb higher tomorrow." —Friedrich Nietzsche

After our successful ascent with Erik, Alpine Ascents International was happy to send me back to Everest in 2002. I'd proved my mettle. From there, I was off, a regular on the roster for Chile's Aconcagua, the Ecuadorian volcanoes, and then back to Everest again. On my third trip guiding Everest, I met Guy Cotter, the owner of the New Zealand mountaineering company Adventure Consultants. Cotter had bought the company after the death of its founder, Rob Hall, in the May 1996 storm on Everest. Chatting with Guy, I asked why Adventure Consultants hadn't returned to its former volume of guiding the other Seven Summits or other Himalayan classics. I could see that the opportunity was there—the guided-mountaineering industry was booming. It just wasn't a priority at that time, Guy said.

Always ambitious, I eventually struck a deal with Guy to be his company's chief of operations. I'd do the marketing, find the clients, and run the trips. I'd help grow the company back into the industry leader it had been. I loved the idea of setting my own schedule—a whole slate of dream destinations awaited me across the globe.

France's Mont Blanc (15,777 feet) was the birthplace of mountaineering, based in the ultra-cool ski-resort town of Chamonix. On off days, there were a dizzying array of personal climbs in the Alps on which to hone my craft alongside the best mountain athletes in the world. Russia's Mount Elbrus (18,510 feet), in the Caucasus Range near Georgia, is technically an easy climb, but culturally mind-boggling. We'd fly into St. Petersburg and take the night train to Moscow. The night train wasn't quite as sexy as it sounds, even in first class. There were four bunks to a berth, and with all our mountaineering gear, duffels were stacked to the ceiling. The train was crawling with cat burglars who'd sneak into the berths at night and lift wallets, passports, and other valuables, so I taught clients how to tie their doors closed at night. I'd spend most of the journey in the bar car anyhow, drinking vodka and telling climbing stories.

In Moscow, we'd tour the Kremlin, maybe catch the ballet, and then fly to the town of Mineral nye Vody. Our Russian and Ukrainian guides would rent us a dacha near the ski slopes on the flank of the mountain for the days before and after the ascent, and lay out spreads of wine, cheese, caviar, and of course, vodka. These dachas were typically owned by oligarchs and were as nice as any mansion in Vail. For me, the hardest part of the Elbrus climb was usually the vodka hangover.

The attractions surrounding Kilimanjaro, Africa's highest point at 19,341 feet, were my favorite. We'd take clients on safari in the Ngorongoro Crater, Tanzania, as part of the trip, booking the most luxurious camps. Staff would place a hot water bottle in the evening to warm your bed up, bring coffee to your tent before dawn, and always have a gin and tonic in your hand for sunset. Seeing lions, leopards, and elephants up close in the wild is the surest way to experience awe I've found, and astonishes every single time.

Between Kilimanjaro trips, I'd fly to Zanzibar, on an archipelago just off the Tanzanian coast. I'd rent a beach hut on the east side for $12 a day or stay in Stone Town, an eighteenth-century spice-road trading town that's now a Unesco World Heritage Site for its amalgamation of Persian, Arab, Indian, and European culture. It was fun to visit the Freddie Mercury Museum there and light a candle to the legend gone too young. Mercury, of the rock band Queen, was born in Stone Town, and his family home is now a museum. Queen cover bands play in bars near the spice market.

One of the strangest episodes of my guiding travels occurred just before a Nepal expedition, at a hotel in Kathmandu. I woke up to fire alarms and smoke throughout the hotel room and hallways. Out on the street in the dark, I realized that the fire department hadn't arrived and that there were hundreds of people who hadn't yet evacuated the sold-out hotel. I ran back in to help, wetting a towel and wrapping it around my face to keep the smoke out of my lungs. The power was out, so I ran down the halls with my headlamp, knocking on doors and telling people to evacuate.

I knocked on one door, yelling in English, "Fire! Evacuate the hotel!" I was stunned when it flew open and there was a pistol in my face, shaking, as though the person holding it was freaking out. "Whoa! Whoa!" I said, as calmly as I could. "There's a fire—I'm here to help."

I could see a small man behind the pistol barrel, looking confused. The towel around my face couldn't have been helping. I pulled it down slightly, and said, "There's a fire," in my most soothing but firm guiding voice. "You have to get dressed and leave."

"What is your name?" he asked, finally, with a German accent, lowering the gun.

"I'm Luis. Grab your pants and your things and let's go," I said.

"Maurice," he said, "please help me. Shine your flashlight over here." He kept calling me "Maurice." The man walked to the closet and to the in-room safe. When he opened it with the help of my light, I could see there must have been 50,000 US dollars stacked inside. I don't know what a single, armed German guy does with $50,000 cash in Kathmandu, but I knew it couldn't be good. He stuffed the money into the wastebasket trash bag and started toward the door.

"You can't go out into the street with a gun in your hand," I said.

"I'm not leaving it," he said, and stuck it into a pocket.

In the hallway, I pointed him through the smoke toward the illuminated exit sign, and then headed down the hallway. "Thank you, Maurice," he said. That was the last I saw of the gun-wielding German, fortunately.

Of course, I also loved the guiding. You are the client's coach, helping them unlock endurance and fortitude they aren't sure they have, and helping them achieve a dream. As at Outward Bound, it can be supremely satisfying to facilitate those experiences for others. It was also fun for me, a young man of thirty, to rub elbows with people who'd succeeded in life. Our clients were most often type who'd risen to the top of their professions, and so had a lot of life experience to share. Executives like the CEO of a cardboard-manufacturing company in Los Angeles, a Swisscom executive, and an oil and gas magnate from Chile all remain friends and advisors to this day.

We'd inevitably spend weeks at a time together, on the trail or weatherbound in tents, passing the time with conversation, and passing issues of *The Economist* back and forth. I loved digging into how their industries worked, the ways the world's economy linked the globe, and how they saw the world evolving. In their most vulnerable moments of suffering through altitude sickness and fatigue, I sometimes saw them in uncharacteristically naked moments. Those times breed trust.

Clients invariably asked me what I was going to do when I grew up, a question asked both for a laugh but also in seriousness. I told them that guiding was all I'd ever wanted. *I think you are going to want more than this,* they often told me. *You seem like a person who needs challenges beyond the physical.* And: *I think you'll end up doing more.*

I was always flattered, but their ways of looking at the world globally, and through the lens of economics, began to rub off on me. I found myself sitting on that beach on Zanzibar, grilling the Dutch proprietor of the beach huts in the same way that the CEOs grilled me: How did you end up here? How does your business run? Does the work suit you? Even then, well before my MBA and my program at the Harvard Kennedy School, I was reflecting on the ways that the outdoor industry fits into society and the economy. From $85,000 guided Everest expeditions to $12-a-night huts on an empty African beach, both are portals to experiences in the natural world that can fuel passion and help connect us to the natural world and to ourselves. I loved how the global outdoor industry is a constellation of millions of small businesses, run by characters ranging from people like my grandfather Kelley to that reclusive Dutchman in Zanzibar.

One of my favorite clients was Len, a Canadian telecom executive whom I met on a 2003 trip to climb 16,050-foot Mount Vinson in Antarctica. I'll never forget my shock upon meeting him in his hotel room in Punta Arenas, Chile, the southern tip of South America, before our flight to Antarctica—he was pulling the sales tags off his crampons, ice axe, and harness. All of his gear, even his down parka, was brand spanking new.

"So, new gear?" I said, with some trepidation. It couldn't possibly be his first climb. The front-office staff surely would have seen his résumé and steered him toward one of our more beginner-friendly expeditions. The Adventure Consultants policy was that anyone on the Vinson expedition had to have considerable experience on a cold-weather trip with glacier travel. Anything in the Himalaya, of course, or Denali in Alaska—but, at a minimum, Washington's Mount Rainier or the Ecuadorian volcanoes. The weather was too extreme on Vinson, and the chance of rescue far too iffy, to bring newbies.

"Yeah, I bought all the stuff on the list," he said with a laugh, "but I don't even know what half of it is." Len was about fifty-five at that time, thick and burly, and brimming with the confidence of someone who has worked his way up from digging trenches for fiber-optic cable to running the company. And here he was, after twenty-four hours of travel to Punta Arenas, planning to get on a plane in the morning to fly off the edge of the earth. And yes, he had slipped through the front-office screening process; he had, in fact, no climbing experience whatsoever. He was as surprised as anyone that he was supposed to have any for the Vinson trip.

"Look," I told him, "I'm really sorry, but I don't think you should get on that plane tomorrow. It can get pretty rough down there. It's two and a half weeks living on the ice, tethered by ropes to other people, suffering brutal cold, cracked hands, a constantly running nose, and a dry cough. If you don't like it two days in, you are basically stuck in your tent. We can't send you home."

That all sounded fine to him, he said. "I'm pretty good at suffering." Looking at him, he seemed like a guy who could handle himself physically. I warned him that he'd have to do exactly *what* I told him, exactly *when* I told him. That can be tough for a lot of

CEOs.

An interesting part of the job was always telling people—some of them twice my age—who were used to calling the shots that they couldn't have what they wanted. We didn't always make the summit, but all of my clients came back alive. As Kurt Hahn said, you needed a readiness for sensible self-denial. Or, a little less clunkily, in the words of Mr. Kenny Rogers: "You gotta know when to hold 'em, know when to fold 'em, know when to walk away, and know when to run." In my guiding career, we did some walking away, and even some running.

Sometimes those conversations were awkward, and my approach, formed by Outward Bound, was often unorthodox for places like Everest. There was one expedition during which I stopped everyone on the glacier between Camps II and III and made the group circle up, therapy-style. People had been splitting into factions, and there was some bullying going on.

"I really don't like some of the behavior I'm seeing in this group," I said. "We're a team and have our lives in each other's hands up here—and the behavior I'm seeing could get someone killed on this mountain. That includes me—my life depends on yours. I'm not going up there if there isn't more trust within the group."

We were sitting on our packs beside the well-trodden groove in the glacier, the trough chipped by thousands of crampon-shod feet. "We aren't going to leave here until we identify the problem," I said. "We don't have to solve it—just make it better."

There were some frowns from the group. "How do we do this?" someone asked.

"We just have to be brutally honest with each other," I said. "This mountain will be brutally honest with you. Let's afford each other the same respect. I'll mediate if you need me to."

Twenty minutes later, after being passed by a couple of other climbing parties who gave us some quizzical looks, we had cleared the air somewhat, and the group was working better.

On Vinson, though, I never had any trouble from Len. He was as physically strong as any client I've worked with, and a quick study on all the climbing techniques. About a week in, we were at a high camp at 12,400 feet, situated for our summit push, when the worst storm I've ever experienced blew in. We were there alone, the first team of the season, having been dropped off by a Twin Otter ski-plane from the Patriot Hills Basecamp 100 miles away. That evening, before the storm, we'd sat and watched the sun swerve toward the horizon, dimming just slightly in the 24-hour Antarctic summer day. It was mind-boggling to realize there wasn't a single living thing in our line of sight. We weren't meant to survive in this environment, and unless you are very careful, you won't. There's a heightened sensitivity in Antarctica, knowing how fragile your existence is.

Then, I felt the pressure drop. There was no weather forecasting in Antarctica in those days, but especially at that altitude I got a small headache because the pressure was dropping so quickly that there was literally higher pressure inside my skull than outside. The wind came in at 40–50 mph, blowing snow into a total whiteout. With the wind chill, it was 80–100 degrees below zero. We were all zipped into our tents by then, but after a few hours, I knew I needed to get out of my sleeping bag, leave my tent, and physically check on every client to make sure they hadn't fallen into hypothermia. The blowing snow was so thick and the wind so disorienting that I tied a rope to a snowstake in front of my tent and anchored the other end to my harness so I could find my way back in the whiteout. In those conditions, it was snowing in each pair's tent, snow forced through the front door and ventilation zippers, and when I crawled into Len's tent, I saw him lying there in his 40-below sleeping bag with a huge grin on his face. Out of the wind and with the hot water bottle at his feet, he was warm enough. "Luis, this is the best thing ever," he said. "What a wild experience."

We got him safely to the summit, on a short rope as they say. Afterwards, he was hooked. "I want to do Everest, so tell me what I need to do, Luis," he told me. We came up with a three-year plan, starting with Aconcagua, Ecuador, a series of routes in the New Zealand Alps to build up some technical climbing skills (and to keep it interesting for me), and finally Denali, a bear of an expedition in its own right. No one had more fun at it than Len.

Like a lot of my repeat clients, I think what Len loved most was the simplicity of the task. I always thought that for my clients, high-altitude mountaineering was their type-A version of "Chop wood, carry water," the Zen concept that one should immerse oneself in a simple task in order to cultivate mindfulness. The single-minded, and usually very difficult, experience of putting one foot in front of the other up an alpine glacier afforded them an opportunity to leave the very complex problem-solving of their regular lives at home. (Incidentally, once the expedition was over was when I saw some of my clients' largest meltdowns. Once the goal was achieved, thoughts of their lives at home would sometimes come crashing in, leading to existential crises.)

Of course, it's also a truism of outdoor adventures—at any altitude—that a hard day's exercise brings a quieting of the mind that allows for the presence to focus on the surrounding physical beauty. A sunset always seems prettier after you've set down that heavy pack.

****

Though I would end up working as a top-end mountaineering guide for twenty years, the first cracks in my dream job appeared on Everest in 2003. It was a bright blue day in May at Camp II, and I was in the sun after the morning's leisurely climb from Camp I. My group was hanging out reading and chatting, and I was sitting with a pair of friends I'd run into there. Willie and Damian Benegas are brothers from Argentina who were descending from a bold, new climb they'd established over six days on Nuptse. Their route converged with ours at Camp II, and we were all in high spirits, teasing Willie for all the gear he'd dropped on the climb.

Just then, we saw a Nepalese worker being helped downhill by the arm by another Sherpa. As the worker walked, he moaned in pain, struggling to breathe. Just below our camp he sat down, seemingly unable to move. We hustled down to see what was up.

He was young—just nineteen years old—named Karma Sherpa, and in serious trouble. "My stomach," he said, "very, very bad."

The friend helping him chimed in: "No eat, drink, shit or piss for three days."

Karma had been cooking for clients for a different guiding company for three days at Camp IV, at an elevation of 26,000 feet. That's a dangerously long time to spend at that altitude.

While I mixed salt and sugar into a water bottle to help replace electrolytes depleted by dehydration, my expedition leader, Willi Prittie, radioed Karma's company basecamp to let them know that Karma needed help descending. Going down in altitude almost always helps.

Frustratingly, no one at Everest Basecamp was available to help Karma. His leader, an American, was himself stuck at Camp IV on the South Col, snow-blind and with a dead radio. Everyone else, it seemed, was conserving energy and manpower for their summit pushes. Willi and I were in the same position, headed to

Camp III with clients in the morning, but a few of our Sherpa staff could walk Karma down to Camp I, where we were hopeful that more help would arrive from basecamp or he would have recovered enough to descend on his own. We could not have been more wrong on both counts.

When Karma had gone just a quarter mile, near where the Benegas Brothers were striking their camp, he collapsed and was unable to continue. Putting their fatigue aside, the brothers ripped an aluminum ladder from a nearby crevasse crossing, got Karma packaged in a sleeping bag and on oxygen, and began to drag him downhill using the ladder as a litter and radioing everyone on the mountain for help. The Benegas boys had limited medical training, and approaching the crevasse-ridden and ice-block jumble of the Khumbu Icefall, they would need to manage the ropes and anchors to safely move Karma downhill. Today, he'd have been rescued by helicopter, but in 2003, such measures were rarely taken.

Willi Prittie and I started a very serious conversation about whether he could spare me to join the rescue. I'd had the most medical training, and protocol dictated that I stay with the victim until I could hand him off to someone whose training superseded mine, likely an MD at basecamp, twelve hours of travel below. Our team would be shorthanded guiding our clients up the mountain. Just then, over the radio, Damian reported that Karma had lost consciousness and was convulsing, vomiting, and unresponsive to verbal commands. Their syringe of the injectable steroid dexamethasone, which can help with symptoms of altitude sickness, had broken. *Could someone please bring another dose, quickly?* Enough was enough. Compassion dictated that I help try to save this young man's life. Willi told me that I was free to go.

I don't remember packing up at Camp II, just running

downhill—running at almost 22,000 feet to try to help a man I had never met. I radioed the rescue team that I was coming with our lead climbing Sherpa, Lhakpa Rita, and from our team at basecamp I also requested IV fluid and a prep kit to be run up by our two fastest Sherpas. "Simply pick our two strongest staff," I radioed our basecamp manager, "and send them, fast."

I made it the mile and three-quarters from Camp II to Camp I in only twenty-seven minutes. Don't ask me how, other than I knew that every minute would count. I arrived on scene and quickly administered the dexamethasone. I tried to do a secondary survey, collecting vitals and general conditions to relay to Luanne Freer, the basecamp doctor.

The problem was, everywhere I looked, Karma's pulse was too light and thready to read. His eyes were rolled up in his head, and to get him to focus on me, I had to rub his sternum with my knuckles, working to elicit a pain response, the lowest level of consciousness. But the worst sign was that his entire abdomen was as hard as a board. It seemed more and more like kidney failure, or septic shock from a perforated bowel or intestine. He had been vomiting bile into his oxygen mask, and it took all five of us to roll him over to clear the mask and his throat.

Eventually, the two Sherpas from our company arrived bearing the IV fluid and a litter so we could move Karma off the ladder. We continued to call for more assistance from other commercial companies on the mountain, but none ever came. A pair of Italian speed climbers on their way down from the summit put their thoughts of basecamp aside and joined in to help. By now, we were in the thick of the Khumbu Icefall, one of Everest's most treacherous sections. Over the three or so miles, the glacier there is fractured into thousands of house-sized ice blocks (seracs) and crevasses, and the going is slow, up sheer walls and across aluminum ladders spanning crevasses. We had to have ropes on the litter at all times as we lowered it over the seracs, lest it tumble into a crevasse, lost forever. On top of that, I would periodically stop the group to check Karma's ever-worsening vitals.

In those days, most people who became that sick at that elevation were left for dead. In this case, though, as I looked at the circle of people around Karma, giving everything they had, I realized that these people were not used to failure, or excuses, so we went about our work with a shared and total conviction. As the sun set, we could all tell that Karma was getting worse. We were reaching the limit of endurance, raising and lowering the litter with no less than five ropes on him at a time, all by headlamp. I was beginning to wonder how to keep the rescuers safe. No one was drinking water or eating; we were losing balance, falling over. There simply was no time.

At 7:15 p.m., in the middle of the icefall, Lhakpa said, "He has passed out again." But as I shone my light on Karma's face, I knew something was terribly wrong. I pushed all the rescuers aside and rubbed Karma's sternum with my knuckles. *Nothing.* Then I checked his breathing and heartbeat. *Nothing.* His eyes were fixed, his pupils dilated.

At that point there was only one thing left to do: CPR. I began chest compressions, and Damien Benegas did the rescue breathing. After ten furious minutes, there was a gentle hand on my shoulder. Willie Benegas told me to stop. It was over. I looked up through the steam coming off all our bodies from the effort and the light from our headlamps and started to cry. We had failed.

Karma Sherpa, nineteen years old, was gone.

It was agreed that we would secure him there overnight, under a serac in the middle of the Khumbu Icefall, and get ourselves to basecamp to recover from the frantic eleven-hour effort. We'd come back to retrieve his body the next day. We silently made our way down the rest of the icefall, watching basecamp glow in the distance and hearing the cheers and laughter of teams finished with their trips, basking in successful summits achieved.

The Sherpa culture has strict rules about cleansing oneself after handling a dead person: juniper smoke, sprinkling with pure water, and throwing rice three times into the air. Once in camp, after all this was done, and the weight of what had happened began to sink in, I had a cleansing ritual of my own: I dropped to one knee and promptly threw up.

The next day, I sat in basecamp trying to recover from all the physical and emotional aches. The first time you crack someone's ribs doing CPR on them, it changes you forever. But I also found myself feeling angry. I was angry that when radioing for help, none came, but when his body was brought the rest of the way through the Khumbu Icefall, hordes gathered to gawk. The BBC, Al Jazeera, and ABC all set up their cameras, dramatizing the danger of Everest. I was angry that someone had ordered Karma to work at 26,000 feet for three days, leading to the inevitable exhaustion and dehydration that had ruptured his stomach. For me, it was the beginning of my understanding of the iniquities of labor in the Himalaya.

In the beginning of Everest climbing, all the way back to the 1920s, Westerners were seen as the "Bara Sahibs," bringing high-paying work to a people who, at the time, were mostly subsistence farmers. The work allowed a very isolated ethnic group—Sherpas—in the Himalayas access to a potentially brighter future. Climbers who felt a special connection to the people and the mountains sought out ways to return and help grow the culture. They brought medicine, education, and higher-order knowledge about how international business was conducted. This was always done with the deepest level of respect and admiration for the communities that Western climbers traveled through and worked with. The glory that came from those expeditions was one of shared effort.

In the commercial era, which began in earnest during the early 1990s, expeditions and the climbing culture got more complicated. The Nepali government realized what a cash cow it had with Everest and surrounding peaks, and the older Sherpas were able not only to secure work for family and friends, but, as pay increased, to start sending their children to school both in Kathmandu and abroad. As this generation returned to work on the mountain, we in the guiding community were in a unique position to help advance the culture even more by imparting positive lessons about how we do business during a new, emerging age of wealthy climbing clientele.

Instead, what was the business lesson we consciously or unconsciously chose to impart?

The bottom line, above all else. Maximize profit. Minimize overhead. Want to advance? *Be the strongest. Do double carries to higher camps and get back in time to serve lunch to the Sahibs.* If one of you dies? *While that is sad, life and our expedition will go on.* Bit by bit, this ethos chipped away at a Buddhist culture that is largely based on principles of service and sacrifice.

Now a new generation of Sherpas has the benefit of deeper self-awareness and education. They can speak multiple languages, often have lived abroad, and understand much about how the Western world works. These Sherpas began to ask questions of themselves and the guiding community. Shouldn't they be receiving a bigger slice of the revenues, for doing the hardest and most dangerous work? Or at least be receiving more respect and better working conditions?

****

The pot that had been simmering with incidents like Karma Sherpa's needless death spilled over in an incident on Everest on April 27, 2013. On that day, a significant group of Sherpas got into a violent confrontation with three Western climbers. Punches and rocks were thrown, and a pair of the world's most famous climbers, Simone Moro and the late Ueli Steck, fled the mountain for fear of their own safety.

I was retired from Himalayan guiding by then, but followed the incident from the United States with shock as texts came in from friends who were on the mountain. Initial reports indicated that there had been some sort of confrontation on the Lhotse Face above Camp II between the three-person Western climbing team of Steck, Simone Moro, and Jonathan Griffith, and a team of Sherpas fixing ropes for commercial guiding operations—the Icefall Doctors. Later that day, those workers and others angrily approached Steck, Moro, and Griffith's tent at Camp II, the same area where our rescue of Karma Sherpa had occurred a decade earlier, to demand an apology. My friend Melissa Arnot Reid, an American climber, ran to warn the three of the approaching Sherpas, some of whom had their faces covered.

When Steck, Moro, and Griffith stepped out of their tent to start a discussion, they were punched and hit with rocks. Arnot Reid stepped between the Sherpas and Steck, who was pushed back into his tent, and Griffith and Moro ran away and hid. The Sherpas demanded that Moro apologize for calling one of the Icefall Doctors a "motherfucker" in Nepali, and when he returned to the tent to apologize, he was also punched and hit with rocks. The Sherpas demanded they leave the region within an hour, and the trio packed up and fled. Even from the earliest reports, it was obvious that without the intervention of Arnot Reid and a few other climbers, the violence could have been much more serious.

Reports trickled in over the next few days that helped clarify the situation. In the days before the incident, there had been a large meeting during which everyone present agreed that no one would climb on the steep terrain above Camp II while the Icefall Doctors fixed lines there, work that would take a day or so. Such meetings and agreements have been standard for decades. But on that April 27, they encountered Steck's team, who climbed past them despite the workers' requests that they not do so, saying that they would be careful. None of the trio had been at the meeting the day before. When the trio dislodged an ice chunk that hit a Sherpa in the face, there was a confrontation on the near-vertical, icy terrain.

There's some disagreement about the details of the initial and later confrontations. The Icefall Doctors say that Steck grabbed one of the workers by the chest in a confrontational way and brandished his ice axe at them. The climbers said that the Icefall Doctors threw chunks of ice at them and that Steck used his hands to defend himself against a Sherpa who rappelled into him from above. The Sherpas say that when they went to discuss the situation with the trio later that afternoon, they were provoked by a Western guide before they reached Steck, Moro, and Griffith's tent. Another account said that a Western guide did knock a rock out of one of the Sherpa's hands while rocks were being thrown at the trio's tent.

What isn't in dispute is that the resentment had been simmering. "It is Sherpas like us who work hard and never get the credit," Tashi Sherpa told *Outside* magazine a few months later. "This incident had been waiting to happen, and it will happen again as long as Sherpas are humiliated."

If 2013 showed strain in labor conditions on Everest, the tragedy in 2014 blew them up entirely. On April 18, in the middle of the crowded Everest spring climbing season, a 64,000-ton block of ice the size of a small office building broke off the west shoulder of the mountain and tumbled directly onto the Khumbu Icefall, the treacherous, broken glacier where we'd had such slow going in the failed rescue of Karma Sherpa. The resulting avalanche killed sixteen people, thirteen of whom were Nepalese workers. While Sherpas, guides, and climbers were still working to find three missing workers, the Nepalese government announced that in addition to the $10,000 of insurance each deceased man's family would receive, they'd be awarded an extra 40,000 rupees—just $415.

That insulting sum was the breaking point for the Sherpas. They knew that the government took in $11,000 in revenue for every Everest permit issued to a foreign climber, some $3.4 million total each year, and that because the enterprise was built literally on their backs as they carried loads up and down the mountain, they should be far better compensated for the immense risks they take. Most workers at that time made between $2,000 and $6,000, depending on their role, in a season—about the same as a Nepalese college graduate would make annually, but with considerably more risk. The Sherpas demanded that the insurance payouts double to $22,000 for the families of each worker who died on the job, and that $10,000 insurance payouts be funded for workers permanently disabled on the job. They also wanted a $1,000 funeral benefit.

"It is just impossible for many of us to continue climbing while there are three of our friends buried in the snow," a worker named Dorje Sherpa told the press. "I can't imagine stepping over them." The body of one worker killed in 2014, Tenzing Chottar, was never found.

When the Nepalese government was slow to respond to the demands after several days of tense meetings at Everest Basecamp, the Sherpas essentially went on strike. Workers began heading home, and mountaineering companies started calling off their expeditions. That week, I published an article on *Outside's* website calling on the mountaineering community to support the Sherpas in their demands against the government, and to go even further than that. Because more Nepalese were starting their own mountaineering companies to compete with Western guiding companies, I wrote that Westerners should "Train them how to be better climbers and how to be better at business. Show them that their brothers, fathers, and sons did not die in vain. Will it affect our bottom line? Probably. Will we have more companies to compete with? Absolutely."

It was the crystallization of my reaction to the injustice of Karma Sherpa's death. I wrote, "In Chinese, the word 'crisis' is composed of two characters. One represents danger, the other opportunity. The danger from this event is that, next year, everything will go back to business as usual. This, in my estimation, would signify that those who perished have died in vain, and would be a further scar on the guiding community and an insult to the Sherpa culture."

These days, conditions for the Nepali mountaineering workers have improved. Many Sherpa guides now make around $10,000 a season, double their pay in 2014. That's a very good wage in Nepal, where the median income is around $800 a year. There are also many more Sherpa-owned mountaineering companies whose owners can do quite well.

There's also no doubt that Nepali climbers as a group are gaining the respect that they've been craving. Arguably climbing's biggest star right now, for example, is Nims Purja, a Nepalese mountaineer who has led teams of his countrymen on two of climbing's most celebrated recent accomplishments. In 2019, he climbed all fourteen of the Himalaya's 8,000-meter (higher than 26,246-feet) peaks in a mind-boggling six months and six days. It takes most climbers a decade to log all these ascents, and fewer than two dozen have accomplished it at all. His feat stunned the climbing world and gained him international fame when the documentary *14 Peaks: Nothing Is Impossible* debuted on Netflix.

Then, in January 2021, Purja led a team of nine Nepali mountaineers to the summit of 28,251-foot K2 in winter, becoming the first to claim the long-coveted first winter ascent. More people have been to outer space—some 400—than have stood on the summit of the notoriously treacherous K2. None had ever been there before in winter. The accomplishment made international news, particularly for the fact that the ten climbers made the final strides to the summit in unison and while singing Nepal's national anthem.

These accomplishments are heartening. Critical for sustainability is the condition that those who have grown up in and near naturally splendid places benefit economically and socially from those places. That goes as much for Kanab, Utah, near Grand Staircase-Escalante National Monument, as it does for Nepal's Namche Bazaar. There's no doubt that mountaineering has raised the standard of living and education for the people native to the Himalaya, and as their power in the Nepalese and global community grows, so does the capacity to protect the Himalayan ecosystem, even in the face of robust tourism.

In 2003, however, such developments still felt far off. After I'd been grieving in basecamp in the days after Karma's death, my camp manager encouraged me to finish the climb. "It is what you are here for, what you are meant to do, after all," he said.

I took my frustrations out on the climb. To catch my group for summit day, I climbed from basecamp to Camp II in a day, then from Camp II to Camp IV the following day, catching my group there as a surprise. They were elated to see me, glad for the reinforcements for the always nerve-wracking summit day. I'd moved faster than I ever had, ascending all 11,434 feet in just three days, triple my normal pace. I'd climbed, in fact, with the capacity of a Sherpa, whose birthright is fitness at altitude. Standing atop the summit for the third time, after having exceeded my own fitness expectations, felt hollow. I was here on the summit, but Karma was dead, and it was hard to see the point.

Chapter 8

CHO OYU

"If you want others to be happy, practice compassion. If you want to be happy, practice compassion." —Dalai Lama

September 30, 2006, dawned blessedly clear on the flanks of Cho Oyu, a 26,906-foot mountain in Tibet. After a week sheltering in basecamp from the storms lashing the peak, I was excited that I could finally begin leading my three clients toward the summit, the world's sixth highest. Two seasons before, I'd become lead guide and director of operations for the famed mountaineering company Adventure Consultants, a heady role for a thirty-four-year-old. I'd been living a rarefied life that would have scarcely made sense to a wheezy, housebound seven-year-old Luis. In the winter, I was ski instructing in Vail, and come spring, I'd be off to the Himalaya or some high-altitude corner of the globe for Adventure Consultants.

I was making six figures to coax CEOs and heiresses, some of whom arrived via their private jets, up towering, glaciated peaks. One client, a professional British socialite, transported us across the globe in her boyfriend's luxury, retrofitted 727 in order to set the women's speed record for climbing the Seven Summits. In between missions, I often reveled in the hospitality of my new friends. A client offered his Chamonix getaway any time he wasn't using it, which was apparently never. You could roller-skate around the white marble living-room floor, and there was a wine cellar and a Porsche in the garage. I wasn't comfortable enough to avail myself of either, but I spent plenty of time ogling the view of Mont Blanc out the floor-to-ceiling windows. Another let me kick up my heels at his ritzy Jupiter Island, Florida, beachside condo. "Just FYI, you might run into the Rock," he said, meaning the famously amiable wrestler turned movie star, who apparently lived two floors up. "He's friendly," he added, probably unnecessarily, though I never did run into Dwayne Johnson.

The perks—including a Rolex one client had hand-delivered to my front door in Colorado—were nice, as was the admiration I got from people in my life, jealous that I got to climb the world's highest peaks for a living. The mountains, however, were why I was still in the game. Their majesty and beauty, and the way climbing put you right in the moment, was what I loved best. From basecamp at Cho Oyu, the round, snow-covered summit dome rose tantalizingly above the dissipating clouds above us. As I walked to our team's commissary tent for breakfast, I knew there was no place I'd rather be.

Ours was far from the only team in camp. Cho Oyu is considered a testing ground for those with aspirations for Everest, just 19 miles west along the ramparts of the jagged, icy Himalaya. Each climbing season, hundreds of people amass at Cho Oyu Basecamp to give it a shot. On that morning, more than seventy tents in hues of orange, yellow, and red were spread across the barren and rocky ground at 18,284 feet, housing climbers from across the globe—France, Romania, Russia, and my trio of clients from England, Belgium, and Australia. Through the impromptu village drifted pungent smoke from burning juniper boughs—part of a ritual performed at the chorten altar by some of the Sherpas working in camp to protect those headed for the summit.

Cho Oyu straddles the Tibet-Nepal border, though our approach to the peak had been from the Tibetan side. We'd flown to Lhasa, and part of the appeal of the expedition, both to me and my clients, had been the sightseeing we'd done of the onetime forbidden city and countryside, militarily occupied by the Chinese since 1951.

We joined throngs of Chinese tourists in the Jokhang Market, searching the locals' faces for signs of repression. The Chinese had notoriously been suppressing Tibetan culture ever since their occupation began, replacing their native Tibetan in schools with Han Chinese and forbidding the education of young Tibetans in Buddhist monasteries. (Since then, things have gotten worse, with the forced migration of thousands of Tibetans, and the installation of a surveillance state that rewards citizens for reporting activism and dissenting views.) Our whole team knew the story of the Dalai Lama's valiant escape from Lhasa to India in March 1959, a seventeen-day expedition through the Himalaya in late winter, mostly traveling under the cover of night. To reach safety and cultural and religious freedom, his entourage crossed high mountain passes much like the one within sight of Cho Oyu Basecamp, the 19,000-foot Nangpa La on the Tibet-Nepal border.

In Lhasa, we'd toured the Potala Palace, the former home of the young Dalai Lama that literally looms over the town center. We wandered in semi-darkness from hall to hall beneath sculptures of grimacing demons and placid, gilded Buddhas. The thing that most caught my attention was the inner sanctum. As I sat and peered out the small windows of the holy leader's former personal chambers, I could imagine the boy Lama gazing out of it in the 1940s. It hit me then that he could never come home, never visit, never see the Potala again.

The morning of the climb, my mind was on logistics, running

through a mental checklist that assured me our gear was in place for the coming four-day ascent. Nearly all of our equipment—oxygen bottles, tents, food, and even the down-filled one-piece suits we'd need for summit day—had already been ferried by our staff of eight Sherpas to camps I, II, and III at 21,00 feet, 23,000 feet, and 24,300 feet respectively. All that was left for me to pack before we set out were extra layers, snacks, and a few talismans I always carried in a small satchel: a bag of rice blessed by the Nepalese Buddhist icon Lama Geshe, and, in a nod to my Catholic upbringing, a St. Christopher medallion. I was excited to get going. Despite a seven-year career climbing in the Himalaya, I'd never summited Cho Oyu.

The only other time I'd been to the peak was five years before, in September of 2001. We'd been busy in basecamp, acclimating for the ascent, when suddenly climbing was rendered irrelevant. We clustered around the radio on September 11, listening to the events unfolding in New York and D.C. and Pennsylvania that bright-blue morning, and it seemed like we were experiencing the end of the world. All anyone wanted to do was go back home to family and friends, and to see what had become of our country.

Five years later, that morning in 2006, pouring myself a cup of coffee in the Adventure Consultants dining tent, there was no way I could anticipate that my Cho Oyu bid would once again be interrupted by a violent international incident.

Twelve days earlier, on September 18, about seventy-five Tibetans had been crammed into the back of a truck in Lhasa. It was a dark night, better to avoid detection by Chinese informants. The Tibetans were refugees, some as young as seven, and each had paid $500 to smugglers to get them out of their own country.

If a Tibetan wants to study the language, culture, or religion of their homeland, they must travel to Dharmasthala, India, the home of the Dalai Lama and seat of the Tibetan government in exile. The problem is that it is illegal for Tibetans to emigrate to India. Those not wealthy enough to pay the necessary bribes must make the journey in secret. At the peak of refugee migration in the early 2000s, some 2,500 to 3,500 did so every year, many of them teenagers looking for a traditional Tibetan education. (These days, the migration is down to a trickle, due, it is believed, to stricter Chinese surveillance.)

On that dark night in Lhasa, the overloaded, overcrowded truck ground past Chinese checkpoints. The smugglers had sternly warned the refugees inside to remain silent—similar to the coyotes who ferry people over our southern American border. After three suffocating days in the truck, the group was dropped beside a trail that led upward into the mountains. There, the group began their hellish ten-day trek on far-too-little food and water, with far-too-little warm clothing. They trudged onward through an unseasonably early winter snowstorm—the same one that was keeping my team pinned down in Cho Oyu Basecamp—drawn on by the idea that once they traversed Nangpa La into Nepal, they'd be safe from oppression.

By dawn of September 30, the frozen and starving refugees could see the snowy, high-altitude pass, just to the right of a glacier spilling off Cho Oyu. On the left side of the glacier were the brightly colored tents of the mountaineers' basecamp. Unfortunately, camped alongside the climbers were a dozen members of the Chinese army, there to monitor the border. Soldiers began scrambling down the rocky slopes toward the refugees, and when the migrants realized the danger, they began to run toward the pass as best they could. The soldiers started shooting.

****

In the large tent we used as a dining room, I was just taking my first sips of coffee when Ang Tshering, the boss of our Sherpa team, came bursting in, shouting, "Very bad, very bad. Soldiers shooting." That's when we heard the gunfire, which seemed sickeningly out of place.

We rushed outside. There were dozens of other climbers and Sherpas gathered at the edge of camp, many pointing toward the Nangpa La pass. There, about 100 meters away, we could see people running uphill through the fresh snow toward the border in two separate lines of a dozen or so each. Nearer to us, Chinese soldiers were kneeling, taking aim and shooting at the runners.

I immediately realized they must be refugees. Nangpa La is a common trading route between Tibet and Nepal, with traders ferrying goods on yaks, paying bribes to the Chinese soldiers to cross the border. But this group had no yaks and carried almost nothing with them.

All around me, climbers emerged from tents into the sunshine, drawn by the gunfire and the commotion. At least 100 people stood there watching, shocked. More soldiers filtered through our camp to take firing positions. I could see the smoke from their muzzles.

It seemed like there was no way the Chinese soldiers could hit the refugees. The Tibetans were too far away; they would make it to freedom. I heard someone say, "Go, Tibet, go." But then I saw another line of soldiers closer to the pass, taking aim and firing.

Some of the refugees had been corralled immediately by the soldiers, but thirty or so continued running uphill in two lines amidst the incoming bullets. One man fell in the snow, and then got up holding his leg and kept going. Farther, just a few yards from cresting a ridge, we saw another figure fall. That was Kelsang Namtso, a seventeen-year-old nun. She never stood up again.

No one knew what to do. We all stood there, dumbfounded. Should we take photos, video? Should we confront the soldiers, to give the fleeing refugees time to make the border? That seemed clearly foolish, standing in an authoritarian nation that was decidedly not our own. I felt powerless, watching more soldiers pushing captured refugees before them through our camp to their own military compound. Other soldiers unzipped the mountaineers' tents, shouting, looking for hiding Tibetans. Up close it was obvious that most of their prisoners were teenagers or younger, and were plainly terrified. It didn't matter that some of the Tibetan refugees had escaped capture, clearing the pass and heading downhill into Nepal. At least one, maybe more, had been killed as we watched.

My first thought was for my clients: I knew this was not a safe place to be. There would be more soldiers, more officials, more questions. Basecamp already felt intimidating and unpredictable. The most dangerous thing in the world is a teenage boy with a machine gun. I knew the safest place was away from here—up on the mountain, out of camp and heading for the summit, where we could let the mushrooming international incident in basecamp settle down. I told my team to get their packs. We'd start climbing immediately. Even at the time it felt like a terrible option, and I still feel shame that I couldn't do more for those starving, terrified kids. There were no heroes on Cho Oyu that day.

Over the next eight hours, we marched uphill toward Camp I, our hearts and feet heavy. We were all shocked. We'd just witnessed a major international incident, a murder.

"We have to prepare ourselves for every single climber getting kicked out of the country for what we've witnessed," I told the clients. "By the time we are back to basecamp, there will be officials everywhere, and more soldiers. The world will know all about this."

Meanwhile, in the camp below, the soldiers tortured their captives, grilling them for information on those who'd escaped. (According to the 2008 BBC documentary *Murder in the Snow*, while thirty of the refugees were captured, forty-one made it over the pass to freedom.) The soldiers also posed for pictures with Kelsang's body, which they left lying in the snow for more than twenty-four hours.

Finally, at Camp II, one of the clients was physically sick from the stress of what we'd witnessed.

"Fuck this climb," she said. "I can't muster the enthusiasm to make the push."

My heart wasn't in it either. The next morning, while the other clients headed for Camp III with my assistant guide, I descended to basecamp with her.

When we arrived that afternoon, on October 2, it seemed like business as usual. I was shocked to see people going about their tasks amongst the tents as though nothing had happened. What had been the global response to the shootings, I asked? People either shrugged or said they didn't know. It was surreal.

Using a satellite phone, I called my friend Tom Sjogren in New York. He and his wife, Tina, ran *ExplorersWeb*, the go-to mountaineering news website of the day.

"Can you believe what happened here?" I asked.

"I have no idea what you are talking about," he replied. "What happened? Where?"

To my horror, not only were there no heroes that day, but three days after the shootings, no one had even reported them to the outside world. Most of the mountaineering parties had satellite phones, but there seemed to be a consensus not to make trouble. The soldiers were still in camp, after all. But worse, I had the sense that some mountaineering companies were more concerned about having their permits for future expeditions revoked by the Chinese. I was furious. I felt that we were all accomplices to a murder.

I said to Tom, "Stay by your computer. I'm going to send you a story that needs to be posted."

Huddled in my tent, I quickly typed out a short report and emailed it to *ExplorersWeb*. I wanted the world to know what had happened, and how we all had stood by and watched it transpire.

"There is a story that happened here on the thirtieth and the first that is not being told," I wrote. "Early morning of September 30, I saw a line of Tibetans heading towards the start of the pass. Then, without warning, shots rang out. Over and over. Then the line of people started to run uphill. Two people were down, and they weren't getting up." In all, the report was just three paragraphs, but I assumed it was enough to break the dam of silence. I wanted people to know, as I wrote, "that people were dying attempting to reach for a better life."

Intimidated by the oppressive secrecy around camp, I asked the Sjogrens to keep the report anonymous. After all, I still had clients I needed to get safely out of the country.

ExlporersWeb posted the report, and within hours both the press and the group International Campaign for Tibet were calling other climbers on the mountain, searching for confirmation and more details.

The next day, I mentioned to my assistant guide that I'd written the anonymous post. The next I saw him, he appeared with Russel Brice, one of the most senior guides in camp. "Are you trying to get us kicked out of the country?" Brice yelled at me. "Are you fucking crazy?"

My assistant guide claimed that the group had been part of a human smuggling ring, transporting girls to India for prostitution.

Shortly after, another expedition leader, Henry Todd, joined them and yelled at me, "You should be fucking hung out to dry for what you did. I think your name has been given to the Chinese." It was an obvious threat. He continued: "I would be careful going out, and don't endanger your clients."

It was shocking to me that these seasoned guides, at least one of whom I'd long admired, were so much more concerned about their businesses than about the lives of oppressed teenagers. This wasn't the climbing community I thought I knew. This wasn't acquiescing to the calculated risks of mountaineering; this was accepting the deliberate killing of innocents. (To be fair, several months later Brice lodged a complaint with the Chinese about the shooting.)

Of course, I was intimidated by the prospect of being detained by the Chinese Army. For the next week, as we slowly moved gear off the mountain and celebrated a few summits for our team, I racked my brain. Should I hotfoot it over the pass into Nepal? Or should I, as one of my more moronic colleagues put it, "give myself up"?

Our trek out and then four-day overland drive with our equipment to Kathmandu was uneventful, but once in the city, my fears returned. Nepal is not under Chinese control, but in 2006 China was helping foment a Maoist uprising in the country, so things felt a little dodgy, even in the bustling backpacker's quarter. I went to the Indian barber below Tom N Jerry Pub in the Thamel district. It's a ritual for me on returning from a Himalayan climb: I get the trim and a straight-razor shave, as well as a little neck and scalp rub. Exiting the shop, I ran into a couple of climbers I recognized from Cho Oyu.

They were two British clients from a different company. They were both policemen, used to some level of conflict and danger, but they still seemed rattled. "Luis, we thought you should know that the Chinese are looking for you," they said. They'd been contacted by the Chinese embassy, and authorities there wanted to interview them about what they'd seen.

"We think we are being followed," they said. "We've just gone to the Thai Airways office to change our flights. We are flying out tonight."

I decided to cover my tracks. Instead of checking into the usual hotel with my clients, I told them, "I'll see you for breakfast." I went around the corner to a different hotel, handed over a fistful of rupees, and checked in under a different name. I texted *ExplorersWeb* the latitude and longitude of the new hotel, just in case.

About this time, the Chinese, apparently unable to keep quiet any longer, started issuing statements. They first reported that there had, in fact, been an incident at the border, but that details were unavailable. The second reported that a group of Tibetans had attacked the border guards there.

By the time the second report reached the press, I was sitting in my anonymous hotel room watching the sunset and thinking, "I have no idea what I've just done." My head was spinning. Had the Tibetans been victims of human smuggling? I'd never had the chance to talk to any of them.

Just then, the phone rang.

I was terrified. I'd only sent my latitude and longitude to *ExplorersWeb* as a worst-case scenario. I'd told no one else that I wasn't in my empty hotel room at the Radisson.

I let the phone ring a few times, figuring it was a mistake by the front desk. The ringing stopped, then started again. I couldn't hide in here forever—the front-desk worker knew I was in the room after all. I picked up the receiver.

"Hello, is this Luis Benitez? This is Kate Saunders, from the International Campaign for Tibet," a woman said, her lilting British accent putting me instantly at ease. The Sjogrens had considered her trustworthy and shared my location. She'd somehow talked her way past the hotel operator to ring up my room.

"Luis, the refugees you saw who successfully escaped made it to the refugee center here in Kathmandu," she said. "The director would love for you to come meet them so you can see who you chose to help."

How could I say no?

The next morning, the driver they'd sent drove us through winding streets on a route I could never duplicate, to a compound chosen for its secrecy from the Chinese government. We drove into a beautiful courtyard, and the first thing I noticed was the feeling of hope. It was a beautiful day. There were Tibetan children laughing and giggling in the courtyard.

The director emerged, ushered me to his office, and asked me to relay my part in the story. As I reached the point where I was talking about the climbers doing nothing, I was overwhelmed by shame and anger all over again. I had simply stood there.

He thanked me for coming, and said I had nothing to be ashamed of, as there were more climbers coming forward now and the world would know the truth.

We toured the center, meeting children in classrooms full of art depicting their lives back home—yaks, mountains, and family. Orange for the sun, and brown for the vastness of the Tibet they'd left behind. We met a doctor in the clinic who told me stories of frostbite and snow blindness from crossing the pass in winter. Most Tibetans prefer the winter crossing, as the soldiers tend not to want to leave their base in the harsh conditions. They had western medicine as well as traditional Tibetan herbal remedies to try to be ready for any issue. Just the day before, he told me, a child had been born to a mother that came over the pass seven months pregnant.

As we turned the corner, there was a group of scared and tired looking teenagers sitting in the corner. "Those are some of the survivors of the incident you witnessed," the director said. They were kids. Young monks, nuns, and assorted other teens. One young nun was in tears off to herself. When I asked the director why she was so upset, he told me something that will imprint the image of her misery on my brain forever: "She is the friend of the person who was killed on the pass. The body you saw? It was her best friend, a seventeen-year-old nun." The young girl had traveled with Kelsang Namtso from their home village of Nagchu, where they'd known each other all their lives. The pair had wanted to have the religious freedom to devote their lives to Buddhism, a practice that one member of each family once traditionally undertook in Tibet.

Kate Saunders had wanted me to go on television to relay what I'd witnessed, but I was frankly scared to do so. Kathmandu didn't feel safe to me, and even if I delayed until I was back home in a few days, the risk to my career felt huge. I'd be jeopardizing the lavish lifestyle I'd gotten used to—the six-figure income, the private-jet rides, hobnobbing with the rich and powerful. I'd also be turning my back on a goal I'd been working to achieve almost since I could remember, the pursuit of which I felt had literally cured me of a debilitating disease. All I'd ever wanted was to own a guiding service and work in the Himalaya.

In that moment, though, seeing those survivors, I knew that I had to do more than help bolster the egos of the world's overachievers by leading them up big mountains. I told Kate I was ready to talk to the press. That one decision led to a domino effect that I had no idea would so significantly alter the course of my life. From starting to work with the International Campaign For Tibet on these complex human rights issues, to collaborating on a BBC documentary about the incident, one thing was clear: my so called simple life as a full time mountain guide would never really be the same.

A few months later, in May 2007, I was at home in Colorado preparing for my sixth Everest expedition when I received yet another surprising phone call. On the other end of the line, calling from Dharmasthala, India, was Lodi Ghari, who explained that he was the Dalai Lama's special envoy, his personal secretary. "His Holiness would like to meet you," he said.

Through the International Campaign for Tibet, I'd been invited to a private audience with the Dalai Lama. It was a huge honor, and I was thrilled. After arriving in Kathmandu a week early for the expedition, I detoured by train to Dharmasthala for the audience and for a press conference on the Nangpa La incident and the plight of Tibetan refugees. After passing through the security checkpoints the Indian government had set up for their distinguished guest, we were ushered inside the Dalai Lama's private residence. With me were Kate Saunders and a Danish physician who'd treated the survivors of the attack. We were all surprised when, instead of the large audience room where His Holiness usually meets delegations, we were instead shown to a small sitting room containing a pair of couches and chairs arrayed around a coffee table. The awareness that this was the same honor afforded to refugees who'd escaped Tibet over mountain passes made the moment a bittersweet one.

After a long wait, the Dalai Lama shuffled in with an aide and a translator. He wore his ever-present mischievous grin and the trademark square, tinted glasses, and limped a little on a bum knee. I stood up, along with everyone else, and I bowed slightly, but he gestured to my seat and in English said, "Sit, sit." He sat beside me on the couch and looked at each of us in turn. Sitting beside His Holiness, I had the odd, floating feeling you get when you see someone or something you've seen in the media your whole life—like a celebrity or the Statue of Liberty. It felt like being teleported into a dreamworld.

The translator told His Holiness who each of us were, and he gave attention in turn. "You have done a very brave thing," he said to me in English. "Has it been difficult?"

I told him of my struggles with my profession, of the moral failings of mountaineering that no longer felt acceptable to me—the lives disregarded, the bodies left behind, the murders tolerated. I told him it was difficult to contemplate leaving the career I had loved for so long, and the friends I had made, to speak out. What he said and did at that point has in large part shaped my life from that moment forward. He laughed! He said, "You know MY story, right? I should be in Tibet, not India! So, Luis, you have a choice. Sometimes you don't choose the path; sometimes the path chooses you. It's up to you how you want to show up, what you want to do." Then he laughed again.

The Dalai Lama wasn't judging or offering a strategy; he was simply allowing me to verbalize the challenge, and to discover my own path by saying it out loud. Of course, my struggles were nothing compared to his, and to those of his people. Or a girl who had lost her life because she dared to climb a path toward something better. That was obvious. But having this great man see me and acknowledge my own challenges was empowering in a way I could never have imagined. It was exceptional leadership.

For the first time, I stopped lamenting what I was losing and started to think about what I could do to help, and how my life would be enriched in the process. I knew that my life of being a fulltime guide was well and truly over, and that if I was really going to step into what I thought was possible, I would have to do the thing that I always encouraged my Outward Bound students to consider on their courses. When you realize you are capable of doing more, of being more, then it really does come down to what you choose, which fork in the road you elect to take. In that moment, in a beautiful, brightly lit room in Dharmsala India, I literally chose to change the trajectory of my life. I started studying foreign policy, and I spoke out wherever and whenever I could about the atrocity, which led, in 2009, to testifying before the Supreme Court of Spain—or as it's known in Spanish, the Tribal Supremo—which was trying the then-seated Chinese president Hu Jintao for crimes against humanity for the country's policies in Tibet.

I did summit Everest a few weeks later, for my sixth time. I felt the familiar pride of having accomplished a difficult and complicated thing yet again, especially of leading another diverse team to a famous objective. I was proud of the hard work and leadership that had carried us to the literal top of the world. I was also starting to grow into the realization that I could use that leadership for more important things.

Chapter 9

UNUSUAL AS BUSINESS

"What lies behind us and what lies before us are tiny matters compared to what lies within us."
—Ralph Waldo Emerson

A year later, I had another impactful encounter with a Tibetan monk, this one quite a bit more unorthodox. In September 2007, my team was meeting with a client in an office tower in Lower Manhattan. Packed into an enormous glass-walled conference room were 100 newly hired analysts and sales associates for the famous Wall Street firm JPMorgan Chase & CO. Everyone wore name tags. The firm wanted my team of Outward Bound Professional (OBP) instructors to help onboard their staff with a day of team-building exercises, focusing on the theme of "believe in the impossible."

In my introduction, I focused on my mountaineering résumé. I told them that teamwork on Everest operates on the same principles as teamwork in business. Some examples: an ambitious goal can inspire capabilities you couldn't dream you possess; clear communication is critical; attention to detail is the key to success; staying calm under pressure takes practice; and, most of all, you won't get anywhere without a solid, committed team. The last bit, I said, is what we were there for. "During the course of your work, you are going to rely on the person to your left and to your right in times of real difficulty," I said. "Today you are going to start building the trust you'll need to achieve things you never imagined were possible."

Maybe this sounds like I was laying it on a little thick, but I can promise you that our audience bought it. Remember: These were kids who'd just been hired onto Wall Street. They'd likely been dreaming of this day for half their lives. They saw themselves as exceptional, preparing to amass vast personal fortunes—a goal that doubtless seemed as glorious as summitting Everest had to me at their age. And, like a team approaching Everest Basecamp, their spirits were running high. As for me, I was excited to help them on their way, but I also had my own agenda. I was there to remind them of their humanity.

After Cho Oyu, I found that my taste for the business of high-altitude mountaineering was shaken. I decided to return to my moral center: I hired on as a director for OBP. The mission was to bring the Outward Bound principles of personal growth and improved leadership to a professional setting. We worked with organizations ranging from Microsoft to Dartmouth College in settings ranging from ropes courses to whitewater-rafting trips. When Bob Gordon, the head of OBP, recruited me, he'd said, "If you think that our society's moral compass is broken, come help me fix it. Help shape leaders using a pedagogy you believe in."

I thought that all business, not just high-altitude mountaineering, needed more compassion—Outward Bound's crowning pillar—at its core. Can pharmaceutical companies price their products at not just what the market can bear, but at what their most vulnerable customers can bear? Can companies offer childcare so that more women can gain financial independence? Can apparel companies help reduce environmental impacts and raise the standard of living in impoverished countries by sourcing their materials not just cheaply, but responsibly? (A dozen years later, this last question would be part of my job description with VF Corp.)

The idea with OBP trainings was to have fun and empower, getting at questions of morality almost surreptitiously. Each exercise and adventure was a metaphor. "Okay," I'd say, after we'd pinballed haplessly down a whitewater rapid because, rather than heeding the designated captain, each of the eight executives holding a paddle had done whatever they thought best. "What do you all think of followership as a value?" Or, to a pair of co-workers who were about to belay each other across a ropes course 30 feet off the ground: "How are you going to trust each other on the next business deal if you can't trust each other right now?"

That day in the conference room in Manhattan, our main goal was to get these strangers to start working in teams. We'd split them into groups of ten. Their task was to spend the morning navigating the city via one clue to another in a scavenger hunt, building connections that would later blossom into greater trust and alacrity at work. We'd left clues taped under park benches, or with hotel bellhops and magazine stands, and the routes eventually all converged at a spot in Central Park.

As part of the hunt, each team had collected a few skeins of ordinary knitting yarn. Standing in a circle on the grass, I started my spiel by unspooling a skein from person to person around the circle. "This yarn isn't very strong," I said, pulling the strand in two. I encouraged each person to do the same. "One strand of yarn isn't going to accomplish much, but the power of the collective can make something remarkably strong."

We then began tossing the skeins back and forth across the circle, creating a web. "Interconnectivity is the key to any organization or business," I said. "Each connection is like a synapse. All together, you create the remarkable human brain.

Brains aren't just fast computers; they are capable of conceiving remarkable, almost fantastical goals."

That's when I called the Tibetan monk over. He'd been sitting nearby, unnoticed in the hubbub of Central Park. He was wearing traditional burgundy robes, his salt-and-pepper hair cropped short. "This is Psang Tenzing," I said. "He's a real Tibetan monk. He is in New York to help the Rubin Museum with their Tibetan art exhibit, but today he has agreed to help you challenge your belief in what is possible. Using this yarn, we are going to lift him off the ground."

The reaction from our clients was predictably skeptical, but I had everyone lower their strands to the ground. Psang Tenzing walked into the center of the net and sat down, his legs crossed before him. Why a Tibetan monk? It was a whim, really. I could have been the one sitting on the net, but the day before I'd dropped in at the Rubin Museum to see some friends from the International Campaign for Tibet, with whom I'd been collaborating ever since Cho Oyu. I met Psang Tenzing there, and spontaneously wondered aloud if he'd be willing to help me with a teaching. He said he would, but the following day, sitting on a web of yarn amidst a circle of 100 skeptical-looking people with name tags stuck to their sweaters, he looked a little less sure.

"He's a little out of his comfort zone," I said to the group. "This is not something that he usually does. But to achieve truly extraordinary things, we have to leave our comfort zones." With that, I had everyone take two steps backwards, pulling tension on the yarn. Without anyone straining, Psang Tenzing rose off the ground an inch, and with another step back, six inches, and he finally came to a perch fourteen inches off the ground, suspended by a net of ordinary knitting yarn held by 193 people he'd never met. The monk's face sprung into a smile, and he couldn't stop laughing.

I loved those set pieces, and the debriefs, which took on an exciting brainstorming quality and became genuinely moving when people choose to share their feelings. Most often, though, I loved connecting with our clients informally on breaks or in the evening around a campfire. When the ceremony was over, the real work of digesting insights occurred. Also, as with my high-end mountaineering clients, I was as interested in their work as they were in mine. I've just always been curious about other people's lives, and the role of a guide and instructor affords plenty of moments to ask questions.

I was particularly interested in learning how my clients' companies were or weren't incorporating ideas of corporate responsibility and compassion. In those days, almost all of them knew about Ben & Jerry's ice cream, for example. Even when the company was purchased from the founders by the conglomerate Unilever in 2000, the brand's long history of social activism and ethical sourcing had been codified in the contract. Ben & Jerry's operates under a separate board, largely focused on social responsibility. Many of my clients were becoming aware of the outdoor-apparel brand Patagonia, privately owned by its founder, Yvon Chouinard, whose book *Let My People Go Surfing* was becoming a widely read manifesto of morale-boosting corporate culture. Like Ben & Jerry's, Patagonia uses its brand to champion social and environmental causes, but Chouinard also wrote of providing his employees flextime to "catch a good swell, go bouldering for an afternoon, pursue an education, or get home in time to greet the kids when they come down from the school bus."

I wondered if the brands my clients worked for could incorporate any of these practices even if they hadn't been part of the organizations' DNA from the start. The question made for lively discussions, even as many of the people I spoke with pointed out that Ben & Jerry's was a true outlier for its brand strength and that Patagonia was a privately owned company, free from shareholder pressure.

I particularly loved having these sorts of conversations with my Wharton School clients. The business school's storied MBA program offers a Leadership in Mountaineering course that culminates in an actual high-altitude mountaineering expedition. In those days, the expedition was to Cotopaxi, and I'd been hired in 2004 to work the course both for my local knowledge and outdoor-education experience, but then stayed on as the courses moved to Chile because I was passionate about the curriculum.

On campus in Philadelphia, the Wharton students studied leadership principles and read case studies, often about real mountaineering incidents, usually ones that ended poorly. Then, once they arrived in the field, we put the screws to them. The idea was to parse the students' leadership decisions and experiences by using their own type-A tendencies to help ratchet up the pressure that high-altitude mountaineering already provides. We had them take turns leading a ropeteam of four—you can't go alone, as crossing a glacier dictates roped travel lest someone need to be pulled out of a crevasse (an instructor was always second on the line for safety). You have altitude sickness—when do you turn over the lead position? Someone can't continue—does your entire ropeteam turn back or can you coordinate with another team for assistance? How do you work through a critical-thinking matrix when you have a splitting headache and your peers are all vomiting?

Sheer tenacity might get *you* up the mountain, but it is unlikely to get *your team* up there, too. A good team has differing strengths—what if you jettison the person whose genius might later save the day because he stumbled early on, just needing time to adjust to the altitude?

The favorite case study was almost always Shackleton's. Ernest Shackleton's 1914 expedition was meant to achieve the first transcontinental crossing of Antarctica, but accomplished something far more remarkable. After traveling to within a day's sail of their Antarctic landing spot, their ship, *Endurance,* was trapped in the ice for ten months. Shackleton kept his crew's morale high, even while preparing for the ship to be inevitably destroyed by the ice. Once the *Endurance* sank, the crew of twenty-seven men survived a further five months living on the ice, which was slowly drifting northward. When they were just in sight of Elephant Island, between Antarctica and Chile, the ice broke apart, but the crew was ready and took to the lifeboats, rowing and sailing for a week to the island with crewmembers fighting seasickness, dysentery, and despair. After nine days of recovery on Elephant Island, Shackleton and a team of five made a remarkable eighteen-day journey in a lifeboat across the Roaring Forties to South Georgia Island, where help awaited at a whaling station they'd last visited more than 500 days before. It was amongst the boldest and most incredible feats of sailing ever undertaken. Yet the terrible winds and seas landed them on the wrong side of South Georgia Island, leaving them no choice but to make a never-before-attempted thirty-six-hour traverse of the crevasse-strewn island. They made it, which is legendary in and of itself, but rescuing the rest of the crew from Elephant Island took three attempts and more than 100 additional days. In the end, all twenty-seven of Shackleton's crew survived for more than two years, marooned in and on the ice, largely thanks to his courage and leadership.

I loved parsing the decisions with the Wharton students. The

Endurance never should have gotten icebound in the first place—Shackleton ignored the warnings from experienced whalers about pack ice in the Weddell Sea. Yet once he'd made that mistake, he correctly focused not on his initial goal, but solely on keeping each of his crew members alive with their continuously diminishing resources. (It was then the norm for such expeditions to sacrifice more than a few lives to achieve their goals.) Shackleton kept a strict routine of daily duties for all crewmembers to stave off ennui and anxiety. According to all accounts, he set a personal example of purpose and courage in order to set the tone for his crew.

Then, to save weight on the over-ice journey, Shackleton ordered scientific instruments abandoned, but brought one crewman's banjo, which proved a huge morale booster. Shackleton balanced big-picture vision with the ability to see the small details critical to achieving the big-picture goal. Probably more remarkable was his ability to bounce back from failure. In mountaineering, I liked to point out, the best climbers fail constantly, turning back when conditions don't allow for success. But they live to climb another day.

One of my favorite stories from the Wharton trips was an "anti-Shackleton" incident that happened in the mountains of Chile. Our role as instructors during climbing is to sit in the ropeteam and make sure everyone stays safe, but to otherwise never guide strategy; we want the students to exercise leadership and to learn from their decisions. On this particular day, two of our ropeteams had members who were suffering acutely from altitude sickness—from headaches, vomiting, and very slow progress. Each climber had a radio tuned to the same channel, so everyone knew the status of every other team. Suddenly, two students from my ropeteam were trading their sick students for a pair of able-feeling students from another ropeteam.

The newly formed able team summited, but after a halfhearted attempt at ascending, the ill students turned downhill. The debrief that night got pretty nasty, with the students who'd been cut loose laying into their ropeteam members who had essentially betrayed them. I remember one student trying to claim to his peers that he'd had their best interests at heart—he'd wanted to get them down the hill as quickly as possible. No one was buying it. I hope that the remorse those selfish kids displayed that night was real, but the cynical part of me thinks they are more likely CEOs now laying off workers with little to no severance package, so that their bottom line looks better.

Amid intense discussions about business leadership and strategy, it never failed to occur to me how ironic it was that I, a guy who'd never gotten a college degree, was instructing some of the world's best and brightest MBA students. It's not that I thought I knew better or had gamed the system—I just recognized that any organization can be improved by diversity of thought and experience. At thirty-five years old, and an expert in my fields of mountaineering and outdoor education, I also knew what I knew.

At the same time, I had a nagging feeling that I wasn't doing as much as I could. I was an itinerant educator, living on the Front Range of Colorado, leading a loose slate of two- to three-day OBP contract courses and the occasional Wharton courses, and an expedition or two with Soldiers to Summits, the veterans' mountaineering group. It wasn't very different from what I'd been doing in 1999, before my first Everest summit.

****

I was feeling the ache of starting over. Starting over is never easy, whether in your relationships or career, but it's always a little simpler if you feel like you are trading up. I'd quit the high-end guiding business on moral grounds, not because I thought I could do better. I was a little heartbroken—wondering if I should have just kept my mouth shut and maintained my jet-set lifestyle.

Starting over is a subject I often touch on when I speak in public, either in business and organizational consulting or at graduation ceremonies. Like heartbreak, there's no real cure for it. You just have to be patient and have faith that with the right intentions and effort, the path will appear before you, and that it will lead you upward again.

I did get one particularly interesting dose or reassurance in 2009. In July, the International Campaign for Tibet brought me to Madrid for a panel on human rights, and to testify before the Supreme Court of Spain about the Cho Oyu incident. The court was trying a lawsuit against Chinese leaders over the mistreatment of the Tibetan people. The effort was the longest of long shots of course, but still important to demonstrate to the Chinese authorities that the world was watching.

After an emotional day of testimony, the International Tribunal Court (ITC) lawyer who'd sat by my side throughout invited me to a reception that evening. Kerry Kennedy, one of RFK's daughters, was hosting a reading for her recently released book, *Speak Truth to Power: Human Rights Defenders Who Are Changing Our World*.

When we arrived, I was naturally impressed that Kennedy had brought along a ringer to do the reading: the actor Martin Sheen. Here was a person I'd been watching all my life in films, and especially on television. *The West Wing* had been my favorite show.

After the reading, mingling over cocktails, I was surprised to see the ITC lawyer embrace the famous actor. He introduced me, and Sheen mentioned that he'd been in the room for the panel I'd spoken on the day before, so he knew my part in the Cho Oyu incident. We ended up sitting at a table and talking. I told him about the unpublicized testimony before the Supreme Court of Spain.

Maybe it was jet lag, but I couldn't help seeing him as the character I'd loved from *The West Wing*, President Bartlet, the sage and principled leader. As with meeting the Dalai Lama, I felt the uncanny buzz of being face-to-face with a celebrity. Sheen waved Kerry Kennedy over. "Kerry, come meet this kid and hear what he did," said Sheen. "Talk about speaking truth to power."

They were both exceptionally encouraging, and the validation was just what I needed to hear at that point, questioning as ever the decisions I'd made. It turns out that both Sheen and I were staying on the same floor of the same hotel, and by coincidence at the end of the night, we bumped into each other in the elevator on the way up. "I enjoyed talking with you tonight," he said as we stepped off the elevator. "It's not easy doing the right thing, but the sleep does come easier that way." I laughed, but that night, it turns out, I did sleep very well.

That same summer, in 2009, I worked a contract for OBP that opened a new path for me, one that I never would have imagined. In the mid-2000s, Vail was a four-letter word in the ski industry. They were the largest corporate entity in a world of mostly privately owned resorts, collectively running five of the nation's largest ski hills: Colorado's Vail, Beaver Creek, Keystone, and Breckenridge, as well as California's Heavenly Ski Resort. The skiing community, with its nonconforming roots and culture, abhorred the idea that there was a publicly traded company in their ranks. Furthermore, for many, Vail represented growth over values. In the late 1990s, for example, they'd raised the ire of environmentalists by pushing the USFS to allow them to expand the boundaries of Vail resort itself into a pristine area important to a lynx-reintroduction program. In 1998, the dispute erupted in an arson attack by members of the Earth Liberation Front that burned three of the ski area's buildings and four of its chairlifts. The attack drew national press coverage as well as an investigation by the FBI.

Then Vail Resorts announced it would be moving its corporate headquarters from the town of Vail to an office tower in Broomfield, a suburb of Denver. To many, it was the figurative removal of what was left of the ski resort's heart. As fate would have it, they hired OBP—and me as the Rocky Mountain region program director— to help smooth the transition by getting headquarters staff from Denver and operations staff from the mountain towns together for team building. At the time, I was as anti-corporate as the next Gen X ski bum, but I was set on staying true to my goal of bringing heart and soul to corporate culture, so waded right in.

Those days of working to mesh the gears of the old-school mountain-ops crew and the new management went well enough that Vail hired my team again in 2010 to help integrate another set of managers. In that year, Vail was finalizing the $31 million purchase of the remaining 30 percent of Specialty Sports Venture, the retail operation formerly known as Gart Bros. Sporting Goods Company. In preparation for our team-building course, I requested a meeting with Ken Gart to find out about his goals and concerns for the course.

When I met with him in his Front Range office, he told me a little about how he'd come up in the family business. His grandfather had started a hunting and fishing sporting goods store in 1928, almost twenty years before my own grandfather founded Kelley's after returning from the war. Gart Bros had grown into a Denver icon—from the three-story, gothic-styled "sports castle" to its eventual expansion into a chain of hundreds of stores across ski country. As Ken and I traded stories of working the register and the stockroom, I couldn't help but wonder how my life would be different if Kelley's had stayed in the family rather than being sold once my grandfather retired.

Ken's primary concern was that the former Gart Bros. team members who were going over to Vail be treated well and that their experience be heeded. After listening to Ken's goals for the OBP course, I offered a theory. My idea was that he needn't worry too much for his team because in my experience, I said, the outdoor industry unfailingly attracts good people who want the best outcomes for everyone they work with or make deals with. That basic intention almost always leads to good outcomes, at least interpersonally. People can and do make mistakes, but in the outdoor industry they are usually made with the best intentions.

I believe that this common trait springs from the outdoor activities themselves. In sports like climbing, skiing, and surfing, failure is common. You fall often, and get back on the rock/board/bike just as often. In fact, you can't get better if you don't fail. All of life should be like that, but in our culture outside of such activities, we've become failure avoidant, so we either don't try or are shamed for failing. I've found that outdoor enthusiasts are more prone to risk taking and are better able to learn from our mistakes and become better problem-solvers, because in the outdoor community, we give each other permission to fail and to try again. That spirit attracts generous and good-hearted people.

I felt and still feel that way about Ken Gart, who has become a sort of accidental mentor to me. Not only is he one of the wisest and most energetic men I have ever met, but as I had surmised talking to him for an hour, he really does care about his employees, his customers, and the outdoor industry as a whole. Evidence of that is the fact that he took my meeting at all, and then sat there and listened to my opinions. In hindsight, it's sort of comical that a thirty-something whose only real business experience was co-managing Adventure Consultants, a twenty-person organization, would have real wisdom to offer an executive who'd been managing a business employing thousands for most of his adult life. He still takes my calls today, which I'm grateful for. In fact, when Governor Hickenlooper was considering me to lead his Office of Outdoor Recreation, Ken Gart was one of the first people he called.

Another of my accidental mentors has been Mark Gasta, who as Vail's then head of human resources hired me for those contracts, and eventually to work with him full-time. Mark was an army helicopter pilot for almost a decade, working on search-and-rescue teams during Operation Desert Storm and beyond. When it came time to go into the private sector, he understood that what he really likes doing is working with people—teaching, mentoring, leading, elevating. So he went into human resources, and after stints with Target and Comcast, landed at Vail. When I encountered him, I was pleasantly surprised to find a real business professional who also happened to be perfectly in sync with what I valued about outdoor-adventure work: high energy, curiosity, problem-solving, self-discipline, and compassion (in other words, the five Outward Bound pillars).

Vail's issue then was that they were having a hard time hiring and retaining experienced managers and supervisors. As with all resort towns, there are always plenty of young people arriving with college degrees but relatively little work experience. Once upon a time, simply giving every employee a free season pass was enough to fill the ranks of cashiers, lift operators, and ski instructors; however, finding experienced and talented managers to lead those newbies was more of a challenge. Often, some of the most capable employees left the company in search of better pay and communities with more affordable housing. Talented and experienced personnel tend to lose interest in living with seven roommates like newbie lifties tend to do. Likewise, it was also difficult to recruit experienced managers to pricey ski towns.

That's without even mentioning the company's ambitious expansion plans. Vail Resorts has swelled from five resorts when I started work there to forty today. Vail correctly realized that their best bet was to promote from within, and to satisfy their needs, they'd need to supplement their leadership candidates' experience with specialized training. Mark's Gasta's view was that he wanted that training to create not just competent managers but effective leaders—people who would manage in a way that lifts others up. Mountain resorts are meant to inspire their guests, and that sort of attitude must be pervasive in the organization. Mark knew that experiential education was the best way to teach and inspire adults in particular, and once he'd worked with me for the OBP contracts, he knew we would see eye to eye on the project. He hired me to help him create the curriculum.

At first, we essentially ran OBP courses with an eye toward teaching leadership skills. I'll never forget the day we took the entire executive team of mountain presidents, from Keystone, Vail, Breckenridge, etc., up Quandary Peak, a 14,265-foot Fourteener relatively close to Denver. I'd briefed them beforehand about lightning—how the incidence increases later in the day as clouds form over the warming peaks; how lightning can strike under blue skies, from clouds several miles away; how hair standing on end and buzzing trekking poles, tooth fillings, and other metals are reliable signs that a strike may be imminent. We were less than an hour from the summit when strands of hair started rising from beneath our climbing helmets into the air, and Chris Jarnot, the president of Vail, started looking back at me. "Are you going to say anything?" he asked.

No, I said. *You guys are in charge. You have all the tools you need.* His eyes got a little wider, and finally he spoke up. "Hey guys, there's electrical activity. I think we should head down." But Chris had a hard time convincing the hard-charging group, who had eyes focused on the summit. They made the decision to head down about five minutes late, and by then there was enough static in the air and cloud buildup overhead that I directed everyone to start glissading down the nearest snow slope—even though it took us off route—just to rapidly lose elevation. It got, as they say, pretty dang western.

Of course, once we were back down in the safety of the trees, it made for a hell of a teachable moment.

Over the next four years, we built an extensive curriculum composed of online courses with four distinct levels, named for the separate camps on Everest's South Col route. Basecamp was essentially new staff orientation, with basic info about company policies and benefits; Camp I was for supervisors; Camp II was for managers; Camp III was for VPs; and Camp IV was for the C-suite. By the team people got to Camp IV, for example, participants received executive coaching. At every level, there was a blend of online learning and in-person group sessions, but everything beyond basecamp contained training in skills like effective communication, leadership, and conflict resolution. Like all good leadership curricula, it was challenging, and resulted in satisfying personal growth. Over the years, dozens of people have told me how valuable the work was to them.

Naturally, there were naysayers and holdouts. Some

participants balked at learning soft skills because, well, they thought they were soft. That was usually before they'd taken any of the courses, though. The truly intractable refuseniks tended to wash out because we eventually incorporated completion of the curriculum into the performance metrics that determined their financial bonuses. Many of the top personnel also objected, both on macho grounds and on the cost impact to their departmental budgets, but the results eventually spoke for themselves.

With more-formal pathways established, the number of candidates for promotion shot through the roof. As Vail expanded, buying resorts like California's Kirkwood and Northstar and Utah's Park City, there also became more avenues for homegrown talent to ladder up by moving from property to property thanks to the common culture that our trainings helped encourage. Mark credits the better leadership and management fostered by our trainings as instrumental in Vail's rise—the stock price rose, for example, from $15 a share in 2009 to a high of $350 per share in 2021.

Of course, I probably don't have to tell you that our formalized leadership curriculum didn't solve all of Vail's woes. The company still gets plenty of bad press, none more so than during the pandemic, when the number of skiers and snowboarders far outstripped the ability of Vail's resorts to accommodate them. Images of obscenely long lift lines populated social media over the 2021 and 2022 seasons. Realistically, the situation was a perfect storm of overselling the company's Epic Pass, which gives nearly unlimited access to thirty-plus resorts across the continent, along with the same employee shortage that hit nearly every sector of the American economy, exacerbated by a chronic housing shortage in mountain communities worsened by wealthy remote workers coming to live in mountain towns.

However, some of the more specific criticisms of the company came from resort insiders who pointed out that, in an effort to cut costs and satisfy shareholders, Vail had been in the habit of eliminating key resort-based positions. That was part of a larger effort to streamline company operations that had been particularly inspired by operations at Disney properties. Even some of the changes that seem to make sense, like eliminating ticket checkers at each lift by installing RFID passes, had unintended negative consequences. At peak times like New Year's, resort higher-ups used to put on their blue coats and go work a shift on the lift lines themselves. That got them face to face not only with guests, but with their newest employees, and helped them keep tabs on the guest experience and the company culture. But now, that valuable face time had been eliminated. It's telling that the last time I saw Vail's current CEO, Kirsten Lynch, she mentioned that they were working to restore the programs that Mark and I had created, but that had been scaled back to reduce costs.

I worked full-time for Vail for four years. That meant an end to my itinerant-guide lifestyle (with the exception of one or two Wharton and OBP courses each year—Mark pointed out to me that the more visible and active you are in the leadership-development space, the better PR it was for Vail). Rather than chafe at the five-day workweek, however, I flourished. I loved the community of Eagle, just down the road from my office in Vail. I made lifelong friends, and loved the daily access to skiing, mountaineering, paddling, mountain biking, and trail running. Nothing beats a mountain town for work-life balance.

****

The learning curve in jumping from experiential education and guiding to corporate life was a steep one—even with a great boss like Mark Gasta. I was so focused on my work that I paid little thought to my personal life. Every time one of my co-workers tried to set me up on a date, I brushed them off. Until Sara was the one asking. She had a colleague named Katie in mind.

Look, she said, *just come to dinner. There will be a group of us, so it won't be awkward, and I'm making steamed pork buns.*

Truth be told, I showed up that night solely for the pork buns, but once I met Katie, I forgot all about them. I noticed her sparkling smile first, and got to know a bit about her. She was a Midwestern girl—the best kind. She grew up on the Upper Peninsula of Michigan in a serious sailing family and had done some legit long-distance sails, including across Lake Michigan in the Chicago-to-Mackinac races. So I knew she wasn't soft. Best of all, she didn't seem to care about what a big deal I thought I was.

During the time we were dating, Katie belonged to a sailing league close to Eagle. The reservoir where their races were held was serious water, with big, mountain-driven winds. Lightning storms would roll in and strike boats frequently. The water was so cold from snowmelt that if you went overboard, you had an average of three to five minutes before you lapsed into hypothermia.

Her role as a tactician on those racing teams pretty much sums up our relationship. Katie is always the objective, calculated voice to my emotionally driven points of view. I have always relied on her for the "opposing POV"—as much as it drives me crazy, it's the thing that I love and appreciate the most about her.

The life we built together in Eagle was just about perfect. We each had jobs we loved—Katie was managing a luxury hotel in Vail—and we loved our small mountain community, our dogs, and the wilderness playground right out the front door. Bit by bit, however, I became increasingly troubled with how our town was being run.

What happened next is probably the most surprising thing I've done, apart from the decision to work full-time for Vail: I decided to run for public office. As I put down roots in Eagle, I found I had all kinds of opinions about how the community was being run. I found myself complaining to friends about the lack of affordable housing. Or lamenting that, unlike other nearby mountain towns, Eagle had no climbing gym or whitewater park, and that our mountain-biking trail system was underdeveloped. I didn't like that main street was losing shops to the big-box stores up-valley in Avon and Edwards. *Someone should do something about those things,* I'd say to friends at CrossFit or over a beer.

Eventually, some of those friends staged an intervention. *Luis,* they said *YOU should do something about those things. You should run for the Eagle Board of Trustees* (its town council). *You've got things you want accomplished, you are used to public speaking, and you work as a leadership consultant.* I had to concede: they had a point.

So I started campaigning for the 2014 election, which for me was essentially like running a leadership workshop. I'd show up at a small gathering at someone's house, give an intro about my leadership experience (Outward Bound, Everest, business-leadership development), and ask those gathered what their goals were for the community. I'd write those down on a whiteboard. It was like a communitywide check-in. What are we good at? What could we improve? I found that I loved it—connecting with my neighbors, sharing ideas, and building consensus to work to improve this place I was proud to call home.

As I listened, my vision became clearer: to shore up local businesses and the tax base to fill the community's coffers, we needed to be capitalizing on the outdoor-recreation amenities

Eagle was blessed with. I would say, "Eagle should be a recreation destination, not a bedroom community for Vail. We should be building a climbing gym, improving trails. It's good for economics, it's good for our kids' fitness and development, and it's good for the morale of those of us who work and live here." It's a message I've never stopped espousing.

It wasn't long before I was joined in my bid by two other ski buddies in their mid-thirties: Andy Jessen, the owner of Eagle's Bonfire Brewing, and Doug Seabury, who owned a local gear shop and boutique. We shook up the field by campaigning together, mainly at Bonfire, and by using Facebook to campaign, which seemed radical to the old-school townsfolk we were running against. Our opponents campaigned for the status quo—keeping the focus on ranching and the traditional way of life. We were the youngest candidates by a country mile, but to our surprise, all three of us were elected to the nine-person board. In terms of our small community's government, it was a seismic shift.

I'll never forget the day a few months later when I raised my right hand and swore an oath for public service. I think it was the first time in my life that I felt like an adult, taking responsibility for my community and for my industry. I still think that as citizens of our nation, serving in local government is one of the most inspiring, effective things we can do. Our national-level politics are paralyzed by extremes, but at the local level, we can still influence society and make our communities better places.

COLORADO
OUTWARD BOUND SCHOOL

Chapter 10

TO STRIVE TO SERVE AND NOT TO YIELD

"There is more in us than we know. If we can be made to see it, perhaps, for the rest of our lives, we will be unwilling to settle for less." —Kurt Hahn

Eagle's trustees were paid $250 a month to serve. Which made governing the community essentially a volunteer position. I was still on salary with Vail Resorts, but spent my free time studying the board book we received before each weekly meeting. There was a lot to learn—from how to set a town budget to finding tens of millions of dollars to replace an aging municipal wastewater system. I learned Robert's Rules of Order and sat through a debate about whether our new flashing LED traffic sign would impact wildlife. I learned how to maintain a respectful expression during even the most unhinged public commentary.

As new trustees, Andy, Doug, and I stepped on more governance landmines than I can count, but we did get some impactful things done. We got a $2.7 million pedestrian bridge built over Interstate 70 so that citizens could walk or ride their bikes across the highway to the community's primary grocery store. It took a huge amount of effort. *Why,* asked the old guard, *are we spending these millions when there's just three businesses that would benefit from the foot traffic—a grocery store, a gas station, and an Italian restaurant?* Our answer: *Because walkable cities, is why. People shouldn't be cut off from their food source if they don't own a car.*

We also completed a deal to allow a local hotel to rent a wing of their building to Vail Resorts for employee housing. The hotel was losing money all winter because they were too distant (thirty-four miles) from the slopes for ski clientele. Vail was desperate for employee housing but worried that the same commute was prohibitive for their employees, while the older Eagle trustees were predictably resistant to the idea of 80 to 100 young strangers moving to what was still primarily a conservative ranching town. We shored up support by canvassing the business near the hotel—a bowling alley, a pizzeria, and a deli, all of whom knew the young Vail workers would be great customers. Then we convinced Vail's public bus system to extend their winter route to Eagle. In the end it was a win-win-win: for Vail, for the hotel, and for the businesses where the new residents spent their money after work.

My favorite project in my two years as a trustee was working to establish a community whitewater park. The Eagle River originates on the slopes of Fourteeners in the Holy Cross Wilderness and flows westward, passing just north of downtown Eagle before merging with the Colorado River thirteen miles down-valley. When I moved to Eagle, the stretch adjacent to town was in rough shape.

The riverbed had been brutalized by interstate construction—straightened out and filled with sharp debris, it was ugly, a poor fish habitat, and sketchy for boating. Furthermore, its bank was an informal parking lot used by long-haul truckers, littered with cigarette butts, fast-food wrappers, and plastic bottles full of urine. In a feeble attempt to mitigate the refuse, the town had placed a garbage barrel and a Porta Potty there.

Many of us wondered why we couldn't swap out this mangled stretch of river and piss-stained parking lot for a fun set of rapids bordered by greenspace and bike paths. By 2014, there were dozens of examples of such whitewater parks built from rehabilitated stretches of river. In places like Columbus, Georgia, and Oklahoma City, engineers had reshaped the riverbed to create splashy waves, pools, and eddies. In the high-water spring snowmelt, the whitewater parks contained class III and IV testpieces for kayakers and rafters, and at lower summer flows they were mellow class II playgrounds populated with kids on boogie boards and inner tubes, swimming and cooling off. In autumn, the pools were ideal spots for fly-fishing. Year-round, the tidy riverbanks were places to sit and meditate on the sounds of the river flowing by.

In locations like Manchester, Iowa, and San Marcos, Texas, the newly constructed rapids replaced low-head dams—the so-called "drowning machines." Cities like Richmond, Virginia, had made their whitewater parks the centerpiece of their urban-renewal efforts, complete with commercial rafting operations and riverside cafés and breweries. In Colorado, new whitewater parks had been drawing tourists and entertaining locals in Steamboat Springs, Salida, and Golden, and there was even a prime example just twenty miles upstream of us, on the Eagle River through Avon, Colorado, built in 2006. That's where I'd been practicing the whitewater skills I'd first learned as a kid on Ozark rivers like the Current and the Black.

The whitewater park was an idea I'd campaigned on. Like expanding Eagle's mountain-bike-trail network, it seemed an obvious way to improve our community's natural amenities. When newly sworn in, Andy and I brought the idea up to the town manager, and he promptly shut us down. The issue was the highway department. The Colorado Department of Transportation (CDOT) is one of the most powerful entities in the state, and they liked having the frontage-road pullout there for long-haul truckers to rest in. Our town staff didn't want to do anything that would anger

CDOT, or frankly, take a lot of extra work and money. It was up to the trustees to get the ball rolling.

Our group of whitewater-park boosters started by gathering data on the benefits of whitewater parks. We discovered that Golden, Colorado's Clear Creek whitewater park attracts 14,000 users annually and generates $2.2 million in economic impact. A whitewater park built on the Sacandaga River in Saratoga, New York, generates some $3.7 million in economic impact annually, and the Lower Animas River whitewater park generates $18 million a year for Durango, Colorado. More than a million people a year visit the $37 million National Whitewater Center in Charlotte, North Carolina. There, the recirculating river course is the cornerstone of an adventure complex that includes a massive artificial climbing wall, ropes course, ziplines, and fifty miles of trail for running, hiking, and mountain biking. It is essentially a massive theme park, but where the attractions take actual skill and require exercise.

Next, we found a simpler river project to whet the community's appetite. Situated just upstream of our whitewater-park site, the town's boat ramp was in disrepair. But it was adjacent to the shady greenspace of Chambers Park, and could make a good hangout spot for boaters and anyone interested in accessing the river. With a $41,000 matching grant from Great Outdoors Colorado (GOCO), the state entity that distributes lottery proceeds to recreation amenities, we repaired the ramp in 2015. We used the ramp's refurbishing to tell a story to the community about improving the riverfront. It wasn't long after that I convinced the entire board of trustees to drive two hours south to check out the way a whitewater park had revitalized downtown Salida, Colorado.

We also recruited citizens to show up to council meetings to advocate for Eagle's park, and to write letters to the newspaper.

With that groundswell of support, our town's administrators were finally obligated to open discussions with CDOT and to begin the permitting process. In 2017, when Eagle's voters approved the $7 million park by voting in a 0.5 percent sales tax earmarked for the facility, I was no longer in office—though I was on hand for the opening ceremony, in 2019. Instead of a jumble of debris, the riverbed contained four fun rapids with more than a dozen people in boats skittering across the waves. Instead of a sketchy parking lot, there was an amphitheater, greenspace, and kids playing alongside the river. Andy, now the pro-tem (essentially the vice mayor) of Eagle, and I talked about how sweet it would be if he could get a path built directly from the whitewater park to his shop, Bonfire Brewing. It would be the perfect place to unwind after an evening of summer paddling, sitting beside the firepit with a pint of his flagship Kindler brew.

Tragically, that was the last time I saw Andy. In 2021, he was killed, along with two other friends from Eagle, in an avalanche while skiing near Silverton, Colorado. Andy was the epitome of the sort of person who makes the outdoor industry so vital and successful. Once an attorney in Denver, he and his wife, Amanda, gave up on their big-money lifestyle and moved to the mountains to follow his passion: brewing beer. Bonfire Brewing was built around the idea of friends bonding around the firepit out back of the shop. On weekends, he opened the brewing room to yoga classes. His sage advice—legal, social, and otherwise—helped people of all walks of life. As the brewery grew into the town's social hub, Andy got more and more involved in the community until he finally felt compelled to run for public office.

Like so many I've met in the outdoor industry (which so often goes hand-in-hand with craft brewing), Andy wielded his outsized talents to make his community a better place. I miss him dearly.

At least for me, Eagle's whitewater park stands as a monument to Andy. Campaigning for it was also the first time I really started to understand the economic- and community-development aspects of building new recreation infrastructure, the cornerstone to the political power of the outdoor-recreation political movement. Additionally, it was one of the key experiences that got the governor interested in me as a candidate for an idea he had been mulling over.

****

In 2013, the State of Utah created the first office of the outdoor-recreation industry. The idea was to have a person to serve as a convener for Utah's ORec interests, from ski resorts and whitewater outfitters to gear retailers and manufacturers. Like a chamber of commerce, the outdoor-recreation office provided connectivity within the industry and advocacy to government and other interests. The office also sought to attract more outdoor-industry commerce to the state, whether recruiting new companies or improving ORec tourism. The first director was Brad Petersen, a former Intel executive and well-known figure in the outdoor-recreation community. I thought it was a great idea, from where I sat both as an Eagle trustee and a Vail Resorts employee. A healthier outdoor-recreation industry, in my view, meant a healthier society.

Little did I know that our own governor, John Hickenlooper, was having similar thoughts. It's also fair to say that there is a friendly economic rivalry between the neighboring states, and Hick, who'd made his fortune by catching the craft-brewing wave early on, knew a good idea when he saw it. Fiona Arnold, his director for the Colorado Office of Economic Development and

International Trade, said she had just the person in mind for the job. I'd worked alongside Fiona at Vail Resorts, where she'd served as executive vice president and general counsel. That afternoon, I received a Facebook message from Fiona requesting a phone call.

All she told me over the phone was that the governor was considering creating an office of outdoor recreation and wanted to chat with me about it. "Can you come to Denver for a meeting?" she asked. I assumed the governor wanted to brainstorm about the position, or would ask me to put together a search committee for the director, both of which sounded fun to me. I agreed. Who doesn't want to meet their governor?

For me, John Hickenlooper is the archetype of a twenty-first century "purple state" leader. A former oil-industry geologist who made his fortune in brewpubs, Hickenlooper managed the impossible: as Denver mayor and Colorado governor, he was wildly popular as a staunch centrist.

He has a knack, as one writer for *The Atlantic* put it, "for striking a deal and making people like it." As a Democrat mayor of Denver, Hickenlooper collaborated with suburban Republicans on a popular light-rail project for the city, and then as governor brokered a landmark methane-reduction deal between environmentalists and the mineral-extraction industry. He had allies across the political spectrum because he could relate to every Colorado voting block, and he was authentically excitable with everyone.

Ensconced in his office in the marble capitol building on that March 2015 day, though, he cut an exceedingly impressive figure. Fiona escorted me through the ten-foot-high double doors to his office, and we found him working at the head of a conference table. He jumped up to greet me, and I noticed his height, his warm and off-kilter smile, and his crackling energy. We sat and talked, and I was surprised by how much he already knew about my career path—the Outward Bound work, my journey with Vail Resorts, and the Eagle board of trustees. I asked him what he had in mind for the outdoor-rec office, even pulling out a notebook to write it down, and was frankly shocked when he said, "The only way I want this office is if you are running it. We are going to announce it next Tuesday. Write up a job description by Thursday of what you want the role to be."

I was too stunned to say much—I hadn't even considered the role for myself—and the next thing I knew the meeting was over and I was walking into the antechamber with Fiona.

"What do you think?" she said, excited.

My head was spinning, recognizing that this really was my dream job. It was the kind of role my uncles Peppin and Alfonso would be exceedingly proud of me for, the kind of position that Mark Udall, now a US senator, would eventually call to congratulate me about. I also thought instantly of Katie, now my wife and now pregnant, and of the idyllic life full of mountain adventure we'd built in Eagle. I knew that neither of us was in a hurry to uproot and move to the city, sacrificing my corporate salary for a government one (my pay was ultimately nearly halved) with a child on the way. "I'll have to get back to you," I said.

Fiona's eyebrows shot up in surprise. No one, it seems, says no to the governor. "When the governor asks you to serve," she said, "you say, 'Yes.'"

Back home in Eagle, the decision was excruciating. I had seventy-two hours. I had a few mostly sleepless nights, tossing and turning in bed and taking walks outside. I really had to check my motivations. Was I doing this for my ego, flattered by the attention of the governor? Ultimately, I decided that the good I could do in fighting for a better outdoors for all Coloradans was important enough to uproot my family from their comfortable life in Eagle.

Outward Bound's principles remained my moral backbone, and I believed then as I do now that we must each heed the call for periods of service to our society. I'm forever grateful to Katie, though: if she hadn't been sold on the idea, I'd certainly have put family first and declined the governor's offer.

When I made my second trip to Denver that week to iron out details, I brought Hick a couple of beers from Andy's secret stash, a brown ale he'd been working to perfect. It was the right gift—I thought Hick was going to literally cry. He immediately put them into the beer fridge he kept in his antechamber, stocked with homebrews from around the state. Though he'd placed his ownership interest in Wynkoop Brewing Company, the Denver brewery he'd founded in 1988, into a blind trust once elected governor, he was still a brewer at heart. Later, when I told Andy about how the governor had reacted, he was beside himself with pride.

Hick's vision for the office of outdoor recreation was roughly that of the Utah job, a commerce booster for outdoor-rec business in the state—one worth $23 billion in annual economic activity, making it amongst Colorado's largest industries. But he also wanted to use the office to raise the state's profile nationally. Hick is nothing if not extremely proud of his home state and its Fourteeners, ski resorts, and famous mountain towns. "We are Colorado," he said. "We should *own* the outdoor-recreation space." He is also a conservationist, and recognized that the outdoors needs constituents to ensure a future of clean air, water, and wild lands.

My vision for the job had a few more nuances. I also wanted to increase respect for outdoor-recreation work. I'd seen how in other countries, ski instruction and mountain guiding were seen as respectable career options, not just fun filler jobs for recent college graduates. And I'd seen through my leadership-development work that you could use education and training to do that, creating focused and dedicated higher-ed programs like those in finance, aerospace, and mineral extraction. Such programs could also help our industry be more resilient and take the lead in sustainability issues.

I also knew from personal experience that the ORec community was ripe with schisms between user groups. Equestrians hated fast-moving mountain bikers. Hikers hated noisy off-roaders. Trad climbers hated sport climbers, who installed steel bolts in the cliffs. I knew those schisms were keeping the industry from presenting a unified front in advocating for the conditions—clean air and water and natural spaces of course, but also paying for deteriorating recreation infrastructure—that would benefit us all. In 2015, the NPS alone had racked up an $11.5 billion maintenance backlog, starved of funding by Congress. In Colorado, there was an estimated $24 million maintenance backlog on the Fourteeners alone—to say nothing of the state's other trails.

Even more alarming, a scary political trend was developing—that of an intent to sell off public lands. Some saw selling public lands, whether state or federally owned, as a way to increase state revenue. Most recreationists, including myself, saw the idea as an existential threat—especially in the West, the majority of outdoor recreation, from dirt biking to fishing, takes place on state or public land. We believe that public lands are the birthright of the American people, hard-won by heroes like Teddy Roosevelt and FDR. I wanted an outdoor-recreation industry united enough to advocate for the public lands it depends on, regardless of which user group you fell into. I wanted to use the Colorado office to lead the way.

When I outlined my goals for Hick, he grinned and said, "I knew I had the right person for the job. Make it better. Don't make it worse." I laughed, and we shook hands on the deal.

My first order of business was a listening tour of the state's ORec industry. I wanted to understand the breadth and depth of outdoor recreation in Colorado, from river rafting in Fort Collins to bass fishing on Chatfield Reservoir. I was well aware of how outdoor-recreation business functioned in famed mountain towns like Aspen, Vail, and Crested Butte, but what about Pueblo, Buena Vista, and Craig? What did these places share, and what could a more robust ORec industry do for them? I grabbed a state gas card, loaded up my Jeep, and spent the summer finding out. Even more important, I wanted to put the face of the industry out there. It was a page out of Petersen's Utah playbook. "Without presence," he'd told me, "you are nobody."

My goal was to meet with locals who had a stake in outdoor recreation, whether they were business owners or mayors. In Sterling, on the plains in Colorado's northeast corner, I spoke with local leaders who'd supported the 2014 and 2015 Pedal the Plains cycling tours, from the business that had supplied the portable toilets for the hundreds of cyclists who'd converged on the community, to the ranchers behind the farm-to-table meal the three-day tour was so famous for. When Sterling residents told me that the bulk of their tourism came from hunters from Nebraska, I connected them with the Colorado tourism bureau to create ads, slated to run in the fall in Nebraska, touting our state's hunting.

In Durango, I visited on the first day that the Animas River had, after the toxic Gold King Mine waste spill, been declared safe to float again. That summer of 2015, three million gallons of the mine's wastewater had sullied the river that flows right through downtown, imperiling a half-dozen whitewater businesses. The mayor was hosting a float to prove that the river was now safe for business, and Hick wanted me there supporting. I showed up at the put-in and inflated my stand-up paddleboard. When the mayor spotted me, he was blown away that the state government had sent someone, let alone someone who was an actual paddler who understood the river's importance to the local economy.

At the takeout, I brought a cooler of beer to the impromptu BBQ and engaged the business owners on ORec tourism in Durango. Several told me that it meant a lot to have the support of the government, even, they laughed, from a guy barefoot and in board shorts. "We're just glad someone in Denver cares about rafting in Durango," they said.

In Trinidad, near the New Mexico border, I found a community that had recently lost hundreds of mineral-extraction jobs, and met with locals eager to revitalize the town through outdoor recreation. One man in particular, Juan de la Roca, had recently moved to town and opened Backshop Bikes. He'd seen the success of Fruita, and reasoned that Trinidad, blessed with similarly warm, dry weather and the desert terrain that mountain bikers love, could have similar fortunes. However, he and his allies were having trouble getting support from the local government. It was a familiar story, and reminded me of what I'd seen in Eagle. I didn't have a budget to give them money, but I did have connections in the state tourism department and with the lottery-funds-dispersement agency GOCO, and I knew journalists. I sent several down to Trinidad to talk up its cycling prospects under the idea of basically promoting something into existence.

These days, thanks in part to Juan's persistence, outdoor recreation has made great strides there. In 2020, Trinidad State

College announced they'd be teaching trail-building classes geared toward anyone interested in making a living in the booming industry (not to mention building their own trail system with the students' help). That same year, thanks to leadership from locals, Fishers Peak State Park opened at the edge of town, offering a 19,200-acre park created from a single ranch. And, in 2021, the community hosted four separate gravel-bike races, drawing hundreds. The town now even has its own office of outdoor recreation, styled after the state office, to facilitate and promote sports ranging from cycling to waterskiing.

After the 2,500-mile tour, my next order of business was to create an advisory council that would capture the ORec community's diversity. I invited business leaders like Kim Miller, the owner of Scarpa North America, which sells the Italian ski, alpine, and climbing boots, and Auden Schendler from the Aspen Skiing Company. I invited staff from nonprofits like Conservation Colorado and American Whitewater, and leaders from government agencies like Colorado State Parks and Colorado Parks & Wildlife.

I wanted the council to be a place where recreationists could dialogue with those representing the public lands where they recreated, as well as the conservation groups dedicated to protecting those lands. There has long been friction between land agencies and the public over the types and amount of recreation permitted. How many rafters is "too many" on a river—and should there be a permit lottery put in place? Are e-bikes an appropriate use in Wilderness?

I wanted the council to be a place where leaders could have these discussions outside the cauldron of the public process. I also wanted the council to be a place to build trust within the outdoor community, to help reduce factionalism. Bird hunters and bird watchers should want the same thing: abundant and healthy habitat for birds. Dirt bikers and mountain bikers should similarly both want open lands with pristine vistas for their trails. I wanted to give those groups more opportunity to dialogue and build relationships.

We first met for a weekend retreat at the COBS Basecamp in Leadville. It was a place where I'd led dozens of team-building courses and witnessed countless breakthroughs.

One of the most illuminating conversations the council had was spearheaded by Don Riggle, of the Colorado Trails Preservation Alliance, an off-road-motorcycle group. Don was a great guy—a Vietnam vet, a ski patroller at Copper Mountain, and a passionate outdoorsman. His knees were shot from years of hiking and skiing, and so now the way he accessed the outdoors was via his motorcycle. I used to tease him that e-bikes and e-motorcycles were going to upend his community. He rolled his eyes. *I have nothing against e-bikes or any other bikes,* he said, *but you guys aren't paying your fair share.*

"What do you mean?" someone asked. Motorcycles and other off-highway vehicles (OHVs) have to get a sticker every year from the state, he told them, the same way that boats do. Boat stickers help pay for marinas and boat ramps, and OHV stickers pay for trails and trailhead facilities. Mountain bikers don't have to buy a sticker. "Shouldn't they be paying for the trails they use? Will e-bikes? They'll cover nearly as much ground in a day as a motorcycle, and bring far more people onto those trails," Don said. It was a great point.

I'd long thought about how we needed taxes on outdoor gear like tents and sleeping bags similar to the one set for firearms and ammo by the Pittman-Robertson Wildlife Restoration Act. I'd not thought about how OHVs like motorcycles and four-wheelers also paid to play via their registration stickers, while mountain bikes did not. I was chagrined by the fact that a few of the organizations I loved were partly responsible for blocking such rules. The International Mountain Biking Association (IMBA) fights registration stickers for mountain bikes. The Outdoor Industry Association, which to that point had done more to coalesce political action in the outdoor-recreation industry than any other organization, had been formed for the express purpose of fighting backpack taxes. It was a troublesome incongruence for me, one that I knew needed to change eventually if we were going to form a more united and committed coalition.

In those early days on the job. there were also a few Chamber of Commerce aspects to my job. Most significant was when I testified to keep two of our best homegrown companies in the state. The outdoor-gear manufacturer Big Agnes and exercise-nutrition company Honey Stinger were both headquartered in Steamboat, the hometown of Bill Gamber, a co-founder in each business. The companies were each experiencing exponential growth, and steadily adding employees. They'd outgrown their headquarters and had bid on a local hotel building for that purpose. The hotel, though, was owned by the City of Steamboat, which was also considering a bid from another business to use the property for employee housing. If they couldn't procure the hotel, Big Agnes and Honey Stinger felt they'd have to leave Steamboat for a location with more room to grow—and they had their eye on Utah.

At a Steamboat town-council meeting, I lobbied on behalf of the state for Big Agnes and Honey Stinger to get the contract. It was critical to keep manufacturing jobs in the state, I said. In a resort town like Steamboat, the skilled design, manufacturing, and marketing jobs the two companies provided served a diversifying function to the town's tourism-based economy. *We can't let these jobs go to Utah,* I said.

When I'd first landed the Colorado job, one of the first people to call and congratulate me had been Brad Peterson of Utah's outdoor-recreation-industry office. At the time, we'd agreed that although Colorado and Utah had state administrations from opposing political parties, our goals were exceptionally aligned. Like me, Brad believed that a thriving ORec industry was good not just for Utah, but for the planet. It would be great for us not to work against each other, particularly where locating businesses was concerned. Eventually, we formalized an agreement that we would not poach companies from one other's states, though fighting to keep a business was wholly appropriate, no matter where it was looking to move. Ultimately, Big Agnes and Honey Stinger lost the hotel contract to the higher bidder, but found a suitable building in Steamboat the following year—and the significance of their relationship to their community was made that much more explicit in the process. As for the agreement between Colorado and Utah, that would be similarly tested in the years to come.

Chapter 11

THE EDUCATION OF LUIS BENITEZ

"Striving for success without hard work is like trying to harvest where you haven't planted."
—David Bly

By October 2016, I'd settled into the job as Colorado's ORec director. When I say "settled," I mean I had a handle on the work, but my private life was another matter. We'd welcomed our daughter, Sofia, in mid-August, and she was everything we could have hoped for. I join the chorus of fathers everywhere who share that their world blossomed with the birth of their child. I've never loved anyone more.

Sofia was a colicky baby, though, and her distress at her acid reflux was heartbreaking, and sleep shattering. Lying flat was often torturous for her, and in those instances we held her upright to allow her to sleep. Because I was traveling so much for work, I'd take night shift when I was home so Katie could catch up on her own rest; on those nights, I logged a few hours of sleep at best. Driving into the office, I was terrified I'd nod off at the wheel, or begin speaking in non-sequiturs in meetings.

It was on just such a bleary-eyed morning when I approached Hick's office in the state capitol, wheeling a shiny new e-bike. I'd recently returned from a whirlwind trip to Germany, where I'd convinced the e-bike manufacturer Haibike to relocate their US headquarters to Colorado. As a trophy, their local sales rep wanted to loan the governor one of their cruisers, so we brought it to the capitol. Getting into Hick's inner sanctum required navigating four separate offices, each guarded by a staffer and state troopers with their Smokey the Bear hats tilted low over their beefy foreheads. Standing in front of the final doorway beside the Haibike rep, I was so jetlagged and sleep deprived that I stood there for several seconds after Hick's secretary waved me in.

But when we wheeled the bike in, Hick was thrilled to see us. He, the secretary of state, and some state senators were clustered head-down around the conference table, poring over something that looked important. Hick looked up, a delighted smile on his face. "Look at this thing!" he said, jumping up.

We tried explaining the battery tech to him as the senators looked on somewhat annoyed, but all Hick wanted to know was how to power the bike up. He threw a leg over and told one of his aides to hold the side door open—the one to the main atrium adjoining the capitol rotunda. Then he was off, riding the bike right out the door, skipping all the layers of security and wheeling through a startled tour group shuffling through the rotunda.

Startled out of my daze, I ran after Hick alongside his chief aide and a state trooper, all of us pleading with Hick to be careful as he lapped the rotunda, dinging the bike's bell. I loved working for Hick. We always had fun together, and I still consider him, to this day, to be one of my greatest friends and mentors.

Hick is always enthusiastic because he's a curiosity-led problem-solver, and the solutions he sees are actionable because they usually involve how commerce plays a role in just about everything. As a businessman, he believes that a rising economic tide floats all boats, and it wasn't a coincidence that his tenure as governor coincided with a period of tremendous prosperity for the state. Like me, he believes that the commerce surrounding recreation will enrich the lives of Colorado's citizens both financially and socially. That means recreation and tourism, but it also means building public amenities like whitewater parks, and ensuring that every citizen lives within ten minutes of green space.

Meanwhile, we both believe that a way to counter the hateful factionalism that has arisen in our society is to offer people something better. It is absolutely true that many Americans feel like they have been left behind. Some of us have been alienated for centuries, whether because we were enslaved or expelled from our homeland, or because of our cultural beliefs or the color of our skin. More recently, others feel hard done by corporate interests or shifting cultural norms. Both sides in these conflicts suffer from the fear of trying because of a presumption of failure. But offering our communities improved financial circumstances, opportunities to improve our health by being outdoors, and the practice of achievement that comes with outdoor recreation can turn this negative trend around. And our industry is a tool that can do that. We can and do lead the way.

Another thing I respect about Hick is that he never turned his back on any Colorado citizen, no matter their ideology. Whether their livelihood came from the mineral-extraction industry or from educational institutions, or whether they preferred snowmobiling to cross-country skiing, he understood that you'll never win someone to your side by alienating them. He never shied away from the parts of the state that disagreed with him. He never, for example, turned down an invitation to address Grand Junction's Club 20, an increasingly conservative civic group, as some Colorado liberals have. Hick knew that even if people disagree with you, you still need to show up and listen, or you'll create a political vacuum that extremists will happily rush in to fill.

Hick always used the term topophilia—the love of a place and the ways that place shapes a person. Hick has been formed by Colorado, the purpleness of its politics, and the prosperity of its diverse economy. It is easy for him to be so optimistic about Colorado because he loves it so much. When he decided to run for president, I found an obscure textbook called *Topophilia*—the same one he'd doubtless borrowed the term from—and gave it to him. "Don't forget the place that shaped you," I said. I feel the same way not just about Colorado, but the wild places and people who make up the outdoor-recreation community across the globe. It is easy for me to feel optimistic about its capabilities because of my deep love of it. Topophilia thru and thru.

It was obvious to Hick that he had a zealot on his hands, and so he allowed me to visit other states to spread the word. Not long after I got the job, Washington State created a similar position. I then traveled to the great state of Montana to see if we could make it a foursome.

In the summer of 2016, I had a meeting set with Montana's governor, Steve Bullock. Walking into the Montana capitol, it was hard not to feel intimidated. A Montana native, Bullock also graduated from Columbia Law School. He's tall, and wears cowboy boots that make him even taller. I couldn't believe I was about to have yet another audience with a state governor. I had to remind myself that I'd done far more dangerous things than this, like descending icy knife-edge ridges half out of my mind with sleep and oxygen deprivation.

I also knew Bullock was the perfect audience for my message. A moderate in a conservative, rural state, Bullock was popular for his understanding of rural and outdoors issues—the USFS, NPS, and BLM are all massive presences in Montana. His chief of staff, who'd brokered the meeting, was Tracy Stone-Manning, who is now the head of the BLM.

Governor Bullock got right to it. "Why should we create one of these offices of outdoor recreation?" he said.

I'd come armed with statistics from the Outdoor Industry Association's 2012 economic study. I told him that the ORec industry in Montana created $2.4 billion in spending a year, representing 5.1 percent of the state's GDP. That was bigger than the construction industry at 2.4 percent, and mineral extraction—including oil and gas—at 2 percent. The last fact was pretty arresting—mining has had a long and checkered history in Montana, particularly for copper and asbestos. "Outdoor rec is an industry that deserves stewardship in Montana," I said.

"Why isn't this for the tourism department?" the governor asked. "Or parks and rec?"

This was the crucial question from a governance standpoint. The state's tourism department is for marketing, not for helping build and maintain facilities like trails and boat ramps that benefit locals as well as tourists. Likewise, parks and rec doesn't work to support outdoor-rec manufacturing businesses, I said. Montana has a strong manufacturing sector starring companies like Simms, the excellent fly-fishing equipment company. An office of the outdoor-recreation industry can facilitate each of those things.

"So are you responsible for all this stuff?" asked Bullock.

"Yes, I'm the air traffic controller for all of that," I said.

Governor Bullock leaned back in chair and said, "Huh." I knew he'd gotten it. What I learned later is that at that moment he was already selecting his director, a dynamo named Rachel Van de Voort.

Rachel is a fourth-generation Montanan, the daughter of a

hunting and fishing guide. She herself was a former whitewater-rafting guide and executive at the hunting-rifle manufacturer Kimber America. In other words, she was the perfect person to represent Montana's ORec industry. Even more than her résumé, though, Rachel's personality suited her for the role. She is warm and congenial, the ideal personality to build connections between industries, agencies, and the public. The first time I met her at a conference, I asked how the meetings were going. "It'd be a lot better if we were talking about this stuff sitting around a campfire passing a bottle of whiskey," she laughed. I couldn't have agreed more.

Rachel's work was instrumental in Montana, as she found ways to make a difference that wouldn't have fallen to anyone else in state government. In one instance, she puzzled out where to build new river-access points on rights-of-way owned by the state. River access for fishing is a big economic driver in Montana—stats show that $50 million in investment in such spots has yielded $900 million in economic activity in the state. Where road bridges have been replaced, there is often an adjacent strip of state property that can become an access point for boaters and fishermen. There are hundreds of such spots in Montana, and Rachel coordinated the highway department and the state's fish, wildlife, and parks department to figure out which ones would provide the most benefit for floaters and anglers. If she hadn't done it, no one else would have.

****

I made visits to promote state offices of outdoor rec to North Carolina, California, Michigan, and even Puerto Rico. The state offices were almost always a fairly easy sell. It was a low-cost way for the government to support commerce—generally just adding a single new staff person—and it followed a model that already existed. Most states have similar directors for other industries: agriculture, mineral extraction, tourism, etc. (In Colorado, I worked just down the hall from the state director of the aerospace and defense industry. He was a retired general, and every time he walked by my office, if I saw him, I would rise from my desk. He would laugh and say I was one of the few people in the private sector who recognized you may take the uniform off, but respect remains the same.) Furthermore, the state ORec offices would help governors keep tabs on an exceptionally broad and diverse sector of their economies. The outdoor-recreation industry is a constellation of small businesses, from quirky hotels to single-person guiding companies, and the resources they rely on— trails and ski slopes and rivers—are often governed by dense bureaucracies like fish and game departments or the USFS. It pays to have someone experienced to liaise between these very different entities.

In Michigan, my meeting was organized by Heart of the Lakes, a land-conservation org, and also attended by the state's Department of Natural Resources and the Parks and Recreation Division. I loved that such groups were seeing the value of the office and that it wasn't a top-down directive from the governor. Thanks to Katie, Michigan had become my second home state. Our wedding had been on Mackinac Island, and each summer we spent a week up at the family house with Katie's parents on the shores of Long Lake. (Katie's mom insists on sleeping in a tent with her grandkids.) I was proud when Michigan eventually created their office in 2019.

Hick also brought me along to the annual National Governors Association meeting a few times to promote state outdoor-rec offices. At one point, Rachel VandeVoort and I were on a panel in Hawaii with the directors from Utah and Wyoming. At one Outdoor Retailer trade show, I huddled over drinks with Marc Berejka, the director of community and government affairs at REI, the massive gear seller known for its proactive environmental stances. Marc was long my partner-in-crime in the state-offices movement, and then later while I worked for VF Corp. He supplied the money from REI, and I did the song and dance. At the time, we had ORec offices in eight states, and I remember him saying, "We have to get to thirteen. Like the original thirteen signatories of the Declaration of Independence, because we are starting a revolution."

Marc was right—it did feel like a movement, and I started thinking about ways to capture that momentum for the good of my industry and to further the goals I'd set out for myself when I'd taken the job: to improve the industry's voice for conservation and access, to improve workforce development, and to help more people get outdoors for their improved health and well-being. Those thoughts would lead directly to the creation of the Confluence of States, an agreement between state offices that I would later craft with the help of one of my University of Denver MBA professors.

After about a year working for the Colorado Office of Economic Development and International Trade, I started thinking that if I was going to be helping guide one of Colorado's largest economic sectors, it would make sense to know a bit more about economics. I decided to get my MBA. The problem was, I'd never even gotten my bachelor's.

I'd grown up in a household where education was perceived as the key to unlocking fiscal security and freedom. For one thing, my mother was a teacher. Secondly, it was an immigrant story. My father had left South America to get his aerospace-engineering degree, the only one in his family to leave Ecuador, let alone get an advanced degree.

As I was the firstborn son of the firstborn son, going back multiple generations, my parents believed that my academic path was set: undergrad at a good university, then straight on to law school where I could excel and later support the family with any legal needs they may have.

By high school, it was obvious, at least to me, that I wouldn't be following that path. The weekends spent hunting, climbing, and paddling now invariably included Fridays, and though I excelled at the art of applied physics in climbing anchors, and was developing an intuitive sense of hydrology through kayaking, my scientific curiosity ended at the classroom door. When I announced to my parents that, instead of college, I'd be studying for my International Federation of Mountain Guides Association exams in Europe and be supporting myself in the meantime by working for Colorado Outward Bound, it didn't go well.

My mother's exact reply was: "You are going to throw your future away to become a glorified camp counselor?" I honestly thought she'd understand—her father had just an eighth-grade education because his family had needed him to work the fields in Arkansas. Yet with the help of his wife, a CPA, he'd run the ever-expanding Kelley's Sporting Goods, rubbing elbows with St. Louis' leading industrialists and politicos. "You do what you love and the rest will come," PawPaw had always told me. Maybe she hadn't received the same counsel from him. "This is your fault," I overheard her saying to my grandfather, about me declining to go straight to college.

I knew from my work with the Wharton programs that the MBA would be invaluable to me. For higher education to be effective, it needs to happen at the right time, and for the right reasons.

I'd never have learned a thing as a reluctant 18-year-old college kid, but now, working every day at the top of government and with business owners and CEOs, I was eager for the specialized knowledge.

Wharton would have welcomed me, but I couldn't afford it. In my own city, however, was the University of Denver. Its prestigious MBA program was also the alma mater of Mark Gasta, my friend and mentor from Vail Resorts. He encouraged me to meet with the business school's dean, and to my surprise, I felt like the dean was recruiting me. He'd seen, he said, some of the media coverage of my new position as the director of the state outdoor-rec office, and believed someone with my experience would add to the cohort. He didn't flinch when I mentioned my lack of a BA. He said that it wasn't uncommon for students with deep professional experience to be granted special permission to enter an MBA program. He was even prepared to offer me a scholarship, which I'd sorely need on my government paycheck.

"It will be tough," he warned, "to keep up with the students who've already worked in finance, law, or traditional business." I knew I'd have to outwork everyone in my cohort to keep pace, but hard work had never discouraged me when I had a goal in mind.

The program was both difficult and valuable. Double-dipping, I used my class time to further projects at the state office. When supporting infrastructure development from bike paths to trail segments, I consulted students who'd worked in finance to better understand the ways a municipality could pay for the work. Before we developed the Colorado Outdoor Rx Report, I consulted cohort members who'd worked in the health-care industry to build a case for the health effects of time outside. When recruiting new states to the outdoor-rec-office movement, I used a market competitor matrix from class to demonstrate what the offices were optimally positioned to focus on—supporting tourism economies, for example, rather than recruiting tourists.

My final project was a fifty-page paper examining whether GDP was the best way to measure the outdoor-recreation economy. At that time, the U.S. Bureau of Economic Analysis (BEA) had been charged by Congress to officially measure the outdoor-recreation economy. It would now be stacked against industries like the financial sector and transportation, a victory for those of us interested in using those figures to further the industry's political aims. It was mind-boggling to me that the federal government had yet to recognize or count a multibillion-dollar sector of the economy.

As a thought experiment, I considered Bhutan's policy of measuring its government's success via a Gross National Happiness (GNH) index rather than GDP. Wouldn't such an index be better at capturing not just the outdoor-recreation industry's economic activity, but also added values like public health and conservation? In some ways, that thesis paper led to the book you are reading.

Through the long nights balancing school and work, my new daughter, Sofia, provided the motivation. Despite the lack of sleep, I savored every moment with her. I marveled at her curly blonde hair and deep hazel eyes, and how she responded to my voice and fell asleep in my arms as I told her stories about climbing and her family.

I've always believed that a life of service to others was one of value; I just never knew until Sofia was born how much being in service to your family mattered more than anything. Having Sofia helped sharpen my focus. I worked harder because clean air and water mattered more. Access to public lands took on a deeper level of importance.

As a parent, I also worked to increase her love for those lands by fostering her sense of curiosity. We looked not just for animals but at unique rocks we'd find on the ground, and I'd tell her a story about how they'd formed, whether the rocks were sandstone laid down in an ancient river delta or pumice spewed up by a violent volcano. I loved examining the snow that fell in our backyard with Sofia, sparking her interest in the different types we found, whether crusty and windblown, light and powdery, or her favorite, wet and heavy. It was her favorite for one reason—such snow was ideal to make snow cones (make a snowball, and then pour condensed milk and cherry syrup over the top). Too dry, it wouldn't consolidate well, and there'd be no snow cone that day. These days though, she loves that light snow for a different reason—it's the best snow to ski.

As she has gotten older, I am continually amazed by her curiosity, her compassion, and her eagerness for everything there is to do in the outdoors. From rowing our raft to rock climbing to camping in our backyard, she is always asking for the next adventure. I don't know if she will choose a career in the outdoors, but regardless, the tapestry of time spent outside will be an intrinsic part of who she is. I've been energized to work for that on her behalf.

****

Once I'd received my MBA, another educational opportunity arose—one that I could scarcely have dreamed of. A colleague mentioned, almost offhandedly, that I might enjoy studying at the Kennedy School of Government at Harvard. He might as well have said I should consider traveling to Mars for the weekend. When I started researching the program, though, I became excited.

The Kennedy School offers an Executive Certificate in Public Policy—the field I found myself working in—to professionals who complete three modules of courses within three years, with a week on campus followed by three months of work online. The draw for me was getting to interact with some of the brightest public-policy minds on the planet, and learning alongside some of the most motivated students anywhere. Many of the professors had set public policy through roles in the White House. I wanted to have conversations on that level, and if the job I'd chosen was to make a difference in the world, I knew I'd find ways to make it so at the Kennedy School.

I never expected to get in—and didn't have a way to pay for it if I did—but I figured I'd apply, miss the cut, and that would answer the question for me. Then one day, sitting on top of the mail pile, was an envelope from Harvard. To my shock, I'd been accepted. To my even greater shock, I was able to convince Fiona, my boss at the state, to pay for the first part of the program, citing it as professional development. The guy who'd never earned a bachelor's degree was headed to one of the most prestigious academic institutions in the world.

I took courses like What is the Cutting edge of Economic Development, and Applying Behavioral Insights to the Design of Public Policy. The teacher of the latter was the behavioral economist Cass Sunstein, advisor to President Obama and co-author of *Nudge,* a book about how individuals and organizations make decisions. For most, those decisions are typically poor, but the book seeks to teach individuals and society to make better ones. My question going in was, how could we nudge governments and the business world into caring more about access to the outdoors, and by extension the outdoors itself?

The thesis I brought to Harvard to test was that we should

focus on two things: economics and quality of life. The 2018 BEA data had arrived, showing that at $373 billion in economic impact, outdoor recreation was a bigger force than either legal services or mineral extraction, including oil and gas. Another case study was from Everest: How Nepal's regional economy had greatly benefited from climbers and trekkers, while Tibet's, on the mountain's northern border, had not. The reason: China never let its residents make the economics of Everest a priority, whereas the Nepalese government embraced it.

Secondly, we needed to brand access to outdoor recreation as a quality-of-life amenity. When people relocate, they make decisions based on things like the quality of jobs and schools, as well as access to culture, all of which governments invest in. Increasingly, people are using access to recreation as a major criterion, too, whether it's proximity to a surf break, a ski slope, or a climbing crag. Goldman Sachs understood that when they established a regional headquarters in Salt Lake City, and the residents of Fruita understood that when they scratched mountain-bike trails out of the open range adjacent to town. Smart public policy oriented toward growth, I argued in class, would be to support recreational amenities. I couldn't have felt more emboldened when some of the smartest people in the world agreed that I was onto something.

Shamelessly, I also took advantage of my Harvard-student status to peruse some of the personal effects of one of its most illustrious alumni. The Houghton Library had a trove of Teddy's Roosevelt's correspondence and journals, but to access them from their deep and guarded storage, you must first fill out a lengthy questionnaire. I wrote that I was studying the need to posit public lands as our people's birthright, as TR had done, and that we needed to argue for public lands as a commercial boon, pointing out that legacy to those Americans who believed otherwise.

Most of TR's journals require the use of special cotton gloves to handle, not to mention the disapproving glare of a grand, matronly curator standing over your shoulder throughout. The vigilance was well worth it. It was one of the biggest thrills of my life to flip through his boyhood journals, full of drawings of flowers and birds, and one memorable sketch of a riverine habitat—the first glimpses of an emerging naturalist. I also pulled his journal from ranching in the Badlands, with its hasty scrawls, the notes that led to his book *Wilderness Hunter,* which in turn led to the formation of the Boone and Crockett Club. Nothing transports you back in time like seeing the actual handwriting of a legendary figure.

Harvard's rich educational opportunities inspired me, above all, to work to extend the same to others in my industry. I hadn't needed a college degree to work as a mountaineering guide, but as I rose through the ranks, I saw that the profession was viewed with much more esteem elsewhere than in the United States. Here, the profession is often seen as a stopgap job before a more "serious" career. In other parts of the world, it is a serious profession, capable of providing a living on par with that of an engineer or a nurse.

As it should be—guides practice complex decision-making, balancing their expertise in glaciology and meteorology to ensure their clients achieve their goals safely. That's without mentioning the leadership theory and financial acumen operators need to make a profit running a staff of two dozen in foreign nations known for labyrinthine bureaucracies.

Even if a guide were to make a good living, as I had, there is the problem of longevity. Adventure guiding of all kinds is hard on the body, and few make it to retirement age still performing at a high level. Where do they go from there if they don't have other training or advanced degrees?[10] In a different vein, as I'd seen at Vail Resorts, the industry needed educational opportunities for employees to develop additional expertise, like working in finance or accounting or human resources, without having to shift to entirely different fields. When I'd done my statewide listening tour, meeting with business leaders, every one of them pointed to the need for more workforce training and education.

So I started talking to every university in Colorado that would listen. The Colorado Mountain College associate-degree programs in the ski and outdoor industries were terrific, and I'm honored to hold an honorary associate's degree from CMC, but we needed more options, especially in post-graduate degrees.

The break I was looking for came from the mayor of Crested Butte. He had heard my call for action toward academia in the media, and wanted me to come down for a visit. I arrived during the offseason. The ski resort was closed, and many stores and restaurants were on hiatus, so when the mayor suggested a restaurant I knew to be closed, it had the air of a secret meeting. I walked in to find the mayor, the president of Western Colorado University, and the school's director of development. No one else was inside. I was impressed that they'd picked a spot where there could be so few distractions. I got right to it: I wanted to see the first-of-its-kind MBA focused specifically on the outdoor-recreation industry.

There was a moment of silence, and then to his credit, without flinching, the university president agreed that it should happen at his school. The program was established in 2018. The school

---

10. It's a similar problem for many of those leaving the military's special forces. Friends who have served in the Rangers and Navy SEALS programs describe their frustration translating their resumes to the civilian world despite real expertise in operating multi-million dollar equipment and leading highly skilled teams in extremely stressful environments.

was expecting eight or nine students that first year. They got twenty-three, taking a slate of courses in financial management and capital budgeting, but also studying things like supply-chain sustainability and how outdoor-rec businesses impact local natural resources. By 2019, the program had a waitlist.

Such academic programs are spreading like wildfire. In 2020, Colorado Mesa University added an Outdoor Recreation Industry Studies program to their bachelor's-degree offerings. In 2021, the University of Colorado Boulder added a master's in economics of the outdoor recreation economy. That program is entirely online, and allows students the opportunity to take as many or as few credits as they like at a time, perfect for folks who are also holding down a job as they study. Then, in 2022, my alma mater, the University of Denver, launched their pioneering, all-online Leadership in Outdoor Recreation Industry program, combining courses from the business school, the law school, and their school of global public policy. It's a program I'd have loved to have been a student in.

Why is it so important that outdoor-industry leaders have the chance to complete such a degree? Take a pair of exercise/athleisure tights, of the sort made by almost every outdoor-apparel company. A stone-cold capitalist would only need to worry about selling as many pairs of tights as possible at the highest possible price while bringing them to market for the lowest possible cost. Any business school can set you up for that. However, like other outdoor-rec-focused master's programs, the University of Denver's will instead home in on the questions of whether those tights can be made durably with recycled materials. Then what about the question of whether the fabrics are using toxic "forever" chemicals? Law courses might weigh in on whether the company could be held liable for the effects of those chemicals once the tights are in the landfill, or even better, whether the company could help get laws passed so that the rest of the apparel industry stays in step with ORec companies trying to eliminate such chemicals.

What about the question of whether the tights are made with fair labor, and whether the factories may be in violation of American or European trade policies? The law school and school of international studies can provide tools there. And what about the trails the tights are used on? Should the company be helping protect access to them for the good of their market? What about helping ensure there's clean air to exercise in on that trail? Outdoor-industry companies should be looking at the so-called cradle-to-grave effects of their business, whether its manufacturing or service. It's the evolution of an industry that has traditionally merely been seen as making fun stuff and providing exciting experiences.

I'm particularly proud of the University of Denver program, and not just because I'm an alumnus of the business school. It was made possible in part by my work with the VF Corp. I set up the meeting between the university and the company's CEO, and helped broker the $3 million gift VF Corp made to help get the program running. It just made sense—VF Corp, who moved their headquarters to Denver in 2019, would inevitably benefit from a better applicant pool in their home community.

There are now dozens of academic programs around the country focusing on the ORec industry, ranging from Oregon State University to West Virginia University to Arkansas's John Brown University. Again, it's hard not to revel in the irony that a guy who slacked his way through high school and never got a bachelor's degree became the biggest booster for academia to take his industry seriously. The most important thing for me about the new programs, though, is the ability for those educational opportunities to be hyper-targeted. Education is best taken when the student wants and needs the information—usually once they have an idea of *why* they need it. An executive working in accounting at a bike-helmet company doesn't need to take an accounting course, but she may be eager to take a course in marketing, so that she might someday rise to a CEO chair someplace. It will only make our industry more efficient and effective to keep such candidates in our community.

Even better, when today's young Luis, a social misfit who has found his salvation in outdoor recreation, sits down with their parents to tell them that he isn't going to law school but is instead pursuing a career in the outdoor-recreation industry, he will find plenty of college programs that would make sense to him—and, more importantly, to his parents.

Chapter 12

THE BATTLE FOR THE OUTDOOR RETAILER SHOW

"Some men are cowards, but they fight the same as the brave men, or get the hell slammed out of them, watching men fight who are just as scared as they are. The real hero is the man who fights even though he is scared." —General George Patton

The North and South Six Shooter peaks are a pair of sandstone towers set 1.5 miles apart, rising 1,400 feet above a red Wile E. Coyote desert landscape in Southern Utah. From certain angles, they look like a pair of old-time revolvers perched atop rocky cones. The first time I climbed them was in the 1990s, with my friends Nancy Crane and Mike Dehoff, on a break between sections of the Outward Bound semester course. On that day, I was most of the way up the first section of the North Six Shooter when I found myself stuck and sweating with stress. I was supposed to transfer my hands and feet from the crack I was jamming into a higher crack to the right, but I didn't want to. The new crack was a bit wider—too wide for my feet or fist, when twisted sideways, to support my weight. I'd have to cram an arm or knee into the crack, which always felt very insecure, like you'd just fall off the wall.

It was embarrassing—I'd climbed much harder-rated routes than this but was used to more solid rock than this Six Shooter sandstone, which seemed to crumble to dust if you rubbed it too hard. Dehoff called up from below in the singsong he reserved for teasing his friends: "How's it going up there, Luis?" I looked down. Dehoff could plainly see me hesitating. His giggle rose up from the ground, both chiding me for my hesitation and reminding me that the route was well within my abilities. Eventually, I gathered my courage and just climbed, trusting my experience. It was the sort of leap of faith that I love about climbing, and I was rewarded with the view from the top.

As I stood on the sedan-sized summit, the flood of endorphins soothing my jangly nerves made the view that much sweeter. To the north rose the mesas of Canyonlands National Park; to the west, the Colorado River was ensconced in its precipitous gorge; and to the south, red-and-white-striped canyons zagged all the way to the San Juan River.

Dehoff and I were such good friends because of an incident that had happened on that very river just six months earlier. One of my students, a twenty-year-old college kid, had become hypothermic while sitting in an inflatable kayak in 45-degree water in an all-day rainstorm. She hadn't eaten enough, and her body ran out of fuel to create heat. She was suddenly too lethargic to even speak, and we struck an emergency camp, got her out of her wet clothes and into a sleeping bag, and rewarmed her in the bag with sock-ensconced bottles of hot water until she was conscious again. Dehoff had been the leader of that river trip, and these sorts of stressful emergencies can be very bonding for the rescuers.

Such heightened experiences can also bond you with a place, and the accumulation of the river rescue, other backpacking trips into the national park, and that day's climb of the Six Shooters had made that landscape as special to me as the Johnson Shut-Ins back in Missouri. It was essential text in the story of my life. I was glad there were so few roads or signs of development visible to the naked eye.

Twenty years later, on December 28, 2016, President Obama designated virtually all of that southward view as the 1.35-million-acre Bears Ears National Monument. It was a day of celebration for the outdoor-recreation community, which had been advocating for the designation for years. Bears Ears contains some of climbing's most classic sites, including the Six Shooters and the massive walls of Indian Creek. It also contains hundreds of miles of spectacular wilderness canyons beloved by hikers and backpackers. The outdoor-apparel company Patagonia, in particular, had thrown its weight behind lobbying the public for the creation of the monument, producing a short film, an interactive website, and other promotional efforts.

More importantly, the new monument represented a significant first—its borders were determined in conjunction with five Native American nations who have ancestral ties to the territory: the Hopi, Navajo, Uintah and Ouray Ute, Ute mountain Ute, and Zuni. The monument was created less for recreation than to preserve the landscape and archeological sites that the Indigenous peoples hold sacred. President Obama had created Bears Ears with the 1906 Antiquities Act (first signed into law, of course, by Teddy Roosevelt), which had been intended to preserve archeological sites, but this was one of the first times that such sites were being protected specifically for the sake of Native Americans. The climbing and hiking communities had been proud to join the Native American community in securing the sublime landscape. In a long history of injustice, it was a tiny step in the right direction.

Others were less pleased. The Republican Party establishment in Utah, in fact, was livid. They were still angry about President Clinton's 1996 designation of 1.7 million acres of Utah as Grand

Staircase-Escalante National Monument. Anti-public-lands Utahns, including most of the state's Republican politicians, had called it a "Federal land grab." The designation had precluded coal-mining opportunities on the Kaiparowits Plateau, and it stirred up the deep-seated anti-federal-government sentiment held by many Utahns. They immediately began lobbying the incoming Trump Administration to dismantle both monuments.

Enter Peter Metcalf. Peter was the founder and CEO of the Salt Lake City–based gear maker Black Diamond Equipment and a staunch conservation champion. Though he'd retired from Black Diamond in 2015, his new position as director of the Salt Lake City branch of the Federal Reserve Bank gave him even more cachet in the Utah outdoor-recreation industry. On the day that Obama designated Bears Ears, Metcalf was at the press conference where Utah's governor, Gary Herbert, and the entire Utah Congressional delegation declared their intention to do everything in their power to block the new monument. "It was an all-out war on the monument and the public lands, and I thought 'enough is enough,'" Metcalf told the press.

Metcalf's exasperation, along with that of legions in the outdoor-recreation community, had been simmering for years. In 2016, it felt as though all public lands were under attack. The so-called Sagebrush Rebellion of the 1980s had been recently rekindled with efforts not only to fight public-land protection, but to actually sell them off. Bills had lately been introduced in states like Arizona, Idaho, and Wyoming to demand the federal government give its holdings to the states, who would then sell off parcels to increase their budgets and promote the exploitation of resources to enrich their citizens.[11] In 2015 alone, thirty-five such

---

11. These were the same ideas that Teddy Roosevelt had fought against when he battled to protect the Grand Canyon in 1903.

state bills were introduced. Similar bills, with laughable titles like the Disposal of Excess Federal Lands Act of 2015, were being introduced into Congress in Washington, D.C.

The most eye-popping embodiment of the anti-public-lands movement had been the forty-day armed occupation of the Malheur National Wildlife Refuge in Eastern Oregon in January 2016. More than two dozen militants took over the ranch with the goal of advancing their fringe position that the federal government was constitutionally required to turn over most of the lands under its management to individual states. The somewhat incoherent doctrine, too convoluted to detail here, was based on a home-cooked interpretation of both Mormon scripture and a religious take on the US Constitution. One of the occupiers was ultimately killed by law enforcement before the occupation was broken up.

Anti-public-land politicians in Congress had also been working to kill off the Land and Water Conservation Fund (LWCF). The federal fund had been established in 1965 to help pay for recreational amenities nationwide and was derived through federal royalties from offshore oil and gas extraction. The LWCF had paid for some $18 billion in land acquisitions and recreational facilities since its inception, ranging from baseball diamonds to picnic tables to bike paths. Every single county in the nation had been the beneficiary of LWCF-funded projects, but the anti-public-lands politicos objected to the fact that some funds had been used to purchase inholdings in national parks and other modest federal land acquisitions. From my point of view, these critics were tragically cutting off their nose to spite their face.

Metcalf's idea to strike a blow for Bears Ears and public-lands protections was to threaten to move the Outdoor Retailer (OR) show. Held in Salt Lake City for twenty years, OR was the outdoor industry's indispensable event. More than 20,000 people crowded into the convention center each summer and winter, wandering a vast grid of booths built to reveal every company's top-secret coming attractions—racks of impossibly light down parkas, cases of glittering climbing hardware, and gadgets like stoves that charge a smartphone with a twig fire. Displays included rain booths built to demonstrate waterproof apparel and movie-set ice-cream parlors handing out free scoops on behalf of gear brands. One year, the footwear brand Keen set up a Ferris wheel just outside the convention center. In the evenings, brands threw private parties with musical acts like Parliament-Funkadelic and Macklemore. The show brought some $45 million in spending to Salt Lake City each year.

The first time I'd attended, I was there to try to score free gear for our 1998 Gangapurna expedition. I got in on a borrowed access badge, and though very intimidated, talked my way past the receptionist at the three-story North Face booth by name-dropping Pete Athans, one of the company's most iconic sponsored climbers, whom I knew from Outward Bound. He loaned me his own yellow The North Face down climbing suit there at the show.

On January 10, 2017, on the opening day of the Winter OR show, Metcalf published an op-ed in *The Salt Lake Tribune* calling for the show to leave Utah if the state's leaders didn't change their stance. "We should respond with our dollars, with our conventioneers, with our money, and take this show to a state that is much more aligned with our values," he wrote. Patagonia founder Yvon Chouinard followed with his own press release supporting the proposal, but Governor Herbert was unmoved. On February 3, he signed a state bill asking President Trump to rescind Bears Ears, and Patagonia announced its boycott. Arc'teryx followed suit, as did a half dozen other outdoor brands.

It's hard to convey what a big deal the industry rebellion was at the time. Brands had millions invested in the show, and the Salt Lake event had become the industry's moral marketplace. Seemingly nearly every conservation and outdoor-recreation nonprofit attended looking to line up funding and support for their cause. It was at OR that the Outdoor Industry Association (OIA) grew from just a trade-issues lobbying group into a more forceful advocate for public-lands protection and greater inclusivity. Maybe most important, it was the community's annual reunion. Friendships began, grew, and were maintained at OR.

The rising anti-conservation tide felt like an existential threat to the outdoor-recreation industry and community, though. Public lands, especially in the West, are an essential condition to outdoor recreation. Like the notably pro-LGBTQIA+ film and television industry boycotting the state of Georgia over its anti-LGBTQIA+ laws, it didn't make sense for the outdoor industry to financially support a state hostile to its interests either.

On February 16, Metcalf organized a call between Utah Governor Herbert and outdoor-industry CEOs, including Patagonia's Chouinard, Outdoor Research's Dan Nordstrom, and REI Jerry's Stritzke, to see if they could find a solution. I wasn't on the call, but the head of the OIA, Amy Roberts, texted me during the meeting. "He thinks we are bluffing," she said. They weren't. After the call, the OIA announced that OR would leave Salt Lake City after the upcoming summer event. Emerald Expositions, the show's actual for-profit owner, acquiesced. *You are either on the bus, off the bus, or under the bus,* we told them. *Don't stand in front of it.*

Where would the show end up? Eight cities, including Denver, Orlando, Florida, and Anaheim, California, submitted bids to Emerald to host the show. Many of us worried that it might go to one of those latter two cities, which had huge convention centers and a strong convention industry but no meaningful connection to the outdoor-adventure community, and no nearby mountains or wildlands to try out the new gear in. The fear was that if OR went to a city none of the participants wanted to visit, they'd just stop going. The event would wither, and so would our political momentum. When we realized that Emerald Expositions was about to launch a public offering that would eventually net them $264 million, the danger that Emerald would simply send OR to the highest bidder felt very real.

It made sense to many of us that Colorado should land the show. It wasn't just the boost it would provide for our economy; it was that Colorado was positioning itself as a very pro-public-lands and pro-outdoor-recreation state. Chimney Rock National Monument and Browns Canyon National Monument had been welcomed in Colorado 2012 and 2015 respectively. When the Trump Administration was reviewing national monuments to shrink, Hick met with them to defend Colorado's seven national monuments. "Our public lands are a fundamental part of our identity as Coloradans and as Americans," he told the press. Hick and I wanted Colorado to be the symbolic heart of America's embrace of public lands and outdoor recreation. Per my job description as the director of Colorado's Office of the Outdoor Industry, I was the one to lead the effort to land OR.

I got to work. I convinced a handful of industry CEOs, like Outdoor Research's Nordstrom (who ironically had his company HQ in Seattle, Washington, another contender for the show) to write an open letter to the industry supporting a move of OR to Denver. Next, there were huge logistical problems to navigate. For one, Denver's convention center and hotel sector were booming, and for many of the dates OR needed, the city already was already running an 85 percent hotel occupancy as far out as 2031. If that couldn't be sorted out, OR in Denver was a nonstarter. Richard Scharf and Rachel Benedict at Visit Denver faced down that problem by convening twice-weekly meetings with more than thirty downtown Denver hotels to find the 6,500 hotel rooms they'd need for the Outdoor Retailer show on the peak nights. I was also in constant contact with Emerald representatives about our efforts.

Emerald believed that the Colorado Convention Center wasn't large enough to house the 900,000 square feet of floor space that OR required. So Scharf reconfigured the OR floor plan, creating space for the show without resorting to outdoor event tents. They also brought the trade unions to the table to help negotiate and lower costs for attendees—an unprecedented move for the Colorado Convention Center. I felt like I was living an episode of *The West Wing,* with teams working around the clock to solve a crisis. My wife was home with our restless baby, and she wondered aloud more than once if this was how our lives were always going to be.

Richard, Rachel, and I realized that logistics alone wouldn't be enough to sell Emerald. I told the two of them to pack a bag for California. We were heading to Emerald's HQ. There, at their nondescript Orange County office-park building, we made a request: come to Denver and do a walk-through of the convention center. No attorneys, no press, just us talking about our vision. Surprisingly, they agreed. I had an idea about how to express that vision, but we'd have to act quickly.

A week later, Richard and Rachel and I were waiting at the Colorado Convention Center when the limo we'd hired to pick up the Emerald execs at the airport arrived. Emerald's lead, Darrell Denny, was by my side as we walked toward the building and I told him my story: of a kid with little hope of a future who found his voice and his confidence in the outdoors. How our companies weren't just selling "gear"; we were selling the very idea that people were capable of doing more than they thought possible. I told him that Denver could deliver on that dream, that promise. I shared that it was ingrained into most who lived in our state, and that I was going to prove it.

Faintly, from down a long and wide hallway, we could hear music and cheering coming from the main floor of the convention center. Curious, Darrell turned and walked toward it. We followed in silence. As we came through the doors, there stood as many state and city and convention-center union employees as we had been able to muster, all cheering. There were hundreds, all decked out in their favorite outdoor gear, with tents and camp chairs set up, and people riding around on mountain bikes and sitting in kayaks. The Colorado band OneRepublic's song "The Good Life" was blaring in the background. It was pure Colorado pride, from people who treasured the opportunity to host the OR show. I looked over at Darrell, who actually had tears in his eyes, and I knew we'd won.

Finally, on July 6, 2017, at a morning press conference at Civic Center Park in Denver, we were able to announce that Outdoor Retailer had signed a five-year contract with the City of Denver to host the show. The outdoor industry applauded, knowing that this was the right decision, though without ever understanding just how much work it had taken to pull off. Some summits go easy, some go hard.

****

With the OR show safely in Denver, I next turned to a process that I hoped would capitalize on some of our momentum. There were now four other states with director of outdoor recreation positions like mine: Washington, Montana, Wyoming, and Utah, with Oregon, Vermont, and North Carolina in the pipeline. To many, the positions were an unexpected revelation, boasting direct access to their state's governors. What's more, many were from deeply conservative states, a rare glimmer of bipartisan consensus.

Wouldn't the power of the state outdoor-rec offices be magnified if we were formally pulling in the same direction? Yes, and I realized, politics being what they are, that it was important to get cooperation between state outdoor-rec offices set down in writing. Those thoughts were the genesis of the Confluence Accords.

I bounced the idea off Rachel VandeVoort of Montana as well as the other state directors. The five of us held monthly phone calls to share best practices, and the group loved the idea. I also got great feedback from my Colorado advisory council. Drawing inspiration from Outward Bound's pillars, I began devising our own, consisting of the areas in which government could do the greatest good for the ORec industry, and therefore society.

Conservation and stewardship were the obvious place to start. Outdoor recreationists have a clear responsibility to care for the land and water where we recreate, as well as the ecosystems we share these resources with. It was also important for our offices to be leaders in helping the public, private industry, and government understand why healthy lands and waters for recreation were so vital to our society. I'd been hard at work on the education and workforce-training piece, and knew that Colorado couldn't be the only state nurturing those programs and opportunities. Along with that, our offices and industry needed—through education and training—to foster and develop greater diversity within the community and industry.

Economic development was the primary consideration behind the creation of our offices. It was important not just to provide prosperity, though; we should also be leaders in sustainable business, for the sake of the wildlands and of fostering diversity, because the outdoor community should be for all. Lastly, I wanted to reduce adverse competition between our states (i.e., poaching one another's businesses) so that our cooperation could continue without rancor.

The fourth pillar really felt like the most powerful. By 2018, my deputy director Janette Heung's work on the Colorado Outdoor Rx Report had solidified for me the understanding of the benefits of outdoor recreation and time outside. If we as state directors could lead the way in facilitating getting outside for people of all backgrounds and persuasions, we'd be doing real good for society. And if we could lead the way in communicating the connection between time outside and healthy ecosystems, we'd be doing real good for those ecosystems. It was a virtuous circle that Kurt Hahn, Outward Bound's founder, would approve of.

I didn't want to be the Accords' sole author, though. I knew there'd need to be a buy-in process from the states, ideally from multiple individuals within each state. I decided that a constitutional convention was in order. I envisioned delegates from each of the eight states, from different sectors of the outdoor-rec community: business owners, nonprofit staff, state-park employees, etc. I envisioned people haggling over the language of the Accords and proposing amendments. I knew the process would be empowering. Then I wanted each delegation to take the Accords home, to gather input and establish agreement. I wanted each state's governor to literally sign off on the Accords. I wanted them to mean something.

I set our convention for the first Outdoor Retailer held in Denver, in January 2018. In the meantime, I wanted to create an organization—the Confluence of States—to support for communication between the states, as well as support new directors with materials they'd need to get started. (I knew we'd be adding more and more states to the Accords, and wanted them to be as "plug and play" as possible.) Furthermore, I didn't want any one state to control the leadership.

To create the Confluence of States, I knew I'd need help from people with experience in administering ORec organizations. I turned to Nathan Fey, at that time the western director for American Whitewater, and to Jason Bertolacci, the Colorado director of the International Mountain Biking Association, asking them both to help me begin constructing governance documents.

On January 24, 2018, in a massive conference room above Denver's Center for the Performing Arts, my vision became a reality. Arrayed at eight tables, each with a sign displaying the state's name, were 100 delegates, ready for the First Outdoor Recreation Confluence Summit. We didn't allow anyone into the summit who wasn't attached to a specific state. I had to turn down my friend Marc Berejka, from REI, because he represented an interstate business. This was about building power from the state level up.

None other than Governor Hickenlooper was set to open the event. "You are starting on this grand expedition," the governor said. "The rapids will be many; the passes will be tall."

The stakes had never felt higher. In addition to the Trump Administration's war on the national monuments, it was working to dismantle the Environmental Protection Agency. It was censoring scientists and gutting regulations critical to protecting our health and environment, including the Clean Air Act, which had made life easier for millions of asthmatic kids like me. It was still fighting the Land and Water Conservation Fund. We needed everyone possible to stand up for clean air and water and access to public lands, and here, fortunately, were dozens of people ready to do just that. Hick concluded his short introduction by extolling them: "The best and brightest are in this room," he said. "I have every confidence in your ability."

At that moment, I felt incredibly proud. I was the child of an immigrant, a poor student in his youth, yet was standing next to one of the most powerful people in the nation, preparing to effect change in my government. I thought of each of my grandfathers and how I'd explain to them what I was doing, and how proud each would have been.

It was my turn to speak, I stepped up to the podium, leaned into the microphone, and began: "The Confluence Summit at its core is just that—a convergence of ideas and ideology, much like rivers flow together and gain strength. This journey, this process, is something that no one state can or should have to do alone. Our strength, our potential, lies in our ability to rise together.

"I get it, we come from different political stripes, yet I am sure we can all agree that our industry and our culture is one of the few economies out there that consistently crosses political divides."

I broke down the format of the day. Each of the states had had months to pick over my draft of the Accords, and I'd asked them to arrive with objections and suggestions. The day would be broken into four sessions for each of the four pillars, and we'd litigate every word of the document until it was acceptable to all.

Once we got going, there was plenty of horse trading, especially between delegations representing liberal and conservative state administrations. States would send emissaries between their tables until a compromise was reached. I would call for occasional check-ins from the stage to stay on task. Then we would ask each state to rise with their top comments and have the others in the room offer their thoughts, and then basically close conversation on the pillar before moving on to the next one. By the end of the day, we had enough consensus that we could head home to our respective governors with high confidence.

Six months later, at Summer OR, the eight state directors met on the roof of a hotel overlooking the Colorado Convention Center for the official signing. The sun was shining, and the Rocky Mountains rising abruptly from the plains just west of town were plainly visible. As the eight of us sat facing the media, we each signed our documents one by one with ceremonial pens I'd had made. The first signatories were Vermont's Michael Snyder, North Carolina's David Knight, Oregon's Cailin O'Brien-Feeney, Utah's Tom Adams, Washington's Jon Snyder, Wyoming's Domenic Bravo, Montana's Rachel VandeVoort, and myself from Colorado. As the last pen was laid down, I felt such a wave of emotion, relief for all the cobbling together, coercing, and cajoling I'd performed to make this day happen, but more so for the significance of the moment.

I saw my experience laid out in parallel with the evolution of our industry, from a dirtbag Outward Bound instructor making $75 a day in the 1990s and living out of the back of my truck to a high-earning professional guide, and then to someone who had the time and foresight to help move his entire community forward to a more mature place. I'd managed to create an indelible mark on my community and my society in the form of these signatures and those of our governors.

More important was what it signified. The point was to do real good, to help protect the places we love to play, to advance the fortunes of people less fortunate than us, and to help stem the cultural acrimony that seemed to worsen every day in our nation There was real power here–if you totaled the recreation economies of all eight states, it represented $53.9 billion in consumer spending I knew that no other industry in the United States had created its own constitution between states. And very few industries had crafted a declarative statement about who they were as a community, who they served as an economy, and what they wanted their place in society to be. You weren't seeing "This we believe . . ." from the auto industry or tech. We were going way above the bottom line.

THE CONFLUENCE ACCORDS

The process of drafting the accords, like our Constitution and Bill of Rights, took time and political will. We established a working group in Colorado to create the original draft, and used our advisory council to help shape the initial document. Then we went to the other state directors, who in turn engaged their advisory councils, which sharpened the language even further. In the end, we knew that this would be a working document, open to amendments and ratification, yet with the right construct would stand the test of time. Here are the accords, in their entirety:

We, a growing confluence of states with a shared passion for the outdoors and a commitment to cultivating a strong outdoor recreation economy, believe that outdoor recreation is core to the very character and quality of life we should all enjoy.

The outdoor industry is a powerhouse of meaningful job creation, and a driving force of our Nation's economy. Our industry is an economic multiplier, creating a unique quality of life in rural and urban areas, attracting new businesses and professional talent to our communities.

While each of our states is unique, our shared commitment to facilitating everyone's love of place through inclusion and diverse outdoor experiences has the power to unify communities, to bridge societal divides, and to improve the mental and physical health of all people.

COMMON PRINCIPLES

The outdoors is the wellspring of adventure, camaraderie, and solace, inspiring us to both explore new places and set down roots. Whereas nature is the backbone of the recreation economy, we are committed to fostering conservation and stewardship values, ensuring environmental quality, and restoring sustainable access to the outdoors for current and future generations.

Therefore, the undersigned representatives for the outdoor recreation sector do hereby adopt and commit our states to the following common principles:

01.CONSERVATION & STEWARDSHIP

Work with the public, private, and nonprofit sectors to advocate for conservation and stewardship of land, air, water, and wildlife, and for public access to them.

Facilitate public-private partnerships to enhance public outdoor recreational access, infrastructure improvements and conservation efforts.

Educate and empower the public on the importance and interrelatedness of a healthy environment, outdoor recreation and a vibrant economy.

02.EDUCATION & WORKFORCE TRAINING

Engage with educators to support environmental and outdoor learning opportunities for early and life-long outdoor activity, career development, and advocacy for outdoor recreation.

Promote workforce training programs for technical training, skill mastery, and business opportunities across the spectrum of outdoor industry careers.

Promote interest, participation, and diversity in the outdoors for all, supporting opportunities for early and life-long outdoor learning.

03. ECONOMIC DEVELOPMENT

Collaborate with all stakeholders to establish and improve sustainable outdoor recreation infrastructure and funding.

Engage federal, tribal, state, and local governments, as well as local and regional economic development organizations to attract, retain, and expand business and market the outdoor recreation economy.

Address barriers to businesses' success in the outdoor recreation economy.

04.PUBLIC HEALTH & WELLNESS

Address social determinants of health by increasing outdoor recreation opportunities for people of all backgrounds and abilities.

Partner with health & wellness stakeholders to determine shared values and common goals, build relationships, and generate innovative partnerships to fulfill shared visions.

Assist in quantifying impacts of access to outdoor recreation and related social determinants on healthcare outcomes and costs.

On October 4, 2019, four more states joined the Confluence of States. New directors from Maine, Michigan, New Mexico, and Virginia signed onto the Accords in a grove of yellowing aspen foliage in Utah, at that state's annual Outdoor Recreation Summit, a conference open to all and designed to help outdoor workers and businesses thrive, and communities to develop outdoor-rec infrastructure and access. Then, in May 2022, Arkansas, Maryland, and New Hampshire joined the Confluence at the annual National Governors Association Outdoor Recreation Learning Network Annual Policy Institute. As of this printing, we are up to twenty states with offices of outdoor recreation, with more on the way.

The state entities vary tremendously. Most of them employ fewer than five people, but Washington's is just a single person: a senior policy advisor to the governor. Utah's moved from the Office of Economic Development to the Department of Natural Resources and employs forty people. They also doled out more than $27 million in grants to communities and orgs to foster outdoor recreation.

Most states have similar grant programs and do myriad things to promote ORec participation and opportunities. New Mexico's outdoor-recreation-industry office created an internship program for high school students to work with ORec employers and established the first-of-its-kind Outdoor Equity Fund, which helps get underserved youth outdoors by providing outdoor organizations with grants—$2 million worth so far—to create programming for them. Michigan's office is coaching small outdoor-rec businesses in marketing and business development, and Oregon's office is leading the charge to create a card that adventurers can buy to guarantee they won't have to pay for their rescue in case something goes wrong in the backcountry (while raising vital funds for county search-and-rescue teams). They are also working with the legislature to shore up rules that protect private landowners from liability if adventurers are hurt on their lands. Some timber companies, for example, have opened their lands to mountain bikers for riding, but it would be a tragedy for the rest of the community to lose that access in case one injured rider's insurance company got overly litigious.

The Confluence of States continues to supply a template for the new states, assuring they will be joining a movement with ethical standards. It also holds annual get-togethers for the directors to help share best practices. As I pointed out to Governor Bullock when I first pitched him on the idea, the offices accomplish things no trade group or parks and rec department could, finding projects that would otherwise fall through the cracks between private industry and public office.

****

Standing on the hotel roof in Denver in 2018 with my fellow signatories a year after Peter Metcalf's boycott, moving OR from Utah felt like a mixed bag. It didn't change Utah's policies toward Bears Ears or Grand Staircase-Escalante national monuments. Six months after the decision to move, in December 2017, the Trump Administration ruled that they were going to shrink Bears Ears by 85 percent and Grand Staircase-Escalante by 47 percent. Unsurprisingly, the revised borders allowed for coal-mining opportunities on lands once within Grand Staircase-Escalante and for uranium mining on lands that had been within Bears Ears.[12] To the Native American community, it was a literal

---

12. There was some bitter irony in this move. Trump's Interior secretary, Ryan Zinke, had taken to riding around on a horse with a cowboy hat on and calling himself a Roosevelt Republican. Yet this poser hadn't seemed to have studied Roosevelt at all. He apparently had no idea that Teddy Roosevelt had loved using the Antiquities Act to preserve public lands from development.

desecration of their sacred sites. Furthermore, the move had hurt small businesses like restaurants in downtown Salt Lake City, a

part of the state that was largely pro-public lands.

On the other hand, the battle over OR was a galvanizing moment for the ORec industry. It showed that brands would put their money where their mouths were to support public lands and, even more importantly, would unite for common goals. Being united raised hope that we could make progress in other areas too, like improving access to outdoor recreation for LGBTQIA+ people as well as representation and opportunities for those same peoples within the outdoor industry itself. Though halting, there has been real progress. It's rare to look at catalogs and websites for outdoor-rec companies and organizations and not see better representation of women, people of color, and people of all sizes. Most publicly traded ORec companies have diversity, equity, and inclusion officers at the VP level, which means they have a seat at the highest table. Such positions are not seen as a nice-to-have anymore, but rather as a need-to-have.

By 2018, outdoor-rec brands were also becoming more comfortable pushing their way to a seat at the political table. The OIA was already much more politically active—in 2013, they'd hired a full-time conservation lobbyist based in Washington, D.C., the indefatigable Jessica Wahl Turner. She had been out front in efforts to re-authorize the LWCF and had been a major player in passing the 2016 Rec Act through Congress. The act had required the Bureau of Economic Analysis (BEA) to measure the size of the outdoor-recreation industry. We knew it was a sizeable economic force from the OIA's own studies—some 2 percent of the entire GDP—but needed the official, unbiased measurement to overcome the naysayers. "Nothing really can replace federal economists recognizing our economy as part of the GDP and that we actually have official statistics to point to," OIA's Amy Roberts told the press at the time. "That will help us when we go in on lands management decisions in terms of the importance and benefits to the U.S. of preserving places to play."

When the outdoor community nationwide united against Trump's national-monument review, it brought a ton of attention to the larger efforts to sell off public lands. So much so that Utah Congressman Jason Chaffetz decided to repudiate his own house bill—the Disposal of Excess Federal lands Act of 2017, which would have directed the federal government to sell off 3.3 million acres of public land. Backlash came from outdoorists of all stripes, including from sportsman's groups like Trout Unlimited, the National Wild Turkey Foundation, and Backcountry Hunters & Anglers. "For Mr. Chaffetz," said my friend Land Tawney in a widely shared video, "you've kicked the hornet's nest, and the army is amassing." That was effectively the end of congressional bills to sell off federal public lands.

Then, in February 2018, the BEA numbers arrived. The agency had teased out our industry's contribution to the entire American economy, separating money spent traveling to national parks from money spent visiting the Statue of Liberty, and distinguishing the impact of making and selling backpacks for lugging books to school from backpacks for lugging tents and sleeping bags along the Appalachian Trail. Their verdict: the industry's gross impact was $637 billion, or 2 percent of the GDP. It was bigger than oil and gas extraction at 1.4 percent and legal services at 1.3 percent.

Heading to D.C. to lobby for conservation and recreation opportunities, industry leaders and outdoor recreation nonprofits like the Access Fund and American Whitewater came proudly armed with those numbers. I myself made more than twenty trips to Capitol Hill to advocate for outdoor recreation in my role with the State of Colorado and then while representing the VF Corp. As in my meeting with Montana's Governor Bullock, armed with these BEA numbers, lawmakers paid attention. I often followed the OIA's Jessica Wahl Turner from office to office, meeting with staffers working for New Mexico Senator Martin Heinrich, Alaska Senator Lisa Murkowski, and Virginia Senator Tim Kaine, if not the lawmakers themselves.

It wasn't a coincidence that more conservation victories followed. In December 2018, two federal laws created new Wilderness in the staunchly conservative states of Tennessee and Arkansas. The Tennessee Wilderness Act protected 20,000 acres of the Cherokee National Forest, while the Flatside Wilderness Enhancement Act added 640 acres to the popular 9,541-acre Flatside Wilderness near Little Rock. In both cases, the sponsoring lawmakers cited the economic benefits of outdoor recreation.

Those laws were just an appetizer for 2019's stunning John D. Dingell Jr. Conservation, Management, and Recreation Act. The massive omnibus bill protected more than 2 million acres in 18 states, including the creation of 1.3 million acres of Wilderness n Utah alone. It designated ten new segments of river as Wild and Scenic, and added acreage to Acadia, Death Valley, and Joshua Tree national parks, amongst dozens of other positive conservation provisions. Most importantly, it permanently re-authorized the LWCF, something conservationists had failed to do for a decade (in fact, the fund had been allowed to lapse the year before). The act had been introduced into the Senate by the Alaska Republican Lisa Murkowski and had passed there by a remarkable vote of 92-8.

Not a year later, Congress passed the Great American Outdoors Act, which took LWCF reauthorization a step further. The venerable fund had provisions for spending up to $900 million every year on recreation and conservation projects, but only rarely did presidential administrations allocate that much. The new law guaranteed that all $900 million be allocated every year. Furthermore, the law provided $9.5 billion to the NPS to help reduce the system's notorious maintenance backlog. Many hailed it as the most significant conservation legislation since the Clean Water Act and Clean Air Act and Wilderness Act passed in the 1960s. As with the previous year's John D. Dingell Act, it passed through Congress with a massive, rare-in-these-times bipartisan support.

There are two epilogues to insert here. The first is that the Biden Administration reversed Trump's decision on shrinking the two Utah monuments. The second is that in 2022, the OR show moved back to Utah. In Denver, the show had been bigger than ever—until the Covid-19 pandemic struck. After two shows in 2020 and 2021 were canceled entirely, attendance at the August 2021 and January 2022 events shrank to less than 8,000 apiece, down from OR's 2018 heyday of over 20,000. It wasn't just the coronavirus—the show's primary function was becoming obsolete. Outdoor Retailer was originally created to show off future products to retailers who would write orders on the spot, but for supply-chain reasons too wonky to discuss here, that is no longer the case. Outdoor Retailer has instead become a very expensive marketing event targeting a very small audience: shop owners. Even before the pandemic, dozens of brands like Arc'teryx and Columbia had decided the massive costs were no longer worthwhile, and had abandoned OR.

Utah offered lower costs—the SLC venue is smaller and has no trade unions—so Emerald saved money and so did the brands exhibiting. The move saddened me greatly because Utah politicians still remain largely hostile to the values our industry is cultivating: conservation and inclusion. Their laws against transgender-youth participation in sports are just one policy that infringe on the rights of the LGBTQIA+ community. Some thirty-four outdoor-rec companies agreed with me, including my own VF Corp and REI, and have declined to attend the show in Utah. On the other hand, I have high hopes for an event beginning in the summer of 2024. My successor at the state ORec office, Conor Hall, along with Visit Denver, is working with *Outside* magazine to create a festival that would serve both the core of the outdoor industry, in the form of a trade show, and the general public, with music, running races, and climbing competitions. It will be something like a hybrid of OR and South by Southwest, and organizers plan to draw 10,000 people, with plans to hit 70,000 people by 2027. Time will tell if the idea is successful, but as of now, our industry and community are still searching for a gathering place where all feel welcome.

Chapter 13

THE ZOOM BOOM

"There is good government when those who are near
are made happy, and when those who are afar are
attracted." —Confucius

In June of 2020, the world was in the grips of the Covid-19 pandemic and the news cycle felt like a forty-car pile-up: overflowing morgues, violent protests against race-related police killings, murder hornets. At least our family could go outside. We did, every day, hiking and running on the trails near our home in the Rockies foothills, snuggling up beside campfires in our backyard firepit, and even camping out in the backyard. Being outside kept us sane. We even became more bonded as a family because we were so deliberate about pursuing those adventures—with schools, restaurants, gyms, and other normal pastimes shuttered, there just wasn't much else to do.

As the weeks wore on, we noticed more and more people on the pathways and trails doing the same thing. People who never went hiking and cycling were doing so, if for no other reason than to meet with friends and family at a socially safe distance. I was proud to be working in an industry that could help bring relief to a nation, even if my work was now from my basement and my meetings were all on Zoom.

It wasn't long before the trails and campgrounds were more

crowded than they had ever been. In fact, they were being trashed. National and state parks saw record visitation, and there were not enough staff to manage the crowds or even serve concessions. The experience suffered, as did the park facilities and ecology. There were crumpled beer cans in parking lots and scorched earth from bonfires in meadows. Outhouses were overflowing, and worse, people afraid of the outhouses were defecating on the ground and covering it with wads of white toilet paper. We saw these "blooms" everywhere we looked every time we went hiking. Friends from across the country reported the same things, from the famous Tetons to once hidden gems like Kentucky's Red River Gorge.

Wealthy remote workers began migrating to outdoor-recreation-rich communities across the country, driving housing prices sky high and displacing residents. Communities like my former hometown of Eagle, Colorado, and Livingston, Montana—the gateway to Yellowstone—remain brimming with frustration. In Maine, according to a report by the state's housing authority, in every county except one, "the average household price is unaffordable to the average income household." Maine's growth is from out-of-staters looking toward the state's great outdoor recreation and landscape. We'd been advocating for recreation-driven migration for years to shore up rural economies, but this was too much too fast. The "Zoom Boom" has brought the congestion and prices of the cities to the trailheads of mountain towns.

In those early days of pandemic social distancing, I also couldn't help but think of the people who weren't able to take advantage of the healing power of nature—either because they live in urban places without access to nature or lack the experience to feel comfortable there. I was really aware of my privilege, living near open space, having a backyard where I could safely camp. We can hardly expect people who don't even have a park near their homes where they can watch a sunset to go spend the night in the woods. Those access issues had been a problem for decades, but the national health crisis of the pandemic brought the disparity into much sharper focus. The only thing that brought me solace was that it was part of my work to help ease that disparity.

In March of 2019, I'd left my job with the State of Colorado and begun working for the VF Corporation, a 120-year-old holding company that owns thirteen of the outdoor industry's most iconic brands, including The North Face, Timberland, Vans, and Dickies. My position was vice president of global impact and government affairs. I was also running the corporation's foundation for charitable giving, and a big part of our philanthropy centered on more equitable access to outdoor recreation.

In 2018, I'd begun conversations with Steve Rendle, VF Corp's CEO. Steve confidentially let me know that he was thinking of moving VF's headquarters from Greensboro, North Carolina, as well as many of its brands, to a new, more central location, and Denver was on the short list. I asked him why he would consider Denver, and, in my role of the state's outdoor-recreation-industry director, his answer filled me with joy. He said that he recognized the focus Colorado had put on the ORec industry and how it was held up as an important part of the fabric of the community and cultural identity of the state.

I went to work overtime connecting him with the state's economic-development team, helping the team draft the pitch to sell a move as monumental as what Steve was describing. In the midst of these conversations, I asked Steve with whom I should be liaising at the company for questions about its government policy. I also asked him how VF handled philanthropy. Did they have a foundation or other charitable-giving mechanism? He got a somewhat pained expression on his face. "No, Luis. Those two vital functions are very much in their infancy with us," he said.

I was dumbfounded. How could a Fortune 250 global company not have these things? I said as much. I talked about the work I did at the state, how the focus on the intersectionality of policy and philanthropy—however you defined it—led to real and measurable impact. Through my study of both history and behavioral sciences, it had become evident to me that people want to care about these things.

He smiled and said something I never expected to hear: "Luis, the pieces you are describing sound very much like a role we could use. Why don't you write a proposal and let's discuss it?"

I was starting to see a pattern in my life. This would be the third job in a row where I would be given the opportunity to chart my own course. This leads me to believe that the future, our future, my future isn't preordained. The future is what we have the courage to shape it into.

What did my job entail? With the emergence of environmental, social, and governance (ESG) investing and reporting, many companies are starting to focus on their global impact. McDonald's, for one, has a Chief Global Impact Officer (CGIO) role. For instance, in this example, consider McDonald's sourcing beef from Brazil. The CGIO doesn't just worry about the quality of the beef; they need to be concerned about whether that cow grazed on slashed-and-burned land in the rainforest. Or were the farmers paid fairly and treated well, and did they practice regenerative agriculture? Could the company practice methane capture from their cattle? Finally, could they market and message all these efforts to the public to gain a competitive advantage and thereby help lead their industry to a more sustainable place?

This was in essence the role I created at VF. How could we lead in sustainability and philanthropy to support the things we believed in? Then, how could we spread the message about the work we were doing, in support of our brands? As I proposed all of this to Steve, he had many questions, but one stuck with me the most: It seemed like I already had a job I loved, he said, so why change?

Craving new challenges is a hallmark of being a climber, of course. I felt like I'd met the goals I'd set with the State of Colorado job. There was something else at play, too. There's a saying that people don't leave companies; they leave leaders. In both cases, the leaders who'd hired me for the state job and the VF job, Hick and Steve Rendle respectively, had both moved on. I followed each out the door not long after.

On that day, though, I shared with Steve a fun anecdote: When I was a young and broke mountain guide preparing for my first self-funded expedition to the Himalayas, I'd needed new gear. I'd cold-called The North Face and made my case as to why they should sponsor me. The company gave a young nobody like me everything I needed to stay safe and comfortable on that trip. Their only request was that I climb safely and bring back some good pictures they could use All these years later, this was my opportunity to give back to a brand that had believed in me when they'd no reason to. This is the loyalty and family that our industry creates, trying to provide that equitable access to adventure, one person at a time.

In those fraught early days of the pandemic, I organized a weekly Zoom call with my counterparts across the industry—the government-affairs staff at Patagonia, Columbia, Arc'teryx, REI, and others. I knew that connecting would help all of us, morale-wise, but it was also good to put our heads together to try to solve the big problems of keeping our workers safe across the globe, and to try to untangle the notoriously thorny supply-chain issues caused by the pandemic.

I also stayed busy promoting the outdoor-recreation industry's involvement in conservation politics, helping advocate in Washington. D.C., for the Great American Outdoors Act, which passed amidst the pandemic to overwhelming bipartisan support. All the people clamoring to get outside while social distancing? I know those crowds affirmed for politicians of all stripes the importance of investing in outdoor recreation.

Those governmental victories continued. In 2021, the American Rescue Plan Act earmarked $750 million specifically for travel, tourism, and outdoor-recreation amenities to spur economic development and increase community well-being. The decade of concerted efforts by people like Jessica Wahl Turner, state outdoor-rec directors, and nonprofits like the Access Fund and IMBA to educate lawmakers was paying off. Some of those funds are going to help the city of Valdez in Alaska build hiking trails, while Skowhegan, Maine, is using $4.9 million to build a whitewater park. Utah's National Ability Center is getting $372,000 to expand their instructor pool to help people with disabilities go skiing, cycling, and rafting. And in Ohio, a community severely impacted by the decline of the coal industry is getting $2.4 million to improve a marina, campsites, and trails to help bolster tourism.

The Biden Administration also reinstated the Federal Interagency Council on Outdoor Recreation (FICOR), a partnership between seven federal agencies, including the USFS, NPS, and BLM, that had been founded in 2011 to pool resources to improve ORec opportunities. The number of trails, rivers, and even beaches that traverse lands managed by different government entities—like, say, the Pacific Crest Trail stretching from the Mexican border to the Canadian border—make the council an obvious good. Before it was disbanded by the Trump Administration, FICOR accomplished some important things: they created a common online marketplace, Recreation.gov, for campsite reservations and required permits across all federal lands including national parks, and created a free pass to most federally owned recreation facilities for every fourth-grader in the country, the Every Kid Outdoors program, recognizing that such experiences can be most impactful for people when they are young.

FICOR also assisted the BEA in 2016 and 2017 in measuring the economic impact, figuring out how to parse outdoor-recreation expenditure from more traditional tourism, and sorting out which items sold and manufactured could go into the outdoor-rec pot. Those figures became so important in legitimizing outdoor rec as a pillar of society to many lawmakers.

The Biden Administration has also made great strides in recognizing the injustices dealt to Native Americans, who are so obviously of the public lands where we recreate. I think many Americans don't know what to make of the "Land Back" slogan. It can be polarizing in much the same way "Defund the Police" has been. Looking beneath the strident messaging of activists, though, both slogans convey reasonable sentiments. Could we not allocate some of the money law enforcement spends on armored troop carriers to hire specialists better able to cope with people in mental crisis, many of whom end up injured or killed by police because officers lack the time or training to parse such complex situations? Similarly, could we not go further in repairing the wrongs our nation has done to those peoples who inhabited this land before our nation was formed?

In some cases, that simply means honoring existing legal

judgements. In June 2022, the Department of the Interior, led for the first time by a Native American in Deb Halland of the Laguna Pueblo tribe, transferred 19,000 acres of Montana's National Bison Range to the Confederated Salish and Kootenai Tribes. Courts had ruled the federal government's annexation of the land illegal in 1971, but it had taken fifty years to generate the political will to follow the court order. In New York, the corporation Honeywell turned over 1,000 acres of forestland to the Onondaga Nation as part of a legal settlement with the tribes and the U.S. Fish and Wildlife Service, reached over Honeywell's contamination of Onondaga Lake and tributaries with mercury from its nearby manufacturing plants.

In other instances, the federal government is signing co-management agreements with tribes for national forests, parks, and monuments. Canyon de Chelly National Monument, entirely within the boundaries of the Navajo Nation, is being managed cooperatively by the park service, the Navajo Nation, and the Bureau of Indian Affairs. Similar agreements have recently been forged for Grand Portage National Monument, Glacier Bay National Park and Preserve, and Big Cypress National Preserve, amongst others. Then, in 2022, the BLM and the USFS signed an agreement to co-manage Bears Ears with the five tribes who'd originally worked together to advocate for and define the monument's boundaries. The tribes have submitted their land-management plan for the monument, which will be incorporated into the government's own plan. Furthermore, in 2022 alone, the USFS has created more than eleven agreements for co-stewardship with Native Nations. For example, Alaska's Tongass National Forest will work with the Hoonah Indian Association on foresting programs.

My friend Len Necefer, a climber and member of the Navajo

Nation, sees limits to these agreements because their efficacy will vary from one federal administration to the next. But, he writes, "these wins are symbolic and we must celebrate them as such. What gives me hope is that in just three generations we have seen a transformation of the self-governance of Native Nations in this country and the inertia of these wins [is] not easily stopped."

Len is a former University of Arizona professor who has pivoted to direct work with the ORec industry through his company, NativesOutdoors. The company sells apparel designed by native artists and produces films featuring native skiers and climbers; it also gives away ski-resort passes to Native American skiers to help increase participation. All the while, he serves as a sounding board for those of us in the outdoor industry interested in forging better relationships with the Native American community. When with the state, I worked with him to bring as many of the Colorado tribal nations as possible together to talk about outdoor-recreation opportunities at a daylong meeting during Outdoor Retailer.

***

All of these solutions are great, but they often represent a patchwork of various entities and activists all pulling in different directions, and perhaps not always communicating with each other about a common goal. While it's not a perfect analogue, there is a precedent for ORec leadership at the national, big-picture level: the Bureau of Outdoor Recreation, which existed for fifteen years beginning in 1962. Ever since my MBA, I'd been dimly aware that there had been such an entity. As a Udall Family fanboy, I knew that the Bureau of Outdoor Recreation had been established by Stewart Udall, serving as President Kennedy's secretary of the interior. However, I'd been so focused on the creation of the state offices of outdoor recreation as a path to power that I hadn't thought much about it.

Writing this book led me into deeper thinking about outdoor recreation's role in shaping our nation, and that's when it became obvious to me that we'd need a federal entity shepherding outdoor recreation. When I looked into the history of the Bureau of Outdoor Recreation, I was amazed by the precedent.

For a nearly forgotten agency, its accomplishments were impressive. The bureau was one of the driving forces behind the creation of the Wilderness Act in 1964, lending a key government-insider stamp of approval to the movement championed by Howard Zahniser, Aldo Leopold, Sigurd Olson, et. al. It was a major player in the creation of the National Wild and Scenic Rivers system, and the Rails to Trails movement, in which abandoned railways are converted to recreational paths. The bureau not only studied the feasibility of claiming their rights of ways for trails, but administered a grant program that helped demonstrate how such paths could be established, leading to some of the earliest rail-trails in California, Maryland, Missouri, New Jersey, New York, Ohio, Pennsylvania, Virginia, and Washington.

Of course, its big contribution was the Land and Water Conservation Fund, made into law in 1965. The fund was basically made to bankroll the work of the Bureau of Recreation, which is why the fund works simultaneously at the federal, state, and local level—precisely the spirit and strategy of the bureau.

Like the Confluence of States, the history of the bureau was a bipartisan one. It was established on the recommendation of a fifteen-person panel made up of congresspeople from both the Democratic and Republican parties and a handful of notable private citizens, including Laurence Rockefeller, a University of

Michigan professor, a *New York Times* editor, and a vice president from the timber company Weyerhaeuser. It was founded by Udall's secretarial decree in 1962, and then formally established with the passage of the National Outdoor Recreation Act in May 1963. Udall appointed Edward Crafts, a thirty-year veteran of the USFS, to lead the new bureau.

Craft's charge for the bureau was three-part; first, it worked to improve outdoor-recreation opportunities by coordinating between a host of federal agencies like the USFS and NPS, as well as a few more-surprising agencies like the Department of Health, Education and Welfare, and the Housing and Home Finance Agency. Secondly, it worked as an advisor and funder to state and local governments with technical assistance and funding. The bipartisan panel had been sensitive to the age-old tension between federal and state control.

The other thing it did was to create a host of valuable research on outdoor recreation. My friend Bob Ratcliffe, a forty-year veteran of the BLM and NPS, actually inherited the complete set of the bureau's publications: some twenty-seven volumes the size of an encyclopedia set. Inside were fifteen years of studies and reports, many of them representing the first work linking outdoor recreation to improved health and well-being. Additionally, according to Bob, the bureau's studies contained foundational research on equity in access to nature. That's what led it to working closely with the Housing and Home Finance Agency and the Department of Health, Education, and Welfare—formulating plans to make sure trails and parks were accessible even to those living in dense urban environments. As Bob says, "the Bureau of Outdoor Rec was defining and practicing environmental justice before the term existed."

The bureau was ultimately the victim of anti-conservationist budget hawks in the Reagan Administration. It was vulnerable, according to Bob, because it didn't have a funding source of its own and didn't really create its own policy—it was essentially created as a go-between for other agencies and for the states. Its responsibilities were largely folded into the NPS, some of them ultimately falling to Bob in his position of Division Chief for the Conservation and Recreation and Community Assistance Programs.

What was lost when the bureau closed was the close cooperation between federal agencies in recreation projects and of course any momentum viz. research on the health benefits of time outside. That research has had to be started from scratch in the last two decades, and people like Bob, one of FICOR's architects, had to reinvent the wheel of federal interagency recreation cooperation. That wheel still isn't rolling well. As Bob says, "Had the bureau continued in its mission, the world would have been a better place. The return on investment would have been huge."

In my vision, a national director of outdoor recreation would continue those efforts to foster more equitable access to outdoor recreation, helping fund and support organizations like Latino Outdoors and Blackpackers. It would also further the work of bringing ORec infrastructure to communities where it doesn't now exist in the form of more parks, pathways, and even beaches. Now more than ever, there's money out there for such projects—look at Biden's American Rescue Plan Act of 2021 and his Infrastructure law. Few state and local entities know how to access those funds. Even if they secure the money, people from across the nation tell me, they don't have people to do the work. Again, as we see in Colorado, higher education can help create a skilled-worker pipeline, minting landscape architects and engineers who are drawn to the ORec industry's values. A national director of outdoor rec could be the catalyst for that.

This director could coordinate with state parks to use infrastructure-bill funds to build EV-charging stations. More greenery in schoolyards reduces ADHD, but who is coordinating with the Department of Education to do that? We could supersize the work that the Trust for Public Land is doing. A federal outdoor-rec director could advocate for the benefits of outdoor recreation across all government departments, in the same way that state outdoor-rec directors do in state government. All without a huge staff.

Another source of funding? A small tax on outdoor-recreation equipment, to help fund recreation infrastructure. Such taxes have been very popular in Minnesota, Missouri, Georgia, and Texas. The national director of outdoor recreation would oversee distribution of those funds for projects improving equity, as well as helping with the overuse issues that arose during the pandemic. We must take care of the lands where we recreate, and their existing infrastructure. To do anything less is profane.

As for the issues of overcrowding, we've proven time and time again that great outdoor recreation can happen in the humbler places too. There are whitewater parks in Oklahoma City. There are mountain-biking trails built atop mine tailings in Minnesota. There are via ferratas in abandoned quarries in Ohio. There are bike paths in Brownsville, Texas. All of those facilities have helped bring economic revitalization and improved physical and mental health to their communities. The outdoor recreation in places like Bozeman, Montana, and Asheville, North Carolina, and Bend, Oregon, is a powerful draw, but building trails and cleaning up rivers in other places can help spread some of those visitors and newcomers to other communities.

In the end, we cannot forget the philanthropic mechanisms

that are making it better as well. In November of 2023, the Trust for Public Land announced that they would be transferring 30,000 acres of woodland in Maine that they had bought from a timber company back to the Penobscot Nation. This truly proves that the outdoor recreation industry, our industry, can and is trying to save the world.

EPILOGUE

I am back where it all began, on a high peak in Ecuador. There is a peculiar chill to a high-alpine stone hut at sunset. Outside, I can hear the glacier cracking and groaning. Upstairs, climbers shuffle around. I can hear the clanking of climbing equipment being prepared for our summit attempt tonight and the soft snoring of the other guides in the room off the kitchen. Scattered around at tables are climbers from all over the world, quietly whispering as I sit and watch the steam slowly rise from my cup of tea.

It seems like life has a way of bringing you back to the start, but my experience is that at each revolution of the circle, you have a chance to do it differently—and better. I am on Cayambe. It's a little smaller than my beloved Cotopaxi, but since Cotopaxi is now reawakened into a very active volcano, our group thought it best to shift here, to the one mountain that straddles the equator. On the summit push, you actually cross from the Southern Hemisphere into the Northern.

It's a fitting metaphor for me: the journey back and forth between worlds. The belief I started with in these mountains as an asthmatic boy caught between two cultures continues to define my journey. This time, I am back with an organization that bridges Colorado and Ecuador. The Range of Motion Project (ROMP) is a nonprofit that helps underserved amputees access high-quality prosthetic care in the United States and in Latin America. They've delivered more than 5,000 prosthetic devices to people primarily in Guatemala and Ecuador, and we are climbing Cayambe with a group of adaptive athletes to raise funds and awareness for ROMP's work here in Latin America.

I love what my friend Lauren Panasewicz, ROMP's director of development, wrote about their mission: "As an avid mountaineer, the idea that we can climb mountains to help others take their first steps towards their own summits is a beautiful translation of mobility in real time: vertical feet for prosthetic feet." When we speak of equitable access to the outdoors, ROMP delivers.

I step back into the guiding arena from time to time with groups like this to not only provide a checkup on my skills, but also as a touchstone for my intentions. My thinking has always been that time outside is good for you. The belief that our industry serves the greater good now goes well beyond just conversations around tables such as the one where I now sit; it spans the country and the world, to help people understand that new economies can grow, natural resources can thrive, and the types of education this industry can provide cannot be found in books or a traditional classroom.

That is the answer to the question I get the most: Why must our industry be political? Isn't it enough to enjoy making innovative products that impel people outside? Haven't we come far enough, diversifying the faces and voices in our industry and community? Aren't we enough?

The Andes, much like mountain ranges all over the world,

continue to offer a reflection. A mirror that helps to define how to heal, how to grow, how to learn more about yourself than you ever thought possible. Try walking uphill at midnight in the cold and the wind under the stars at an altitude that has you gasping for air, and you will come to understand the penance you serve while climbing a mountain. Mountaineering has a way of purifying and focusing your thoughts, your intentions. It has a way of inspiring that only the rarest of human experiences can. The pursuit of time outside can lead us to our better selves as individuals and as a society. Meaning, we can always do more, be more, strive to make it better, every step of the way.

I think of the glorious October day in 2022 when I was lucky enough to be on-hand for the designation of Camp Hale-Continental Divide National Monument near Leadville, Colorado. Camp Hale was the training ground for the 10th Mountain Division during the Second World War. It even served as a secret CIA training ground at one point for Tibetan freedom fighters waging a guerrilla war against the Chinese occupation in the high Himalayas. The camp would prove fruitful to the outdoor industry in Colorado, too. After the war, a few enterprising troopers came back to Colorado, and seeing the value in all they had learned about skiing and adventuring in those hills, created many of Colorado's world-famous ski resorts, including Vail, Aspen, and Arapahoe Basin.

Camp Hale was seminal in my own life, too. As an Outward Bound instructor, I taught climbing on the same crags that the 10th Mountain Division used to train their soldiers. In winter, we took students deeper into the hills behind Hale, backcountry skiing and winter camping just as the soldiers had in 1943. Arriving in the forested valley tinged with golden aspen groves that day, I felt profoundly gratified to be there to witness this moment, which had come about thanks to the Biden Administration's validation of the site.

Biden wasn't the first president drawn to the mountains around Hale. After leaving office, President Ford helped establish Beaver Creek Ski Resort, just over the ridge from where we now gathered. His official residence there was the stuff of legends. He would entertain dignitaries from around the world and show them the majesty of "his valley." As the story goes, whenever his wife wasn't in town with him, you could often find the president wandering around the village in khakis and a flannel shirt, with a three-day growth of stubble. Whenever someone would ask after Mrs. Ford, and if she was also in town, he would say, "Look at me—what do you think?"

Waiting onstage were tribal leaders and the entire Colorado delegation, including my old boss John Hickenlooper, now a U.S. senator. As President Biden took the stage, the energy around me was palpable. To one side sat a good friend, Sarah Schrader, CEO of Bonsai Designs. Sarah has settled in Grand Junction, Colorado, and when the oil industry in that part of our state was going bust, she reschooled oil-derrick workers to work for her designing and building ziplines and high-ropes challenge courses around the world.

To the other side of me was a slight and older woman who had tears streaming down her face. I leaned in and asked what was wrong. She then told me the story of her time as a part-time ski patroller in Beaver Creek, and how she worked the rest of the time as a nurse. She was crying, she said, because she'd been a private nurse for President Ford as he got older, yet still insisted on coming to Beaver Creek. She shared that he often talked of trying to make Camp Hale a national monument but that the timing "was never right." History, she said, had a funny way of working itself out.

I marveled sitting there between the next generation of the industry represented in Sarah, and the somewhat unlikely archivist in the woman on the other side of me. And while President Biden's comments were gracious and complimentary to Colorado, I will never forget what came next.

Most presidents at events where security isn't a concern will "work the rope line," connecting with people. In this setting, as the president mingled amongst no more than sixty or seventy people, he seemed to want to talk and enjoy the fresh air a little more than expected. Before I knew it, I found myself face to face with him. I drew Sarah and the nurse into the conversation. I thanked President Biden for coming and for the creation of the monument. As he held onto my hand, the nurse relayed her story about President Ford. This stopped Biden in his tracks. He hugged the nurse, saying, "We know, don't we, how important these places are. I would bring my kids out here to ski, bring my grandkids out here, too. They must know what it is we are fighting for."

As he moved on into the crowd it struck me: This is the why. Especially after the pandemic, everyone recognizes the value of spending time outside, the mental and physical heath bonuses you get by breathing fresh air or by watching the sunset. Standing in that place, it was hard not to feel like we were closing in on creating that larger political voice for our economy and our industry.

The other instance in which I thought we were getting close was at the kickoff rally for Hick's presidential campaign in Denver in 2019. His campaign wasn't successful, though his pivot to the Senate was, but the event was monumental for me because I was honored to be asked to speak at the rally.

One average Tuesday morning, I got a call from a friend on Hickenlooper's speechwriting team. I was halfheartedly listening, trying to catch up on emails, while he regaled me with stories from prepping the candidate and all that was to come. What he said next got my attention, though. "Luis", he said, "we are getting ready for the campaign-kickoff rally, and the governor was wondering if you would be interested in getting the whole thing started."

I almost dropped the phone. What did he mean? Say the Pledge of Allegiance? Welcome everyone? Tell everyone to take their seats? He laughed and said, "No, he wants you to tell the story of the industry, why these things matter, how conservation connects to climate, and to do it all in about three minutes. Get me your draft within the hour." The rally was just one day away.

My speech was ultimately short and sweet, but personal for me. I calmed my nerves stepping up to the podium in Denver's Rotunda that March evening, looking out on a sea of hundreds of lit-up faces amongst the marble columns. "You know, my Abuelito used to say to me in Spanish, '*Cree en los que creen en ti.*'" I translated for the crowd: "Believe in those who believe in you."

Hick had believed in me, and in my mission to make my industry better. Beyond that, he had believed in my vision to make my industry a model for changing the world, which was also part of Hick's campaign mission. That was huge. This idea championed by people like Jessica Wahl Turner, Peter Metcalf, Marc Berejka, and me was now a cornerstone of a presidential campaign. While Hick couldn't quite get there, I believe his message did resonate with the Biden Administration. It's there in the money set aside for recreation and rural development in their laws and policies. And it's there in the idea of the civilian service corps and in the resurrection of FICOR. Imagine if we can make all of this a campaign issues for the candidates in 2023.

The outdoor-recreation industry (and economy) is still growing up, growing comfortable with its political voice, securing its future. Those of us who have "roped up" together to elevate our voice and our efforts have done so knowing that the generation we serve is not our own; our work is for those who come next. Our job has been to crack and hold open the door for the next generation to walk through.

I hope someday to bring my daughter to Cayambe. To show her that amidst the wind and the snow, the rock and the starlight, you have the capacity to discover the truth of your life. It is a truth that will be tested, that will be challenged. Life will bring you to your knees, attempt to make you feel smaller than you are, but as any outdoor enthusiast can tell you, it's not about how often you are humbled, but how well you can rise to your feet again, and through the tempest, keep putting one foot in front of the other while appreciating the beauty of the journey along the way. No one accomplishes this alone. The stories and the experiences we collect through our lifetimes shape the narrative that helps define who we are—as people, as an industry, and I even think as a country.

Looking out the window before trying to get a few hours of sleep, I recite in my head, as I have before every summit push since I was a 19-year-old working for Outward Bound, the final stanzas from *Ulysses* by Alfred Lloyd Tennison. Outward Bound has adopted an augmented version of the epic poem's last line as its motto, one that has defined my journey, and, I think, my industry's journey too.

When I really need inspiration, though, as I do at the start of any big climb, I prefer the hard tolling of the original lines, acknowledging our long journey and the inspiration to understand that the process knows no finish line. My greatest hope is that Tennison's words will illuminate what's to come, for all of us.

Come, my friends,
'Tis not too late to seek a newer world...
...that which we are, we are.
One equal temper of heroic hearts
Made weak by time and fate, but strong in will.
To serve, to seek, to find, and not to yield.

ACKNOWLEDGMENTS

The gratitude for bringing this book to life extends far beyond my capacity for thanks. If we have ever spoken about the magic and power of the outdoors, consider yourself part of this gratitude. For others, first, Fredrick Reimers. Without him, this project never would have come to life-Rico, thank you for being the keeper and the shaper of my voice for all these years. Sequoia, who would have thought, all those years ago, that mountaineering would see us here? Thank you for being the best publisher a guy like me could ask for. Marie Logsden and Buck Stein, for seeing the possibility and who, without even flinching, jumped in to provide the engine to get this book done. Fredrick and I will forever be grateful. Matt Samet, editor extraordinaire. My family, of course, for enduring nights and days wondering if I was ever going to stop writing/editing and come upstairs.

To all the other leaders I have crossed paths with in this industry-Tom Adams, Katherine Andrews, Fiona Arnold, Sam Bailey, Stacy Bare, Christian Beckwith, Rachel Benedick, the Benitez family (Ecuador and the USA), Grace Benner, Senator Michael Bennett, Marc Berejka, Jason Bertolacci, Carrie

Besnette-Hauser, Jason Blevins, Seth Bolster, Gordon Bronson, Todd Burleson, Trent Busch, Chris Castillian, Jenna Celmer, Guy Cotter, Congressman Jason Crow, Stephanie Donner, Senator Kerry Donovan, Paul Duba, Carlos Fernandez, Nathan Fey, Doug Friednash, Brad Garmon, Ken Gart and the whole Gart family, Mark Gasta, Rebecca Gillis, Jose Gonzalez, Anita Graham, Pitt Grewe, Secretary of State Jenna Griswold, Jen Gurecki, Michelle Hadwiger, the incomparable Kathy Hagan, Conor Hall, Mayor Michael Hancock, Kenji Haroutunian, Taldi Harrison, Joel Hartter, Joel Heath, Senator Hickenlooper, Sharon Houghton, Mitsu Iwasaki, the Jacquemin family, Johnathan Jaroz, Corley Kenna, Lindsey King, Trista Kogan, Jim Licko, Patty Limerick, Annelise Lovelie, Kirsten Lynch, Charley Mace, Chris Mattias, Peter McBride, Theresa McKenny, Peter Metcalf, Kim Miller, Mario Molina, Jose Montero and the entire Montero family, Max Nathanson, Dr. Len Necefer and his Meme Machine, Congressman Joe Neguse, Penn Newhard, Dan Nordstrom, Jake Norton, Cailin O'Brien-Feeney, Carolann Oudette, Chris Perkins, Governor Jared Polis, Mahting Putelis, Diane Regas, Steve Rendle, Dani Reyes-Acosta, Don Riggle, Amy Roberts, Brady Robinson, Ramona Robinson, Ambassador Ken Salazar, Steve Sander, Laura Schaffer, Richard Scharf, Auden Schendler, Sarah Schrader, Alyssa Sears and the entire Sears family, Buie Seawell, Nina Sharma, Jon Snyder, Lucas St. Clair, Libby Stockstill, Samantha Swain, Chris Sword, Land Tawney, Biju Thomas, Senator Mark Udall, Rachel VandeVoort, Geoff Van Dyke, Amy Venturi, Jessica Wahl-Turner, Dr. Leroy Walters, Betsy Webb, Erik Weihenmayer and the entire 2001 Everest team, Attorney General Phil Weiser, Ben Wright, Kyle Zeppelin-and to all the clients I have ever shared a rope with, and all the other friends I have ever shared a campfire or tent with talking about what this industry can and should be, mil gracias!

LUIS BENITEZ

Luis Benitez grew up in the Midwest and has been climbing and going into the outdoors since his earliest years. He has worked as a high-end international mountain guide, with six Everest summits to his name; outdoor educator; and, most recently, a policy leader in the outdoor industry. Prior to joining the Trust for Public Land as their chief impact officer-his current role-Luis was vice president for government affairs and global impact at the VF Corporation, which includes iconic brands like The North Face, Vans, and Timberland. Luis also served as president of the VF Foundation.

In 2015, Luis was appointed by Colorado Governor John Hickenlooper to lead the then newly established Outdoor Recreation Industry Office. In that role, he transformed the outdoor industry into a powerful force for economic development, conservation and stewardship, education and workforce training, and public health and wellness. Under his watch, the state's outdoor economy ballooned from $28 billion to $65 billion.

In his philanthropic journey, Luis has helped create two nonprofits: Trekking for Kids, which focuses on service-based expeditions allowing participants to climb and trek while teaching them about local issues like housing and healthcare for disadvantaged youth. And Warriors to Summits, a nonprofit that helps veterans connect with the outdoors.

He has also served as an adjunct in Ecuador and Chile for the Wharton School of Business at the University of Pennsylvania and at the University of Colorado, Boulder's Masters of the Outdoor Recreation Economy program. Luis holds an executive MBA from the University of Denver, with an emphasis certification on behavioral sciences and public policy from Harvard University's Kennedy School of Government.

FREDERICK REIMERS

Frederick Reimers grew up at Keewaydin, a canoe-tripping summer camp in Northern Ontario, where his father was the director. He went on to lead whitewater, mountaineering, canyoneering, and sea-kayaking expeditions for nearly a decade for the Colorado Outward Bound School.

He began his writing career at the Jackson Hole News and went on to staff positions at Paddler magazine and Canoe and Kayak, where he served as editor. He resides in Jackson, Wyoming, with his wife and son, and writes and creates podcasts for outlets like Smithsonian, Ski, and Outside, where he often reports on the economics and politics of outdoor recreation.

ABOUT THE PUBLISHER

Di Angelo Publications was founded in 2008 by Sequoia Schmidt—at the age of seventeen. The modernized publishing firm's creative headquarters is in Los Angeles, California. In 2020, Di Angelo Publications made a conscious decision to move all printing and production for domestic distribution of its books to the United States. The firm is comprised of eleven imprints, and the featured imprint, Erudition, was inspired by the desire to spread knowledge, spark curiosity, and add numbers to the ranks of continuing learners, big and small.

TRUST FOR PUBLIC LAND™

The outdoors are essential to our happiness, health, and well-being.

Quality parks and green spaces are fundamental for sustaining equitable, resilient communities. Access to nature and the outdoors—close to home, in the cities and communities where people live—is a matter of health, equity, and justice. That's why we work alongside communities across the country to create, protect, and steward the nature-rich places that are vital to human well-being.

We're driven by four commitments: equity, health, climate, and community.

USE THE QR CODE BELOW TO
SUPPORT US